Human rights in E
no grounds for cor........y

Viewpoints by **Thomas Hammarberg**
Council of Europe Commissioner
for Human Rights

Council of Europe Publishing

The opinions expressed in this work are the responsibility of the author and do not necessarily reflect the official policy of the Council of Europe.

All rights reserved. No part of this publication may be translated, reproduced or transmitted, in any form or by any means, electronic (CD-Rom, Internet, etc.) or mechanical, including photocopying, recording or any information storage or retrieval system, without prior permission in writing from the Public Information Division, Directorate of Communication (F-67075 Strasbourg Cedex or publishing@coe.int).

Most of the photos provided by the Council of Europe were taken by Sandro Weltin, photographer at the Council of Europe, who has accompanied the Commissioner for Human Rights on several official visits in order to illustrate the situation of human rights in Europe.

Cover photo: Migrants detained in Fylako Centre for irregular migrants, Evros, Greece, December 2008 (© Council of Europe).
Back cover photo: Isabel Nukoaca, 11, explains that a new school must be built in her village, Roma-dominated village of Barbulesti, Romania, October 2010 (© Council of Europe).
Cover design and layout: Documents and Publications Production Department (SPDP), Council of Europe.

Council of Europe Publishing
F-67075 Strasbourg Cedex
http://book.coe.int

ISBN 978-92-871-6916-7
© Council of Europe, April 2011
Printed in France

Table of contents

Foreword 9

Chapter 1: Xenophobia and identity 31
Respecting the other 32
Islamophobia 36
The burqa and privacy 39
Discriminatory stop and search 43
Hate crimes 46
Minority languages 50

Chapter 2: Roma rights 57
European history of repression of the Roma 58
Continued stigmatisation of Roma 61
Ending discrimination against Roma 64
Roma political representation 71
Roma without citizenship 75
Discrimination against Roma migrants 79

Chapter 3: Immigration and asylum policies 83
Rights for migrants 84
The criminalisation of migration 87
The right to asylum 91
Detention of asylum seekers 93
Family reunification ....

Trafficking 102

Statelessness 104

Displaced persons... 108

Chapter 4: Protection against homophobia and transphobia 113

Yogyakarta Principles 114

Homophobia 117

Transphobia... 121

Chapter 5: Rights of people with disabilities 127

Making society inclusive 128

Rights for persons with mental disabilities 132

Discrimination against people with intellectual disabilities............ 136

Chapter 6: Gender rights 143

Gender representation in politics... 144

The pay gap 146

Domestic violence.. 149

Rape 152

Chapter 7: Rights of the child................................... 157

The UN Convention on the Rights of the Child 158

Views of children 162

Children and violence... 166

Sexual abuse of children 169

Children in unsuitable care institutions 172

Children in prison 176

Child migrants 180

Child poverty 183

Chapter 8: Social and economic rights 187

Poverty and marginalisation 188

The global economic crisis and human rights 191

Equality, discrimination and poverty 194

The right to housing 197

The rights of older people 200

HIV, Aids and the right to health 204

Climate change: an issue of human rights 206

Enforcing social rights standards 211

Chapter 9: Police, courts and prisons 217

Police violence 218

The "ticking bomb" argument 222

Final abolition of the death penalty 225

Corruption undermines justice 228

Judges must be independent 233

Lengthy court proceedings 236

Enforcement of court decisions 238

Prison conditions 241

Life sentences 243

Remedies for victims of human rights violations 246
Applications to the Strasbourg Court 249

Chapter 10: Fighting terrorism while respecting human rights 253
Counterterrorist methods and European complicity 254
Intelligence secrecy: no excuse 259
Terrorist blacklisting 263
Terrorism – Lessons from Northern Ireland 267
Privacy and data protection 272

Chapter 11: Gross violations in the past 279
Lessons from history 280
Accountability in post-totalitarian states 284
The International Criminal Court 226

Chapter 12: Media freedom and freedom of expression 291
Blasphemy and hate speech 292
Media diversity 295
Journalists at risk 298
Freedom of assembly 301

Chapter 13: Actors for human rights 305
Human rights defenders 306
The example of Andrei Sakharov 308
Religious leaders 312

Ombudsmen 314
Local authorities 316
Parliaments 320

Chapter 14: Systematic measures for human rights implementation 325
National implementation 326
State budgets 331
Human rights education 334

Chapter 15: International action 339
Foreign policy and human rights 340
The accountability of international actors 346

List of acronyms and abbreviations 351
Council of Europe human rights treaties:
record of ratifications and signatures 353

Foreword

Political rhetoric on human rights in Europe is different from daily reality. Almost every politician is on record as favouring the protection of freedom and justice. Standards on human rights have been agreed at European and international level; many have been integrated into national law; but they are not consistently enforced. There is an implementation gap.

It is this implementation gap that this book seeks to address. It is built on a compilation of separate "viewpoints" or articles which I have written, and later updated, since beginning my mandate as Council of Europe Commissioner for Human Rights in April 2006. I have now visited almost all of the 47 member states of the Council of Europe. On each visit I have met victims of violations of human rights and their families, leading politicians, prosecutors, judges, ombudsmen, religious leaders, journalists and civil society representatives as well as inmates of prisons and other institutions, law enforcement personnel and others. The "viewpoints" written on the basis of these many visits summarise my reflections, conclusions and recommendations.

What I have seen and heard has made me deeply impatient. Of course, it takes time to develop a culture of respect for human rights and to establish institutions and procedures which turn human rights principles into reality. However, progress is too slow; and the disappointment felt by many is more than justified.

There are circumstances which can delay necessary reforms: war or political strife, natural disasters and economic crises. Less convincing are the excuses, which I have heard frequently, that public opinion resists reforms aimed at protecting and promoting human rights. On the whole, people want freedom and justice not only for themselves, but also for others. Politicians have a responsibility; the implementation of human rights is largely a question of political will.

All member states of the Council of Europe have ratified the European Convention on Human Rights, first agreed in 1950. Although this treaty and other human rights standards have been agreed between governments, their far-reaching strength lies in the fact that they have proved so obviously relevant and essential across the decades and across this diverse continent. Whatever the intention was when they were drafted, they have taken on a life of their own.

Civil society groups, individuals and the media in country after country refer to them as decisive in matters perceived as important. For many individuals, they inspire hope and more and more people turn, for instance, to the European Court of Human Rights in Strasbourg. It is this extraordinary response to human rights which has made them special and given them a moral weight which no government can afford to ignore. This popular and moral dimension of human rights is of great import and must be protected.

It is therefore particularly unfortunate that attempts are made to hijack or distort the very meaning of these rights. Key concepts and the language of human rights have been politicised and demeaned in political discourse. Some governments belittle or cover up their own shortcomings while using human rights as a propaganda tool against other states.

It also happens that government politicians – and some media – object strongly when shortcomings in their own countries are exposed by mechanisms set up to verify realisation of agreed international human rights standards. National pride trumps the openness to consider steps to improve.

There is a need to counter hypocrisy and to be more serious about implementing human rights effectively. This requires responding to criticism in a constructive spirit and making a conscious effort to secure the broadest possible support for human rights. A heavy responsibility rests also on international organisations such as the Council of Europe. The fact that the field is so politically sensitive makes consistency and even-handedness even more crucial.

There can be little progress without honest, concrete monitoring. Non-governmental organisations play a pivotal role here, as do the mass media. Ombudsmen and other independent national human rights structures exist nowadays in most European countries: when truly independent, they cast light on problems which have to be addressed.

Reporting about violations is of course insufficient. Monitoring must be followed up with measures of implementation. Three types of action are required of governments: that they themselves respect human rights standards, that they protect people from human rights violations perpetrated by others, and that they take the necessary steps to fulfil rights. All require pro-active efforts. Capacities must be built to ensure that human rights are made a reality in all walks of life.

What matters are results. I believe that we who are serious about human rights should reject simplistic notions. The discourse is not primarily about naming "good" and "bad" governments or establishing a sort of ranking list. There are shortcomings and problems in all countries; those responsible have in all cases an obligation to demonstrate the political will to address them.

The articles in this book are organised in 15 chapters. In the first, "Xenophobia and identity", I describe a sad and growing problem in Europe today: racism, xenophobia, Islamophobia, anti-Semitism, homophobia, transphobia and other phobias directed against others considered "different" by the majority group. Minorities are made targets of hate speech, violence and systematic discrimination.

Extreme right-wing parties promoting hatred against migrants and minorities are now represented in several national parliaments in Europe. In some countries they also directly influence government policies. Several of the established, mainstream political parties have begun to use the rhetoric of the extremists in order not to be outflanked by them – which has lent an unfortunate "legitimacy" to xenophobic positions. The consequence is continued discrimination, segregation, inter-communal tensions and, in some cases, friction with neighbouring countries.

These tendencies appear to have increased with today's global economic crisis: the high levels of unemployment have caused widespread uncertainty. Attempts by governments to initiate discussions about "national identity" have failed when based on a notion that their task was to identify one sole common identity. Instead governments should recognise and build upon the fact that all European states today are multicultural, and that diversity needs to be celebrated and protected through tolerance and positive understanding.

The chapter "Roma rights" describes how the Roma population continue to be victimised as a result of a climate of intolerance. The Roma remain far behind majority populations in terms of education, employment, housing and health standards. They have virtually no political representation. Many Roma live in abject poverty and have little prospect of improving their lives or integrating within wider society.

Many of them lack even personal identity documents. In fact, thousands have no administrative existence at all. They have never obtained a birth certificate, and have not overcome the administrative obstacles placed in the way of being recognised by the state. They often live entirely outside any form of basic social protection or inclusion. Without personal ID they have no access to education and health services.

Racism against Roma people is widespread throughout Europe. In times of economic problems, it appears that the tendency to direct frustration against scapegoats increases – and the Roma appear to be an easy target. Instead of fishing in murky waters, national and local politicians should stand up for and speak out on behalf of principles of non-discrimination and respect for people from different backgrounds. At the very minimum, politicians must avoid anti-Roma rhetoric themselves.

One of my concerns is the need to disseminate information about the history of Roma in Europe since this would allow for a better understanding of what they have suffered in the past. Only a few thousand Roma in Germany survived the concentration camps and the executions.

The survivors faced enormous difficulties when trying to build their lives again, having lost so many family members and relatives, and having had their properties destroyed or confiscated. Many had their health ruined. For years, when some tried to obtain compensation, their claims were rejected. Significantly, the mass killing of the Roma people was not an issue at the Nürnberg trial. The genocide of the Roma – *Samudaripe* or *Porrajmos* – has hardly been recognised at all in European public discourse.

In this chapter, I also quote the Swedish writer and Roma rights campaigner Katarina Taikon, who emphasised that these problems are human rights issues. She stressed that the Roma were not asking for privileges, only the same human rights as others enjoy. "We request the same legal protection against assault which others would get. And we do request that generations of Roma who have grown up without housing and schooling and who have been suffering abuse and discrimination by the state and the local authorities receive recognition and compensation."

The chapter "Immigration and asylum policies" points to the failure of European countries to co-ordinate their approach on migration issues. Some are, for geographic reasons, overwhelmed by the many migrants coming, and "cost-sharing" across Europe has not functioned well. One consequence has been the breakdown of the asylum system in Greece: a fact which did not prevent other European countries from continuing to send asylum seekers to Athens, citing the obsolete Dublin II regulation, a practice which the Strasbourg Court in January 2011 found in conflict with the European Convention.

Governments have focused on measures to prevent people from coming. It is now more difficult for both refugees and economic migrants to reach our borders. In spite of this, men, women and children have continued to try, and thousands have drowned in recent years in the

Mediterranean Sea. The European reaction to these tragedies has been virtually non-existent.

Patrol boats along Europe's southern coasts are now used to intercept and turn back migrants from African countries. Airlines are put under pressure to refuse to take any passengers who risk being denied entry on arrival at their destination. My point is that these technocratic policies are undermining international standards on the right to seek asylum. Asylum seekers cannot even get to a place where they can formally request asylum. Among those stopped in this way have been individuals whose freedom or lives are under threat. A serious human rights deficit has been created.

Those who, in spite of all the obstacles placed in their way, do manage to find their way into European countries face further problems. Irregular migrants who lack the correct papers are termed "illegal" and in several countries are criminalised and often placed in detention. Certainly, states must manage their borders and decide who should be allowed to come and stay. However, there are agreed international standards which must be honoured. The right to seek asylum, followed by a fair adjudication procedure, constitutes a minimum.

It seems not to be fully understood or accepted that irregular migrants also have human rights. Everyone, whatever their legal status, has the right to primary and secondary education, emergency health care, reasonable working conditions and respect for their private and family life. Instead, the insecure legal status of irregular migrants makes them vulnerable to abuse, and when their rights are infringed by officials, employers or landlords, it is often difficult to claim those rights effectively.

The chapter on homophobia and transphobia addresses the problem that lesbians, gays, bisexuals and transgender persons (LGBT) have been the target of extremist violence for generations. Nazi Germany had some 100 000 people arrested because of their sexual orientation and more than 10 000 were sent to concentration camps. It is a bitter irony that some of the old Nazi "arguments" against homosexuals are still heard in public discourse in Europe today.

The real problem is not an individual's sexual orientation, but the reaction of others. Whatever the psychological roots, many people still react aggressively against homosexuals and transgender persons. Sadly, some religious leaders and teachers have also given direct or tacit support to discrimination and homophobia; this further delays the attitudinal change that is so necessary in many countries.

This is a human rights issue. There is a need for action against hate crime and hate speech; to protect freedom of expression, association and peaceful assembly (for example Gay Pride parades); to uphold the right to seek asylum; to ensure non-discrimination in employment, education and health care; as well to protect the right to respect for private and family life.

There are more than 80 million persons with disabilities in Europe. The chapter "Rights of people with disabilities" underlines that their rights are recognised in international human rights treaties, not least in an important UN convention adopted in 2006. However, these rights are still far from being realised, and moving to concrete implementation has been slow. A change of attitude is required – from a charity approach to rights-based action.

There has been some progress in recent years – partly as a consequence of the UN convention and the Council of Europe action plan adopted in 2006 – but current policies still focus largely on institutional care, medical rehabilitation and welfare benefits. Such policies build on the premise that persons with disabilities are victims, rather than subjects able and entitled to be active citizens.

The key message here is equal opportunities: society should be open to everyone. This requires pro-active measures to make society accessible to the needs of persons with disabilities. It should, for instance, be possible for children who are blind or deaf or using wheelchairs to attend the school of their choice.

People with intellectual disabilities are still stigmatised and marginalised. They are rarely consulted or listened to. A great number of people with such disabilities continue to be kept in old-fashioned and inhumane institutions. Efforts to provide housing and other services for them in community-based settings have met with obstacles, and have been delayed.

It is important that people with disabilities can participate in all decisions affecting their lives, both at an individual level and through their representative organisations. Words like "inclusion" and "empowerment" are relevant in this context. Persons with mental health and intellectual disabilities still face problems when they want to take decisions for themselves. Even in important matters, their legal capacity is restricted or ignored.

There is a great difference between taking away from people with disabilities their right to make decisions about their lives, and providing "access to support". The first approach views people with disabilities as objects of treatment, charity and fear. The second places them at the centre of decision-making, respecting their autonomy, and viewing them as subjects entitled to the full range of human rights.

The chapter "Gender rights" recognises that myriad issues might fall under this rubric, but focuses on three systemic injustices against women: their under-representation in political bodies, discrimination in the labour market, including pay-scales, and violations of their bodily integrity.

There are great variations across Europe regarding female representation in politics. Spain and the Nordic countries are ahead of the others. This shows that, where honest efforts have been made to encourage the nomination of more women, the gender balance can be improved. Despite this experience, the argument is still heard in some countries that women are not interested in political power and direct representation. The truth is rather that male politicians have little interest in challenging the status quo and prefer to protect their own positions of power.

The same tendency can be seen in the labour market: there is no excuse for the pay gaps between men and women in the same or very similar jobs. Moreover, women still face a glass ceiling when seeking promotion to higher positions, and job sectors dominated by women are typically paid less than those professions where men tend to predominate. Some of these stereotypical dividing lines are now being overturned – not least through advances in education – but there is a need to reassess the inherent importance of some professions, for example, in the health, childcare and education sectors.

In some parts of Europe, violence against women continues to be seen as solely a private matter. Such "privatisation" of responsibility should not be accepted. Domestic violence is today recognised as a human rights problem and authorities have a responsibility to take action to prevent and punish such abuses. Sexual assault must be seen as a very serious human rights violation. The fact that such abuses are largely hidden is not an excuse for ignoring their existence. On the contrary, it should be a political priority to protect women from this threat. The very first step should be to investigate why there are so few convictions in cases brought to court – and to remedy this failure.

Children make up a large section of the population and constitute the future of society – in more ways than one. However, their concerns are seldom given genuine priority in political terms. This is a key theme in the chapter "Rights of the child". Ministers responsible for children's affairs are often junior appointments and are kept outside the inner circle of power. Children's concerns are often seen as non-political and sometimes trivial.

My starting point is to stress the importance of implementing the UN Convention on the Rights of the Child, which all European countries have ratified. The convention has undoubtedly contributed to considerable progress for children, but problems remain. One relates to the principle that the best interests of children should be considered when decisions affecting children are to be taken. This, in turn, requires that the views of children themselves are voiced and that their views are taken seriously.

Sexual abuse of children is widespread and corporal punishment is still permitted in several European countries. I argue that such treatment violates a child's physical integrity, demonstrates disrespect for their dignity, and undermines their self-esteem. This sense of deeper damage was described by the Polish paediatrician Janusz Korczak who once wrote that "there are many terrible things in the world but the worst is when a child is afraid of his father, mother or teacher".

Children with disabilities have traditionally been put into institutions. This policy is changing, also in former communist countries. The process of deinstitutionalisation must continue, but it must be pursued with care and in the best interests of each child. The same goes for institutions established for children who are orphaned or have been rescued from dysfunctional families. Suitable alternatives must be developed to create a family-based environment for these children, so that the initial tragedy experienced is not further compounded.

I suggest a similar approach to be taken regarding minors who have committed offences. During my visits to various European countries, I have met juvenile inmates in prisons and detention centres. Many have suffered neglect and violent abuse within their own families and have received little support from society at large. Understanding the origins of violence and serious offending in children does not mean condoning such behaviour. Rather such understanding emphasises the importance of early intervention aimed at prevention and clarifies that mere punishment after the fact by way of imprisonment will never be the solution.

Child poverty has increased as a result of the economic crisis. About one quarter of the children in South-Eastern Europe and the former Soviet countries still live in absolute poverty and also in richer countries an increasing number if children grow up in destitute families.

This is a profound problem, affecting a great number of children, and with negative consequences far into the future.

The chapter "Social and economic rights" is wide-ranging, pointing to the large number of people who are poor and marginalised in Europe. They lack influence and opportunities for making their voices heard. They often feel ignored by political parties and elites and, in general, have little confidence in the authorities.

Studies have shown that people who are poor are the most frequent victims of crime, yet they have little confidence that the police will address these crimes. When they are the perpetrators of crime, or alleged perpetrators of crime, they are disadvantaged in the courts when compared to those who can afford skilful lawyers. The poor are over-represented in the prisons.

One category of people who have been victimised by the economic crisis is the elderly. Their needs and rights have often been ignored and sometimes totally denied. Older people often also suffer from a widespread perception that they are non-productive, and therefore somehow worthless in modern society.

Studies show that there is a clear link between human rights and the extent of equality in society. A more equal society is better for everyone, not only for the most vulnerable. Equal societies have less mental and other illnesses, and longer life expectancy than those marked by inequality. Facts about social problems and crime rates demonstrate that inequalities even, or especially, in the most affluent societies create widespread insecurity: everyone is harmed.

In this chapter I have also included articles about the right to health (in the context of HIV/Aids) and the right to housing, as well as about the threats to our economic and social rights which are linked to climate change. The daily lives of many are already affected by the consequences of global warming: desertification, droughts, flooding or cyclones. Basic human rights – such as the right to life, health, food, water, shelter or property – are jeopardised.

The chapter is brought to a close with an article about the importance of enforcing social rights. Only one third of states have shown their genuine commitment to implementing socio-economic rights by signing up to the collective complaints procedure which was introduced in 1995. It is important for trade unions, employers' groups and other civil society organisations to make this valuable mechanism, and the European Social Charter, better known within their communities.

It is not enough for parliaments and governments to ratify international treaties and enact laws for the protection of human rights. These treaties and laws must be given practical effect. Incompetence, corruption and political interference in the system of justice undermine the rule of law and deny rights – that we still have such problems in Europe is highlighted in the chapter "Police, courts and prisons".

Torture and cruel, inhuman and degrading treatment have not ended. There are reports of such violations of human rights in several countries, most often during arrest, transport to police stations or interrogation sessions. The more "sophisticated" methods such as electric shocks and water boarding are nowadays unusual; the pattern is rather one of brutal beating and kicking, combined with serious harassment and threats.

Unfortunately, European governments have also taken decisions to deport migrants to their home countries in spite of a real risk of detention and torture.

The good news is that Europe today is almost entirely a death-penalty-free zone. Russia has not yet abolished this punishment in law, but has consistently enforced a moratorium for more than a decade. The unfortunate exception to this trend is the only country on the continent which is not itself a member of the Council of Europe – Belarus – where death sentences have been passed and carried out, even recently.

Several cases of contract killings of independent journalists, human rights activists or other campaigners have not been properly investigated. While the gunmen in some cases have been identified, those behind the crimes have not been brought to justice. Doubts about the seriousness of these investigations have not been convincingly answered.

Many of the complaints to the European Court of Human Rights relate to excessively slow procedures and to failures of member states to enforce Court decisions. Domestic courts themselves are not functioning as they should in a great number of states, and former communist countries have also been slow to develop a truly independent and competent judiciary. Corruption and political interference are undermining public trust in the system.

In a number of countries, sentences are extremely severe even for minor crimes. Added to that, conditions in prisons and other places of detention are frequently inhuman and degrading. Almost all over Europe I found overcrowding; lack of mental health care; little attention paid to rehabilitation – and consequently, a high level of recidivism. Had it not been for the excellent work of the European Committee for the Prevention of Torture (CPT), the situation would have been even worse.

The so-called "war on terror" created a challenge for Europe. Strong and co-ordinated action was obviously needed to prevent and punish terrorist acts. As I propose in the chapter "Fighting terrorism while respecting human rights", the mistake after 11 September 2001 was not the determination to respond, but the choice of methods: terrorism must not be fought by illegal or "terrorist" methods.

While European governments stayed silent or even co-operated with this "war", more and more detailed and shocking information began to emerge about systematic torture, secret prisons, indefinite detention without trial, extra-judicial executions and other serious human rights violations – all in the name of countering terrorism.

This approach was a flagrant defiance of the core principles of justice on which human rights are built: protection against torture; presumption of innocence; no deprivation of liberty without due process; the right to a fair trial; the right of appeal; and the right to reparation. This policy has seriously harmed the international system for human rights protection; and has not ensured greater security for those supposedly being protected against attack.

I argue that European governments must initiate credible investigations into what went wrong. It is absolutely necessary that the facts about rendition flights and secret places of detention are discovered through proper democratic procedures. The Lithuanian Parliament conducted an investigation which found that the national security service had indeed co-operated with the CIA in preparing a place of detention for terrorist suspects. A prosecutor in Poland is investigating reports of torture in a secret CIA prison, but the authorities in Romania continue to deny that any CIA prisoners were kept on their soil.

An obvious obstacle to uncovering the facts, and therefore making plans to avoid such problems in the future, has been the tradition of confidential co-operation between the security services of different countries. European agencies are afraid that if they reveal what went on previously, they might lose the benefits derived from regular information exchange with their US and other intelligence colleagues. This fear has unfortunately meant that crucial issues about human rights violations have remained hidden.

One lesson from these sad experiences is the vital necessity of establishing effective democratic control over the activities of security agencies. These agencies must not be allowed to operate without oversight – nor, as they have sometimes been described, as a state within the state. The European approach to the "war on terror" exposed double standards but also ineptitude as well as confusion about what human rights standards require.

Another lesson from this period is the need to take care with surveillance technology which is now developing at breathtaking speed. Sophisticated equipment can help in the struggle against terrorism and organised crime, but also raises questions about the right to privacy. Everyone should be protected from intrusions into their private lives, and from the improper collection, storage, sharing and use of such data.

Addressing and establishing an honest account of violations of human rights committed in the past is absolutely crucial, and essential to subsequent efforts to build or re-build the rule of law, bring those responsible to justice, compensate the victims and take action to prevent the recurrence of such crimes. This is discussed in the chapter, "Gross violations in the past".

To establish and acknowledge the truth is also important in a longer-term perspective. Those killed were human beings, not numbers. Individuals who survived, as well as the children and grandchildren of the victims, have the right to know what happened, and to grieve with dignity. The opportunity to remember and commemorate must be ensured.

Coming to terms with history is always important, but it is particularly necessary when massive atrocities and gross human rights violations have taken place. Such crimes cannot be ignored without risking severe consequences. Prolonged impunity or a lack of acknowledgement, especially over several generations, creates bitterness among the victims and those who identify with them. This in turn poisons relations between people who were not even born when the events in question took place.

Historic accounts of mass atrocities have in several cases been extremely controversial and sometimes deeply injured national pride. Facts about what happened, real or distorted, have been made use of as part of a propaganda battle between states or political parties. The truth has been suspended and held hostage during such controversies.

One-sided interpretations or distortions of past events have led to discrimination against minorities, xenophobia and even the resurgence of conflict. New generations must not be blamed for what their forefathers did, or are thought to have done. What is important is an honest search for the truth, sober discussion based on facts, and an understanding that different versions of history exist and must be acknowledged. Only then can the right lessons be learned.

The purpose of journalism is not to please those who hold power or to be the mouthpiece of governments. Instead, I argue in the chapter "Media freedom and the right to demonstrate" that the media have an important role as a "public watchdog". The media's role is to inform the public about relevant developments in society, even when that information may embarrass.

In recent years leading investigative journalists have not only found their sources scared into silence, they themselves have fallen victim to the most brutal harassment and even murder: Hrant Dink in Turkey, Georgiy Gongadze in Ukraine, Elmar Huseynov in Azerbaijan and Anna Politkovskaya in Russia. No effort can be spared in apprehending and bringing to justice the actual killers, as well as those who ordered these appalling crimes.

Media culture is considerably affected by the attitude of the authorities towards journalists asking for information, especially on sensitive matters. The media have a legitimate interest in obtaining and disseminating information about government decisions and actions. The role of the media is vital in ensuring that citizens can exercise their right to know how their elected leaders act on their behalf, and to hold them properly to account. Open access to government information is a democratic principle of the first order.

Defamation is still criminalised in several parts of Europe. Laws are in place making it a criminal offence to say or publish true or false facts or opinions that offend a person or undermine his or her reputation. The mere existence of such laws could intimidate journalists and cause unfortunate self-censorship.

The way frequencies for television and radio are allocated is a test which some governments have failed. State agencies determining these allocations should work according to agreed and objective criteria and not discriminate against applicants whose sympathies they do not share.

Publicly funded media should operate in an impartial manner in the interest of the population as a whole, and as an essential counterweight to the business-driven entertainment media. The "public service" media – often financed from tax money or other common resources – should, of course, not be used as propaganda instruments for those in power. Independence and impartiality are of paramount importance and ought to be protected through agreed guidelines and appropriate procedures when appointing senior staff.

Journalists are not perfect and mistakes are made. Some of these mistakes may harm individuals. There is clearly a tension between ensuring that the media behave responsibly and ensuring that any regulatory controls to monitor their conduct are not exploited to influence content improperly. There have been encouraging results in countries where media representatives have developed codes of ethics and designed their own procedures to enforce professional standards, for instance, through press councils or press ombudsmen.

In such countries, media practices have matured, the right to reply has been enhanced and the public has benefited from better protection against all forms of abuse and media misuse. However, there are also examples where such efforts have not managed to protect the ethics of journalism – commercial interests have been too strong. This is a problem for democracy as a whole.

The final article in this chapter is about obstacles which some local or national authorities raise to prevent public rallies. Though freedom of assembly is well protected in international treaties and also in national legislation, I have received frequent reports about police interventions to hinder peaceful demonstrations.

Parliamentarians, local politicians and authorities, as well as ombudsmen at national and regional levels, can contribute much to ensuring a deeper respect for human rights principles and standards – many of them do but others do not. This is discussed in a chapter I have called "Actors for human rights".

Parliaments adopt laws, ratify international treaties, decide on national budgets, review key strategies and action plans and monitor the performance of the executive powers: they clearly have a major role in implementing human rights. In too many cases this potential is not fully used.

Provincial and local political bodies are also important for protecting and promoting human rights. In many countries, key decisions relating to social welfare, schooling and health care are at least partly taken at the local level. There is a risk that these actors may not be fully informed about the nature and implications of the international human rights agreements which the central governments are under an obligation to uphold. Decentralisation and the localisation of power should provide an opportunity not for diminishing, but rather for strengthening, the protection and promotion of rights.

All European governments now have institutions which receive complaints from the public and monitor issues of fairness and justice in society, including cases of abuse allegedly committed by public authorities. The names and mandates of these institutions differ, but they play an important role as quasi-judicial mechanisms protecting the rights of individuals. Unfortunately their budgets gave been reduced during the economic crisis – when their contributions would have been particularly needed.

Civil society non-governmental actors are crucial for developing a culture of respect for human rights. However, organisations working for human rights, especially those which also monitor and report on human rights violations, are not always well regarded by the authorities. Indeed, some have been persecuted. This has led to initiatives to protect such "human rights defenders".

When the United Nations declaration for their protection was adopted in 1998, the then UN Secretary-General, Kofi Annan, stated the obvious but important truth: "When the rights of human rights defenders are violated, all our rights are put in jeopardy, and all of us are made less safe".

Andrei Sakharov was one of the most important human rights defenders of our time. Even when he was exiled and isolated in an apartment in the closed city of Gorky, he continued to write appeals for prisoners of conscience in the Soviet Union and other countries of the world. He gave Russians and others a strong moral message and leadership, the consequences of which continue to be felt today.

Informed human rights discourse does not only focus on whether a government respects the standards but also on what measures it takes to ensure that rights are protected and fulfilled. There should be a systematic, well-planned approach; this is the key message in the chapter "Systematic measures for human rights implementation".

Progress cannot always be immediate and the fulfilment of many rights also depends on human and financial resources. However, there is a growing realisation that human rights can only be ensured through a consistent policy of "institution building" and through programmes such as developing an independent and competent judiciary, training a professional police force that upholds and respects the law, regularly reviewing legislation and encouraging active independent non-governmental groups to ensure routine scrutiny of those programmes. In other words, a systematic, comprehensive and well-planned methodology is required.

It is important that each country develop a national plan for the genuine implementation of human rights. Such systematic planning ought to be based on consultation which allows non-governmental groups and activists to take part, and includes a focus on efforts at regional and municipal levels.

The first step is to undertake a baseline study to identify existing problems. Domestic non-governmental groups, ombudsmen and international bodies can usually provide information for such a study, as can the media and a wide range of expert authorities. Such data must be collated and analysed in a structured manner for the purpose of planning.

The second step is to draw up an action plan or strategy where the main human rights concerns are identified and appropriate measures to address these problems are put in place.

Thereafter come the crucial stages of implementation and evaluation.

One key aspect of the action plan should be to promote knowledge of human rights. Everyone is entitled to know their rights and how to claim them. Such knowledge is one of the main conditions for the realisation of human rights. However, human rights education in schools is still inadequate in most countries, at all levels. More also needs to be done to ensure that professional groups such as the police, judges, teachers, social workers and journalists obtain a solid education and professional training in human rights. A deeply embedded culture of human rights is needed to effectively operationalise the oft-stated political rhetoric – ensuring that human rights are truly protected and promoted as they must be.

The last chapter, "International action", emphasises that governments must uphold the values enshrined in international human rights treaties in their external relations as well. The United Nations Charter makes clear that the protection of human rights is not only a national but also an international concern and responsibility. This principle has been further confirmed in international and regional human rights treaties, and the European Convention on Human Rights includes the option of bringing inter-state complaints.

There is a compelling, principled argument for acting on human rights concerns in countries beyond one's own. People who are oppressed and silenced – and therefore unable to defend their rights – should be able to count on the solidarity of those in societies other than their own to help protect them. I have met individuals in such situations who have testified to the enormous importance of knowing that people or authorities in other countries are concerned about their fate and will take action on their behalf.

However, for governments to raise human rights issues in international fora, or bilaterally, is often seen as controversial and even provocative. This is partly because the concept of human rights has a moral dimension: those who violate the standards are seen not only as having made a mistake, but as being responsible for unacceptable, unethical acts.

This is why it is so important that governments are sincere and consistent when they criticise others.

It is necessary to record where more needs to be done, and I have tried to do this in the separate articles in this volume. My primary purpose is to suggest remedies for the shortcomings that exist in Europe today, and to put forward practical recommendations which I hope will provoke constructive discussion.

In the course of my work I have met many people – some themselves victims of inhuman violations, or their families – for whom human rights represent still a hope. For them the Universal Declaration and the European Convention have a significant meaning.

The awareness has spread. I have met civil society activists, ombudsmen, journalists, lawyers, teachers, social workers and other professionals who are deeply committed to the betterment of this world and who see human rights standards as a key instrument in this struggle.

Also, I have met leading politicians and government officials who do take their human rights obligations seriously, sometimes under difficult political pressure.

The human rights vision articulated in the ashes of the Second World War is as relevant as ever. There has been great progress but also disappointing setbacks. Human rights express ideals – but these are not unrealistic. They establish core values and standards that are essential to a peaceful, decent and just society in Europe and the world today.

Thomas Hammarberg
Strasbourg, 1 April 2011

Acknowledgements

Maggie Beirne and Margo Picken helped me put the articles in this volume into shape. Their advice on both substance and style was extremely valuable and I am grateful to them both.

Support, as usual, was given by my two closest colleagues at the Commissioner's Office: Isil Gachet and Sandra Ferreira. Without their help much less would have been achieved.

Chapter 1: Xenophobia and identity

Europe today is not free from racism, xenophobia, Islamophobia, anti-Semitism, homophobia, transphobia and other phobias directed against others. Minorities are made targets of hate speech, violence and systematic discrimination. The response from mainstream political parties and other majority representatives has often been meek and confused. They have left the political initiative to extremists and lent an unfortunate "legitimacy" to their positions. This is dangerous.

Photo © Shutterstock.

Respecting the other

Europe today is not free from racism, xenophobia, Islamophobia, anti-Gypsyism, anti-Semitism, homophobia, transphobia and other phobias directed against others. Intolerance has been exacerbated by and found fertile ground in the current global economic crisis. Extremist groups and parties have become increasingly active and threatening, and have succeeded in recruiting supporters from amongst the disaffected, not least amongst young unemployed men.

Minorities are made the targets of hate speech, violence and systematic discrimination. The response from mainstream political parties and other majority community representatives has often been meek and confused. In this way, they have left the political initiative to extremists, and lent an unfortunate "legitimacy" to the claims they make.

This is dangerous. It is crucial to take a clear stand against such hatred and discrimination. However, the root causes of the fear and confusion which extremists manage to exploit must also be analysed and addressed.

The threat of growing unemployment in many European countries is certainly a major factor. Increased migration across countries and borders, as well as the electronic revolution, has contributed to feelings of insecurity among many. The consequences of "globalisation" are difficult to fathom. More and more people appear to feel the need to define their own identity – sometimes aggressively – in a world which is changing so rapidly.

President Sarkozy of France initiated a country-wide debate on the issue of national identity. There have also been calls for national "identity" to be defined in other European countries. Such discussions can of course be helpful – if they avoid promoting one single identity to the exclusion of all others. A definitional process which only manages to define who is included –and, by extension, leaves others to be excluded – is problematic.

The widely respected historian Tony Judt contributed to this discussion in his *The Memory Chalet*:

> *Being "Danish" or "Italian", "American" or "European" won't just be an identity; it would be a rebuff and a reproof to those whom it excludes. The state, far from disappearing, may be about to come into its own: the privileges of citizenship, the protections of cardholding residency rights, will be wielded as political trumps. Intolerant demagogues in established democracies will demand "tests" – of knowledge, of language, of attitude – to determine whether desperate newcomers are deserving of British or Dutch or French "identity". They are already doing so. In this brave new century we shall miss the tolerant, the marginals: the edge people…*

Despite its sad history of discrimination and oppression of minorities and vulnerable groups, Europe has always been and benefited from being an inherently pluralist, multifaceted continent. Our ability to continue to interact positively with one another will surely influence Europe's future. Multiculturalism is a value which must be actively protected.

In this discussion we should avoid equating "multiculturalism" with segregation or the creation of parallel communities without interrelationship. Such definitions appear to be introduced with the purpose of promoting a policy of assimilation – one identity.

I would encourage those taking part in the soul-searching talks on national identity to read (or re-read) a particularly relevant book: Amartya Sen's *Identity and violence*.

Professor Sen observes that the world is increasingly seen as a global federation of religions or civilisations. In this scenario, we ignore all the many other ways in which individuals define themselves. He questions the presumption that people can be categorised into a single overarching system of partitioning.

He is of course right. In reality, we each belong to a number of different categories depending not only on our ethnicity, nationality or faith, but also on our local roots, gender, sexual orientation, parenthood, language, education, profession, social class, politics, age-group, state of health, leisure interests, organisational membership and many other distinctive attributes.

The relative importance of belonging to any one particular group or having any one particular identity can only be determined by the individual him or herself. Though nationality or religion could, for example, be of utmost importance to some, this is not the case for many others.

We know from experience that the imposition by the state or other authorities of one allegedly unique identity – such as that of a particular civilisation or a particular religion – creates a basis for, and can actively encourage, sectarian confrontation.

Sen stresses the risk that a fostered sense of identity within only one group can be manipulated into a powerful weapon with which to brutalise another. Solidarity within any particular group can, and often does, feed discord between groups.

What concrete challenges does respect for others hold for national human rights policies?

- states should actively promote fundamental principles of pluralism, tolerance and broad-mindedness on which democracy itself is based;
- guided by these key values, states should show greater receptiveness to diversity in their own societies and take appropriate measures to allow, and indeed encourage, members of existing minority groups to determine and express their own identities;
- states should create consultative mechanisms, at national, regional and local levels. These mechanisms would initiate and maintain an institutionalised, open, sincere and continuous dialogue with representatives of all non-dominant groups, such as minorities. These consultative bodies should have a clear legal status and be inclusive and representative;
- the defence of social rights is absolutely crucial in order to avoid widening gaps, growing inequalities and further injustice.

Minorities suffer disproportionally as a result of societal inequalities and tend, moreover, to be made into scapegoats when other sections of the population feel alienated or disillusioned;

- practical measures are needed to address discrimination (both direct and indirect) in public and private employment policies. More efforts should be made to recruit minority representatives into key professions like teaching and policing, as well as into political leadership positions;
- greater priority should be given to the role the school system can play in developing tolerance and communal accord. Primary and secondary education should not be segregated, but inclusive. Respect for others should be part of the curriculum, as required by the United Nations Convention on the Rights of the Child;
- human rights should be the cornerstone of policies on migration;
- hate speech and discrimination of all kinds should stop. The marginalisation of Roma deserves special attention (see separate chapter devoted to this particular theme). The problems faced by the Roma remain scandalous and indicate that European governments are not seriously promoting human rights for everyone. An official acknowledgement and apology for past violations would be a good place to start;
- comprehensive anti-discrimination legislation should be adopted and monitoring bodies established to guarantee equality for all;
- positive achievements in promoting equality should be made known. Our dependence on one another, including migrants, needs highlighting.

Different groups should be allowed to fully integrate into society and, over time, demonstrate what they and their culture have to contribute to the diversity of the whole. Curiosity and open-mindedness, instead of fear and suspicion, should be encouraged – alongside a positive and dynamic vision of the future.

Islamophobia

The Swiss referendum banning the building of minarets was no exception: opinion polls in several European countries reflect fear, suspicion and negative opinions of Muslims and Islamic culture. Islamophobic prejudices tend to be combined with racist attitudes – directed not least against people originating from Turkey, Arab countries and South Asia.

Muslims in Europe suffer harassment in their daily life. I have heard reports about such abuses during my missions in all parts of the continent. Non-governmental organisations have described hate crimes targeting Muslims – ranging from verbal threats to physical attacks on people or property.

Islamophobia is certainly not a new phenomenon in Europe. One indication has been the repeated difficulty for many Muslim communities to obtain permission to build a mosque.

However, it is clear that the US-inspired "war on terror" worsened the situation considerably.

The global fight against terrorism generated a style of political discourse which is shaded by racism and xenophobia, including anti-Muslim sentiments. In addition, police actions – including repeated ID controls and intrusive searches – have targeted Muslims or people who look as if they originated from countries with large Muslim populations.

This, in turn, has been interpreted by some right-wing extremists as encouragement to their xenophobic propaganda while Muslims have felt further victimised. This consequence of the anti-terrorism policy needs to be corrected as a matter of priority.

Recent elections in several European countries have seen extremist political parties gaining ground after aggressively Islamophobic campaigns. Even more worrying is the inertia or confusion which seems to have befallen the established democratic parties in this situation.

Compromises are made which tend to give an air of legitimacy to crude prejudices and open xenophobia.

When the German President Christian Wulff in a speech in October 2010 confirmed the obvious, that Islam – like Christianity and Judaism – is part of the national context, this was seen as controversial.

At the same time a survey initiated by Friedrich Ebert Stiftung showed that 58% of the German population agreed that "religious practices for Muslims in their country should be seriously limited". This rejection of the freedom of religion for Muslims is a worrying sign.

Interestingly, there were huge regional differences in the responses to this survey. In the eastern parts of the country – with a much smaller Muslim population – support for the statement was as high as 76%. Distance and ignorance tend to increase suspicions.

This appears to be a general phenomenon: lack of knowledge feeds prejudices. Political leaders have on the whole failed to counter Islamophobic stereotypes. Of course, this became more difficult after the terrorist attacks in New York, Madrid, London, Amsterdam and also Beslan and Moscow. However, the emotions caused by these horrible crimes called for systematic efforts to establish a distinction between the evil-doers and the overwhelming majority of Muslims. These efforts were rarely made.

Neither has sufficient priority been given to analysing what makes some people listen to hateful propaganda against Muslims. Part of the explanation appears to be the same ignorance, fear and frustration which have caused bigotry against Roma and immigrants in general. We have learnt that minorities are sometimes turned into scapegoats by people who feel alienated and ignored by those in power. It is important to seek fuller explanations.

Islam is of course already part of European culture. Muslims on the continent – including the approximately 1.6 million Muslims in the United Kingdom, 3.8 million in Germany, 5 million in France and 15-20 million in Russia – contribute to our economies and societies. They belong. Most of them are in fact born in these countries, the majority are not particularly religious and very few can be characterised as Islamists.

The diverse groups of Muslims are now blamed by politicians in some countries for not "assimilating". However, integration is a two-way process based on mutual understanding. Anti-Muslim bigotry has in fact become a major obstacle to respectful relationships. Indeed, the Islamophobic atmosphere has probably been a factor enabling extremists in some cases to recruit young and embittered individuals who lack a sense of belonging.

A minimum is that governments seek ways to stem outright discrimination. Several surveys have demonstrated that many Muslims in Europe face unfair treatment in employment, education and housing in European Union countries. Young Muslims, in particular, face obstacles in social advancement:

- discrimination testing in the United Kingdom and France has shown that persons with Muslim names or originating from countries with a Muslim majority are much less likely to be invited for a job interview. The unemployment rate among Muslims in several EU countries is higher than for people of other religions;
- available statistics also indicate that Muslims are disadvantaged in the education system; their school performance is weaker than that of other groups. This may partly be caused by other factors than those related to religion – for instance, unemployment, poverty, language and immigration status – but it clearly contributes to a vicious circle of social marginalisation;
- housing is another problem. Migrants, including those from predominantly Muslim countries, generally have poorer and more insecure habitat conditions than others. This, in turn, affects education and employment possibilities.

Discrimination also exists in some European countries outside the EU. I was reminded of this when I visited a mosque in Kiev which was not allowed to build a minaret because people in the neighbourhood might react negatively.

The European Commission against Racism and Intolerance (ECRI) has regretted in its reports the inaccurate portrayal of Islam on the basis of hostile stereotyping, which makes this religion seem like a threat. Laws against discrimination and procedures for complaints now exist in most countries. However, it is not always easy for individuals in minority groups to claim their rights in cases of discrimination. There is a need for support initiatives.

One such project is the co-operation in the United Kingdom between the London Metropolitan Police Service and non-governmental groups, including the Forum against Islamophobia and Racism (FAIR). This initiative seeks to combat crimes against Muslims, to give assistance to victims and to build police capacity to monitor Islamophobia.

In order to tackle the prejudices on a broader front, education systems should provide factual knowledge about Islam (and other religions). The importance of teaching about the religions of "the others" has been stressed repeatedly during the seminars the Council of Europe organised with the participation of religious leaders.

The burqa and privacy

Prohibition of the burqa and the niqab will not liberate oppressed women, but might instead lead to their further exclusion and alienation in European societies. A general ban on such attire constitutes an ill-advised invasion of individual privacy and, depending on its terms, also raises serious questions about whether such legislation is compatible with the European Convention on Human Rights.

Two rights in the Convention are particularly relevant to this debate about clothing. One is the right to respect for one's private life and personal identity (Article 8). The other is the freedom to manifest one's religion or belief "in worship, teaching, practice and observance" (Article 9).

Both Convention articles specify that these rights can only be subject to such limitations as are prescribed by law and are necessary in a democratic society in the interests of public safety, for the protection of public order, health or morals, or for the protection of the rights and freedoms of others.

Those who have argued for a general ban of the burqa and the niqab have not managed to show that these garments in any way undermine democracy, public safety, order or morals. The fact that a very small number of women wear such clothing has made such proposals even less convincing.

Nor has it been possible to prove that women wearing this attire are victims of more gender repression than others. Those interviewed in the media have presented a diversity of religious, political and personal arguments for their decision to dress as they do. There may of course be cases where women are under undue pressure to dress in a certain way – but it has not been shown that a ban would be welcomed by them.

There is of course no doubt that the status of women is an acute problem – and that this problem may be particularly true in relation to some religious communities. This needs to be discussed, but prohibiting the supposed symptoms – such as clothing – is not the way to do it. Dress, after all, may not reflect specific religious beliefs, but the exercise of broader cultural expression.

It is right and proper to react strongly against any regime ruling that women must wear these garments. This is in clear contravention of the Convention articles cited above, and is unacceptable, but it is not remedied by banning the same clothing in other countries.

The consequences of decisions in this area must be assessed. For instance, the suggestion that women dressed in a burqa or niqab be banned from public institutions like hospitals or government offices may result in these women avoiding such places entirely, and that is clearly wrong.

It is unfortunate that in Europe, public discussion of female dress, and the implications of certain attire for the subjugation of women, has almost exclusively focused on what is perceived as Muslim dress. The impression has been given that one particular religion is being targeted. Moreover, some arguments have been clearly Islamophobic in tenor and this has certainly not built bridges nor encouraged dialogue.

Indeed, one consequence of this xenophobia appears to be that the wearing of full cover dress has increasingly become a means of protesting against intolerance in our societies. An insensitive discussion about banning certain attire seems merely to have provoked a backlash and a polarisation in attitudes.

In general, states should avoid legislating on dress, other than in the narrow circumstances set forth in the Convention. It is, however, legitimate to regulate that those who represent the state, for instance police officers, do so in an appropriate way. In some instances, this may require complete neutrality as between different political and religious insignia; in other instances, a multi-ethnic and diverse society may want to cherish and reflect its diversity in the dress of its agents.

Obviously, full-face coverage may be problematic in some occupations and situations. There are particular situations where there are compelling community interests that make it necessary for individuals to show themselves for the sake of safety or in order to offer the possibility of necessary identification. This is not controversial and, in fact, there are no reports of serious problems in this regard in relation to the few women who normally wear a burqa or a niqab.

A related problem arose in discussion in Sweden. A jobless Muslim man lost his subsidy from a state agency for employment support because he had refused to shake the hand of a female employer when turning up for a job interview. He had claimed that his action was grounded in his religious faith.

A court ruled later, after a submission from the ombudsman against discrimination, that the agency decision was discriminatory and that the man should be compensated. Though this is in line with human rights standards, it was not readily accepted by the general public and a controversial public debate ensued.

It is likely that issues of this kind will surface increasingly in the coming years and it is healthy that they should be openly discussed – as long as Islamophobic tendencies are avoided. However, such debates should be broadened to include the promotion of greater understanding of different religions, cultures and customs. Pluralism and multiculturalism are essential European values, and should remain so.

This in turn may require more discussion of the meaning of respect. In the debates about the allegedly anti-Muslim cartoons published in Denmark in 2005, it was repeatedly stated that there was a contradiction between demonstrating respect for believers whilst also protecting freedom of expression as stipulated in Article 10 of the European Convention.

The Strasbourg Court analysed this dilemma in the famous case of *Otto-Preminger-Institute v. Austria* in which it stated that "those who choose to exercise the freedom to manifest their religion ... cannot reasonably expect to be exempt from all criticism. They must tolerate and accept the denial by others of their religious beliefs and even the propagation by others of doctrines hostile to their faith".[1]

In the same judgment the Court stated that consideration should be given to the risk that the right of religious believers – like anyone else – to have their views respected may be violated by provocative portrayals of objects of religious significance. The Court concluded that "such portrayals can be regarded as malicious violation of the spirit of tolerance, which must also be a feature of democratic society".

The political challenge for Europe is to promote diversity and respect for the beliefs of others whilst at the same time protecting freedom of speech and expression. If the wearing of a full-face veil is understood as an expression of a certain opinion, we are in fact talking here about the possible conflict between similar or identical rights – though seen from two entirely different angles.

---

1. *Otto-Preminger-Institut v. Austria,* judgment of 20 September 1994.

In Europe, we seek to uphold traditions of tolerance and democracy. Where conflicts of rights between individuals and groups arise, it should not be seen in negative terms, but rather as an opportunity to celebrate that rich diversity and to seek solutions which respect the rights of all involved.

A prohibition of the burqa and the niqab would in my opinion be as unfortunate as it would have been to criminalise the Danish cartoons. Such banning is alien to European values. Instead, we should promote multicultural dialogue and respect for human rights.

Discriminatory stop and search

Members of minorities are stopped by the police, asked for identity papers, questioned and searched more than others. They are victims of "ethnic profiling", a form of discrimination which is widespread in today's Europe. Such measures clash with human rights standards. Such action also tends to be counterproductive as it discourages people from co-operating with police efforts to detect real crime.

A survey conducted by the EU Agency for Fundamental Rights (FRA) in 2009 indicates that minority groups feel that they are targeted by the police when selecting persons to stop and search. Not surprisingly, many members of minority groups see this behaviour as a sign that they are suspected and unwelcome in society at large.

The report – based on interviews in 14 European countries – showed that one out of every four Muslim respondents had been stopped by the police during the past year and that 40% of them believed that this was because of their immigrant or minority status. Many had been stopped more than once during the previous year; the average was three times.[2]

---

2. www.fra.europa.eu/eu-midis. Interviews were carried out in Austria, Belgium, Bulgaria, Denmark, Germany, Finland, France, Italy, Luxembourg, Malta, Slovenia, Spain, Sweden and the Netherlands.

Stop-and-search is an increasingly serious problem in several European countries since the acts of terror of 11 September 2001. The European Court of Human Rights has dealt with a case concerning the United Kingdom where anti-terrorism legislation confers powers on the police to stop and search individuals without reasonable suspicion.[3] In January 2010, the Court found a violation of Article 8 (right to respect for one's private life) of the Convention. It considered that the powers of stop and search under UK domestic law were neither sufficiently circumscribed nor subject to adequate legal safeguards against abuse.

Ethnic or religious profiling is all too prevalent across Europe. The Open Society Justice Initiative has analysed ethnic profiling in the European Union and found a pervasive use of ethnic and religious stereotypes by law enforcement agencies. Wrong in and of itself, such ethnic profiling also harms real efforts to combat crime and terrorism.[4]

The report established that ethnic profiling is counterproductive. Such practices have resulted in criminals who do not fit the established profile being overlooked and going free. Ethnic profiling also subverts the rule of law by undermining confidence in the fairness of the police; stigmatises entire communities; and alienates many of the very people who could assist the police reduce crime and prevent terrorism. Profiling based on individual behaviour and other such alternatives are to be recommended.

There should be an objective reason why a certain individual is stopped and searched – a reasonable and individualised suspicion of criminal activity. The colour of your skin, your dress or visible religious attributes do not constitute objective reasons.

In 2007 the European Commission against Racism and Intolerance (ECRI) published a highly relevant recommendation on "Combating

---

3. *Gillan and Quinton v. the United Kingdom* (Application No. 4158/05). Hearing held on 12 May 2009, judgment of 12 January 2010.
4. "Ethnic profiling in the European Union: pervasive, ineffective and discriminatory", OSI, May 2009.

racism and racial discrimination in policing".[5] It encourages governments to clearly define and prohibit racial profiling by law. Governments should also introduce a standard of reasonable suspicion to ensure that control, surveillance or investigation activities are carried out only when the suspicion is founded on objective criteria.

Furthermore, ECRI emphasises the importance of training the police on the proper application of the standard of "reasonable suspicion". Police control, surveillance and investigation activities should be monitored to assist in ensuring good practice. This monitoring must include the collection of data broken down on grounds such as national or ethnic origin, language, religion and nationality.

These measures will be more effective if part of a comprehensive approach which should include clear legislation; processes of accountability; effective complaints mechanisms; and active support for rights-based procedures from the senior police leadership.

Such pro-active initiatives are needed in several countries. Indeed, the purpose of another Open Society Justice Initiative project, carried out in 2005, was not only to expose shortcomings in practice, but also to improve relations between the police and minorities through more accountable and effective use of police powers. Positive steps were reported on police training and improved supervision and monitoring of ID checks, as well as stop and searches. These examples can serve as models for others.[6]

The project also assessed methods used during stops and identity checks and whether they disproportionately affected minority communities. The data gathered demonstrated two points. First, that the police were engaged in ethnic profiling – minorities were more likely to be stopped; and, second, that members of minorities were not found to have offended more than the majority population.

---
5. ECRI General Policy Recommendation No. 11, adopted 29 June 2007.
6. "Addressing ethnic profiling by police. A report on the strategies for effective police stop and search project", AGIS 2006 and Open Society Institute, www.justiceinitiative.org.

This was an important finding since those who have defended ethnic or religious profiling have often claimed that minority groups are more likely to be involved in crime than others and therefore increased police intervention was justified.

It is clear that a disproportionate use of stop-and-search powers has a detrimental and negative impact on the community at large. All groups in society need to have confidence in and trust the police. This need is even greater amongst groups which are the targets of xenophobic action or hate crimes. A lack of trust is fostered if minorities feel that they are targeted by the police.

If the police are to secure the community confidence and co-operation they need for their work in tackling crime and terrorism, they must realise they have a vested interest in promoting equality and combating racial discrimination. The police must be trained to work in a diverse environment, and be supported to recruit staff from minority communities. Police often constitute the first line of ensuring respect for human rights, and they need to become active protectors of human rights.

Hate crimes

Hate crimes are a daily reality throughout Europe. Reports show that people suffer violence because they are black, Jewish, Roma or Muslim, or because of their sexual orientation or gender identity. Individuals have been physically attacked in the street, had their windows broken or homes set on fire. Government authorities have a responsibility to put an end to these shameful and serious crimes.

The OSCE's Office for Democratic Institutions and Human Rights (ODIHR), and the non-governmental organisation Human Rights First, have both published surveys on violent acts motivated by intolerance and hatred. The European Commission against Racism and Intolerance (ECRI) presents facts and analysis about such crimes in its country reports with recommendations on how to counter them. All these documents demonstrate the danger of allowing prejudice against others to take root and spread. Unfortunately, the move from hate speech to hate crime is easily made.

One example is Ukraine. In my 2007 assessment report on the human rights situation there, I referred to racist attacks, to violence against Roma people and to a worrying trend of active anti-Semitic movements. Racist criminals were usually arrested when found, but often quickly released by the police, who had reportedly taken bribes. In other cases, the attacks were judged not to be xenophobic, but merely the criminal actions of hooligans, and were therefore given a more lenient response.

There are similar violent hate crimes in a number of other countries. In the Russian Federation, extreme right-wing groups have committed a series of hate crimes, in some cases even murders, against members of ethnic, religious and national minorities. In recent years, people from the Caucasus, not least Chechens, have been targeted. The law is clear and sees such racist and anti-Semitic motives as an aggravating factor, but this is not always followed through in the judicial process. The problem remains even after the government has spoken out against racist and anti-Semitic violence.

In Italy, Roma people have been at the receiving end of violence in recent years. Physical attacks and arson have often followed bigoted speeches by some politicians, and xenophobic reporting in some media outlets. The Roma community as a whole has been made a scapegoat for crimes committed by only a few, but politicians have demonstrated little moral leadership in trying to stem this wave of anti-Gypsyism.[7]

Across Europe, a mix of Islamophobia and racism has also been directed against immigrant Muslims or their descendants. This has increased considerably since 11 September 2001 and subsequent

---

7. Typically, no term describing negative attitudes towards Roma – similar to, for instance, anti-Semitism in relation to Jews – has been widely accepted. One problem is that local terms for Roma themselves have differed and that some of them have been clearly derogative in themselves. "Anti-Ziganism" and "anti-Gypsyism" have been the more common terms and the Council of Europe, after consultation with Roma representatives, has decided to use the latter term.

government responses to terrorism. Muslims have been attacked and mosques vandalised or burnt in a number of countries. In the United Kingdom no less than 11 mosques were vandalised after the London terrorist bombings on 7 July 2005; in France, five mosques were set alight or damaged with explosives.

Gay Pride events have been attacked in several European cities, including Bucharest, Budapest and Moscow. In Riga, extremists hurled faeces and eggs at gay activists and their supporters as they were leaving a church service. Some years ago a Swedish hockey player was stabbed to death in Vasteras after he had made known that he was homosexual. In Oporto, Portugal, a group of boys killed a homeless Brazilian transgender woman and left the body in a water-filled pit. These incidents are only the tip of an iceberg.

Some of these assaults have been committed by bigoted individuals, but many bear the imprints of neo-Nazi groups or other organised, extremist gangs who tend to be simultaneously racist, anti-Semitic, anti-Roma, anti-Muslim, anti-Arab and homophobic. Such gangs often also target foreigners and persons with disabilities.

The seriousness of such crimes, and the duty of governments to take action to stop them, has been underlined by the European Court of Human Rights. In one judgment (*Nachova and Others v. Bulgaria*, 6 July 2005), the Court underlined the importance of effective investigation in cases of racially motivated violence:

> *Racial violence is a particular affront to human dignity and, in view of its perilous consequences, requires from the authorities special vigilance and a vigorous reaction. It is for this reason that the authorities must use all available means to combat racism and racist violence, thereby reinforcing democracy's vision of a society in which diversity is not perceived as a threat but as a source of enrichment.*

In the same judgment, the Court stressed the duty of governments to take all reasonable steps to unmask any racist motive and to establish whether ethnic hatred or prejudice played a role.

What steps can be taken to prevent and react to cases of hate crime?

- governments should establish co-operative relations with minority communities and invite proposals on measures to be taken to prevent and act upon hate incidents that have taken place. Such measures will build confidence within the community and reassure citizens that reports of hate crimes are taken seriously. This, in turn, will increase reporting hate crime to the authorities;
- anti-discrimination bodies should be established with a broad mandate and the authority to address hate violence through monitoring, reporting and assistance to victims;
- steps should be taken to monitor and collect data on bias-motivated crimes and the circumstances giving rise to them. There is an information vacuum in several countries due to a lack of adequate and disaggregated official data, which must be remedied. The European Union Monitoring Centre on Racism and Xenophobia – a forerunner of the Agency for Fundamental Rights – reported in 2006 that, among European Union countries, only Finland and the United Kingdom had what could be considered "comprehensive" data collection systems on racist crime;
- access to complaints procedures needs to be improved for individual victims and for groups acting on their behalf. Victims are often reluctant to – or fearful of – making a direct complaint to the authorities, so many assaults go unreported. Extra effort is therefore needed to reach out to representative groups to ensure effective reporting of hate crime;
- the judicial response to hate crime must be severe. In several countries, the bias motivation is indeed seen in law as an aggravating factor, and this in turn increases the penalty available to the courts. In others, hate crimes are defined as distinct crimes requiring severe sentencing. But there are still member states which lack explicit penalties. In some the definition of hate crime is limited to some victim groups only. Violence against persons because of their sexual orientation or disability is, for example, not included in the hate-crime legislation of several countries;

- existing hate-crime laws must be enforced in order to increase their deterrent effect. The procedures should be well documented and made public.

There is also a need to invest more energy in prevention – to inform and educate in order to address the ignorance and fear which often underlies xenophobia and intolerance. The Strasbourg Court has emphasised the special responsibility teachers have in the promotion of tolerance throughout society. The Council of Europe has produced excellent teaching material (see in particular the campaign "All Equal – All Different"). Modern school curricula in member states should include education about other religions and cultures to counter intolerance. The media also have a responsibility not to become a vehicle for the dissemination of hate speech or the promotion of violence.

Sadly, some politicians use their platforms to foster and exploit prejudice. They neither stand up for human rights, nor encourage a better understanding of and respect for those in society who are different. They thereby "legitimise" intolerance which in turn allows for hate speech and even hate crime. Such politicians do not deserve to be re-elected.

Minority languages

Language rights have become a contentious issue in several European countries, and also between neighbouring states. As some governments take steps to strengthen the standing of the official language(s), national minorities are concerned that their linguistic rights are being undermined.

The spelling of names in passports, the naming of streets and other places, the language used in schools, language requirements when communicating with the authorities and possibilities to establish minority media are issues minority representatives are raising throughout Europe.

The redrawing of the political map in Europe over the past 20 years has made these problems more acute. Nationalistic tendencies, combined with confusion and insecurity about "national identity", also appear to have encouraged extremists to promote a xenophobic discourse, often targeted against minorities.

This requires mature political leadership. Language is essential for social organisation and even the very functioning of the state. However, language is also a central part of an individual's identity, which may have a particular importance for members of minorities.

Language disputes have arisen in situations where minority groups are present in such large numbers, or have such strong political representation that the state language is perceived to be under threat. An argument made for the controversial 2009 amendments to the Law on State Language in Slovakia was the importance of ensuring that Slovak-only speakers would be able to understand all official communications, even when residing in areas primarily populated by the Hungarian minority.

The Venice Commission was asked to give an opinion on the amendments and stated that the protection and promotion of the state language is a legitimate concern. However, this must be balanced against the protection and promotion of the linguistic rights of persons belonging to national minorities. The commission suggested that "the obligation to use the official language should be confined to genuine cases of public order needs and bear a reasonable relation of proportionality".[8]

Disputes over language are not a new phenomenon and standards have been developed in a number of international and European human rights treaties about how best to resolve such disputes:

- the Framework Convention for the Protection of National Minorities (FCNM) is a Council of Europe treaty which, *inter alia*, protects and promotes the language rights of persons belonging to national minorities. It has a monitoring body

---

8. Opinion adopted by the Venice Commission, 15-16 October 2010.

to assist its implementation by state parties – the Advisory Committee;

- the European Charter for Regional or Minority Languages protects and promotes languages as a threatened element of Europe's cultural heritage. Implementation is monitored by the Committee of Experts;

- these standards are complemented by the European Convention on Human Rights, which prohibits discrimination on grounds of, for instance, language (Article 14). The case law of the European Court of Human Rights in Strasbourg is also highly relevant;

- the OSCE has also developed standards which are promoted by its High Commissioner on National Minorities. One important document is the Oslo Recommendations regarding the Linguistic Rights of National Minorities (with an explanatory note);

- the United Nations International Covenant on Civil and Political Rights states that persons belonging to minorities shall not be denied the right, in community with other members of their group, to use their own language. Less binding but highly relevant is the UN Declaration on the Rights of Persons Belonging to National or Ethnic, Religious and Linguistic Minorities.

These treaties and recommendations state key principles and define governments' obligations. As the nature of the problem differs greatly from one country to another, the standards must be interpreted to meet the intended purpose and achieve the appropriate balance. There has to be a "margin of appreciation" – to use the language of the Strasbourg Court – when applying them. This margin should, however, not be used to avoid the obligation to respect the human rights of persons belonging to minorities.

The conclusions of the various international monitoring bodies and the case law of the Strasbourg Court provide important guidance for political decision makers.

Personal names

The Strasbourg Court has stated that "the name is not only an important element of self-identification; it is a crucial means of personal identification in society at large". In one case it decided that the refusal of the authorities to accept the preferred spelling of a person's name violated the right to respect for private life as provided for in the European Convention (Article 8).[9]

These principles are also relevant when the state and minority languages are based on different alphabets or scripts. When visiting Lithuania in 2009, I learned that the spelling of Polish names in passports and other official documents had become a controversial issue. The government submitted a proposal which would have been a constructive step towards fuller respect for minority rights, but unfortunately parliament voted against it.

Local names, street names and other topographical indications

The Advisory Committee on the Framework Convention concluded in the case of Lithuania that the absence of bilingual public signs in certain areas was incompatible with the convention. There appeared to be a contradiction between the Law on the State Language and the Law on National Minorities which ought to be addressed.

In my own report on Austria, I addressed the controversy around the possibility of displaying topographical signs both in German and in Slovenian in certain municipalities in Carinthia and recommended the implementation of the judgment of the Austrian Constitutional Court on this issue. The judgment protected the principle of bilingual signage in areas where there was a significant number of persons belonging to a national minority.

Such an approach also means that local authorities, even when dominated by minority representatives, should accept use of the official language in parallel with the minority one when necessary. Persons

---

9. *Guzel Erdagöz v. Turkey,* judgment of 21 October 2008.

belonging to the majority in the country should not be discriminated against when they live in a region where they are in the minority.

Education

Minority-language education is essential for protecting language rights and for maintaining languages. Governments should ensure that persons belonging to minorities have adequate opportunities to learn the minority language and even to receive instruction in this language. Bilingualism should be encouraged for all.

The right to adequate opportunities for minority-language education should be implemented without prejudice to the learning of the official language or being taught in that language. The Advisory Committee and the High Commissioner on National Minorities have both stressed the importance for all – including minorities – of the right to quality education in the official language.

This is essential in regions where individuals belonging to national minorities have poor or no command of the state language(s) and as a result are excluded from wider community life. The Advisory Committee has discussed this problem in relation to Estonia, Georgia, Latvia and Moldova, among others.

In most European countries the teaching of and through the medium of the Romani language is almost totally neglected – even where there is a significant number of Roma inhabitants.

Contacts with authorities

The possibility to communicate with the authorities in one's own language is another concern voiced by persons belonging to a minority. This right cannot always be fully realised in practice where human and financial resources are limited. However, the Framework Convention and the Charter both state that, when there is a real need, governments should endeavour to enable such communication as far as is reasonably possible.

Many states have chosen to regard the numerical size of a minority in a given area as the relevant factor for recognising certain language rights, and they have established minimum thresholds for this purpose. These should, however, not be set too high: the Advisory Committee, for example, has deemed a threshold set at a minimum level of 50% to be unreasonable.

In recruitment policies, public administrations should not demand proficiency in the state language beyond what is necessary for the post in question. Access to employment for persons belonging to national minorities must not be unduly limited. In parallel, a constructive approach is recommended, for instance, through offering applicants from national minorities an opportunity to be trained in the state language. At the same time, administrations should recognise the value of recruiting civil servants with knowledge of relevant minority languages, as this will enable the authorities to better serve the whole population.

Such positive measures are especially important when the government decides to take steps to actively protect and promote the official language. Sanctions to enforce laws on the state language should be avoided. The focus should rather be on the need to harmonise such legislation with laws protecting minority languages; only in this way can one avoid policy contradictions arising and guarantee that the language rights of all citizens are respected.

Media

The possibility of establishing minority-language media is often another concern for persons belonging to national minorities. The media should ideally reflect the plurality and diversity of the population as a whole. State regulation of the broadcast media should be based on objective and non-discriminatory criteria and should not be used to restrict the enjoyment of minority rights.

Persons belonging to national minorities should have access to national, regional and local broadcast time in their own language on publicly funded media. Quotas for broadcasting time in the official language(s) should not prevent public or private broadcasting in minority languages. The Advisory Committee has found a number of negative examples of this type of quota.

The decision in Turkey to open a 24-hour television channel in Kurdish is a positive example. This initiative was seen as a signal of a changed attitude towards a minority whose rights have been repressed for years. I have been informed that there are similar plans for the Armenian language.

The basic lesson we ought to have learned by now is that human rights concerns can only be effectively addressed through a serious assessment of the genuine needs of minorities. Too often authorities have not listened carefully to minority concerns when policies are being developed. It is important that governments maintain close contact and regular communication with persons belonging to national minorities and that they seek a thorough and continuing consultation – a constructive dialogue.

Chapter 2: Roma rights

In many European countries the Roma population is still denied basic human rights and made victims of flagrant racism. They remain far behind others in terms of educational attainment, employment, housing and health standards and they have virtually no political representation. Their exclusion from society feeds isolationism, which in turn encourages prejudice against the Roma among xenophobes. More effort is needed to break this vicious cycle.

Photo: Swedish writer and Roma rights campaigner Katarina Taikon with refugee children after a positive government decision on their asylum request (© Rosa Taikon).

European history of repression of the Roma

Only a few thousand Roma in Germany survived the Holocaust and the Nazi concentration camps. They faced enormous difficulties when trying to build their lives again, having lost so many of their family members and relatives, and having had their properties destroyed or confiscated. Many had their health ruined. For years, when some tried to obtain compensation, their claims were rejected.[10]

For these survivors, no justice came with the post Hitler era. Significantly, the mass killing of Roma people was not an issue at the Nürnberg trial. The genocide of the Roma – *Samudaripe* or *Porrajmos* – was hardly recognised in public discourse.

This passive denial of the grim facts could not have been surprising to the Roma themselves. For generations they had been treated as a people without history. Their suffering was rarely recognised – and if recognised, quickly forgotten.

The history of repression against the Roma precedes the Nazi era and goes back several hundred years – following their migration from the Indian subcontinent. The methods of repression have varied over time and have included enslavement, enforced assimilation, expulsion, internment and mass killings. The Roma have been routinely stigmatised as unreliable, dangerous, criminal and undesirable. They were the outsiders who could easily be used as scapegoats when things went wrong and the locals did not want to take responsibility.[11] In Wallachia and Moldavia (today's Romania) the Roma lived in slavery and bondage for centuries up to 1855 when the last Roma slaves were finally emancipated.

---

10. The term Roma and/or Travellers in these texts refers to Roma, Sinti, Kale, Travellers and related groups in Europe and aims to cover the wide diversity of groups concerned, including groups identifying themselves as Gypsies.
11. The Council of Europe has published fact sheets on Roma history: http://www.coe.int/t/dg4/education/roma/histoculture_EN.asp. The University of Graz is a project partner: http://romani.uni-graz.at/romani.

In Spain more than 10 000 Roma were rounded up in a well-planned military-police action one day in 1749. The purpose according to a leading clergyman who advised the government was to "root out this bad race, which is hateful to God and pernicious to man". The result was devastating – deportations, detentions, forced labour and killings destroyed much original Roma culture.

In the Austro-Hungarian Empire during the 18th century, rulers applied a policy of enforced assimilation. Roma children were taken from their parents, and instructions went out that no Roma were allowed to marry another Roma. The Romani language was banned. This policy was brutally enforced and use of the language was to be punishable by flogging.

Fascists in the 20th century also turned against the Roma. In Italy a circular in 1926 ordered the expulsion of all foreign Roma in order to "cleanse the country of Gypsy caravans which, needless to recall, constitute a risk to safety and public health by virtue of the characteristic Gypsy lifestyle".

The order made clear that the aim was to "strike at the heart of the Gypsy organism". What followed in fascist Italy was discrimination and persecution. Many Roma were detained in special camps; others were sent to Germany or Austria and later exterminated.

The fascist "Iron Guard" regime in Romania started deportations in 1942. Like many Jews, about 30 000 Roma were brought across the River Dniester where they suffered hunger, disease and death. Only about half survived the two years of extreme hardship before the policy changed.

In France, about 6 000 Roma were interned during the war, the majority in the occupied zone. Unlike other victims, the Roma were not systematically released as the Germans retreated. The French authorities saw continued internment as a means of forcing the Roma to settle.

In the Baltic states, many Roma were killed by the German invasion forces and their supporters within the local police. Only 5-10% of the Roma in Estonia survived. In Latvia about half the Roma population were shot. It is estimated that the vast majority of Roma in Lithuania were also killed.

In fact, all countries in Europe were affected by the racist ideas of the time. In neutral Sweden, the authorities had already encouraged a sterilisation programme targeted at the Roma as early as the 1920s, and this continued until the 1970s. In Norway also, pressure was exerted on Roma to be sterilised.

The Nazi regime in Germany defined the Roma (including the Sinti) as "racially inferior" with "asocial behaviour" which was doomed hereditary. This reflected old and widespread prejudice in both Germany and Austria. The Nürnberg race laws of 1935 deprived the Roma of their nationality and rights as citizens: they were interned in labour camps and sterilised by force.

An earlier plan of Nazi racists to keep some of the "racially pure" Roma in a sort of anthropological museum was forgotten. Some Roma, not least children, were singled out for Josef Mengele's cruel medical experiments. A policy of forced sterilisation was implemented, often without anaesthesia.

The systematic murder of Roma by Nazis started in the summer of 1941 when German troops attacked the Soviet Union. The Roma were seen as spies for "Jewish Bolshevism" and were shot by the German army and the SS in mass executions. In all areas occupied by the Nazis there were executions of Roma people. Figures are uncertain, but it is estimated that far more than 100 000 Roma were executed, including in the Balkans where the killings were supported by local fascists. The Ustascha militia in Croatia ran camps, but also organised deportations and carried out mass executions.

In December 1942, the Nazi regime decided that all Roma in the "German Reich" should be deported to Auschwitz. There, they had to wear a dark triangle and a Z was tattooed on their arm. Of all camp inmates, the Roma had the highest death rate: 19 300 lost their lives there – 5 600 gassed and 13 700 dying of hunger or disease, or as a result of medical experimentation.

It is still not known how many Roma in total fell victim to the Nazi persecution. Not all Roma victims would have been registered as Roma, and the records anyway are incomplete. The fact that there were no reliable statistics about the number of Roma across Europe before the mass killings took place makes it even more difficult to determine the precise number of Roma casualties. Council of Europe research has concluded that it is highly probable that the number was at least 250 000. Other credible studies indicate, however, that there may have been 500 000 Roma who lost their lives, and perhaps many more.

The Roma victims of the Nazi era were forgotten for many years. The struggle by survivors to obtain compensation received a very minimal and very tardy response. There have been a few positive exceptions. In 2003, the Romanian Government established a commission on the Holocaust to document the repression and killings in Romania during the fascist period. After long delays a memorial site for the Roma victims is now being prepared in Berlin close to the building of the Bundestag.

Truth commissions ought to be established in a number of countries. Ideally, there should be a Europe-wide review of the mass atrocities against the Roma during the 20th century. A full account and recognition of these crimes might go some way to restoring trust among the Roma towards the wider society.

Many Roma continue to see the authorities as a threat. When required to register or to be fingerprinted they fear the worst. This is all the more understandable when they explain how they see similarities between much of today's anti-Roma rhetoric with the language used in the past in Europe by Nazis and fascists. That inflammatory racist language, as well known, made way for the mass killings of their people in the 1930s and 1940s.

Continued stigmatisation of Roma

President Sarkozy of France declared "war" on crime in summer 2010, following incidents of violence involving some members of the Traveller community (*gens du voyage*). However, the main focus

of the government's campaign was soon directed against Roma from Romania and Bulgaria.

The Roma were collectively stigmatised as criminals in strikingly sweeping statements. It was decided that some 300 unauthorised settlements were to be dismantled and Roma irregular immigrants to be returned to their country of origin, if necessary by force. Changes to the law were proposed to facilitate and speed up these actions.

In fact, such expulsions were nothing new in France: thousands of cases had occurred in previous years though they had received much less publicity. And France was not alone. Italy, for instance, had also rounded up and deported a considerable number of Romanian Roma in 2008.

What caused a particularly strong reaction this time from many quarters – including the Council of Europe and the United Nations – was the blatant use of anti-Roma rhetoric accompanying the government campaign. In France, as in Italy, the Roma community as a whole was linked to criminality. Their presence was described as a threat against "public security" – a legal term which is normally used for extraordinary situations when the peace and survival of the state is considered to be at stake. The fact that this message was official, and came from the government itself, did not facilitate a constructive exchange.

The alleged link between the Roma and crime – an often repeated refrain in the hate speech against this minority – can be rebutted and the misunderstandings sorted out. Of course, some Roma have been guilty of theft. Some have also been exploited and instrumentalised by traffickers. Socially marginalised and destitute people are in most countries over-represented in criminal statistics – for obvious reasons.

These problems should be taken seriously and appropriate criminal and preventive measures taken. However, these problems offer absolutely no excuse for stigmatising all Roma – the overwhelming majority of who are not in conflict with the law. It is a crucial ethical principle that a whole group should not be blamed for what some of its members might have done.

The consequences of xenophobic statements by leading politicians should not be trivialised. Some distorted minds may understand such statements to be authorising retribution and even physical attack. The unfortunate rhetoric by some candidates in the course of the 2008 Italian election was followed by ugly incidents of violence directed against Roma individuals and camps. The cold-blooded murder of six Roma, including a 5-year-old child, in Hungary in 2008-09, was committed in an atmosphere fuelled by hate speech.

Anti-Gypsyism is now again being exploited by extremist groups in several European countries. Mob violence against Roma individuals has been reported from, for instance, the Czech Republic and Hungary. It is sobering that the Canadian authorities have granted asylum to Roma refugees from these countries on the grounds that they faced grave risks.

The state representatives whom the Roma tend to meet most often are the police. During my missions, I have been struck in several countries by the signs of bad relations between Roma communities and the police. Many Roma have given specific examples of how the police failed to protect them against assaults from extremists. Even worse, there have been cases where police officers themselves have initiated violence.

One such incident occurred in Košice in eastern Slovakia in April 2009. A group of Roma children was apprehended. They were taken to the police station and forced to strip and then slap one another violently in the face. Thanks to the media this particular case came to public attention.

The EU's Agency for Fundamental Rights (FRA) published a study in 2009 about how Roma and other minorities feel about their situation in society:[12]

- one in three of the Roma interviewed stated that they had been stopped by the police during the past 12 months and half thought

---

12. The FRA survey focused on seven member states: Bulgaria, the Czech Republic, Greece, Hungary, Poland, Romania and Slovakia. In each of them, no less than 500 Roma respondents were interviewed.

that this had happened because they were Roma. Many of those stopped had experienced this several times, on average four times;
- one in four interviewees stated that they were victims of personal crime at least once during the past 12 months, and one in five responded that they had suffered racially motivated personal crime including assaults, threats and serious harassment;
- a clear majority – between 65 and 100% depending on the country – did not report such crimes to the police. They did not trust that the police would want or be able to do anything.

Anti-Gypsyism is widespread throughout Europe. In times of economic problems, it appears that the tendency to direct frustration against scapegoats increases – and the Roma appear to be an easy target. Instead of fishing in murky waters, national and local politicians should stand up for and speak out on behalf of principles of non-discrimination and respect for people from different backgrounds. At the very minimum, politicians must avoid anti-Roma rhetoric themselves.

A number of concrete steps can be taken. Past atrocities against the Roma should be included in history lessons in schools. Key professions, such as the police, should be trained about the need to protect Roma against hate crimes, and be disciplined if they themselves misbehave.

Most important is the need for elected politicians to demonstrate moral leadership: they must encourage, and live out in practice, a commitment to respect and promote human rights for everyone.

Ending discrimination against Roma

In many European countries the Roma population is still denied basic human rights and made victims of flagrant racism. The Roma remain far behind others in society in terms of educational attainment, employment, housing and health standards, and they have virtually no political representation. A number are stateless or have no identity papers. When attempting to migrate they are

discriminated against and are often refused entry or expelled. Their exclusion from society feeds isolationism which in turn encourages prejudice against the Roma among xenophobes. More effort is needed to break this vicious cycle.

The social marginalisation of Roma is no longer a hidden problem. A number of international organisations have developed programmes to address the issue. For example, the UN Development Programme has promoted the "Decade of the Roma Inclusion 2005-2015" in co-operation with various governments – primarily in the Balkan region. The OSCE Office for Democratic Institutions and Human Rights (ODIHR) in Warsaw is giving technical assistance to implement practical programmes for inclusion and the European Commission has provided considerable funding to support such efforts.

Evaluations of the results so far have been disappointing. Some aid programmes have not been well designed and have failed to engage with the Roma themselves. It is clear that these problems run deep, and cannot be resolved in a few years.

Nor is there one simple, single solution. While anti-Gypsyism is a threat to all efforts to ensure that Roma enjoy their rights, several acute social problems are interlinked. If as a child you do not receive sufficient schooling you will be disadvantaged in the job market. If you cannot get a job you cannot improve your housing. Poor housing conditions in turn affect one's health and also the education of one's children. And so the vicious cycle persists across the generations.

In other words, a comprehensive programme is needed to tackle all these problems simultaneously. However, there is one aspect which must be given particular priority if the cycle of disadvantage and exclusion is to be broken, and that is good education.

Education

Many Roma children remain outside national educational systems altogether. Even among those who do enrol, there is a high drop-out rate, and educational achievement is generally low. One explanation for the educational problems faced by Roma children lies in the high illiteracy levels among their parents.

This is the core of the problem and requires more analysis based on relevant data, clearer policies and determined action. It is important in particular to recognise the value to subsequent educational achievement of preschool education. Improving support at an early age can be of great assistance in later years for children coming from a background where there is a limited tradition of studying.

Unfortunately not all preschool education is free of charge. Such schools may also not exist in Roma neighbourhoods, and transport can be expensive and cumbersome.

The improper placement of Roma children in special schools or classes for pupils with intellectual disabilities is another major problem. I have visited schools in several countries where Roma children were placed almost automatically in special classes for pupils with learning problems. This happened even when it was recognised that the child was obviously capable. This discrimination is unacceptable.

Roma segregation in education was addressed by the European Court of Human Rights which delivered a landmark ruling in the case *D.H. and Others v. the Czech Republic* on 14 November 2007. In the *D.H.* case, the non-governmental European Roma Rights Centre demonstrated to the Court that Roma students in the Czech Republic were 27 times more likely to be placed in special schools than similarly situated non-Roma. The Court found that this pattern of racial segregation violated the European Convention (Article 14 on non-discrimination and Article 2 of Protocol No. 1 on the right to education).

The Court noted that the Czech Republic was not alone in this practice and that discriminatory barriers to education of Roma children were present in a number of European countries. The Court has made other rulings in this area. In June 2008 it found Greece in violation of the non-discrimination provisions of the European Convention on Human Rights (*Sampanis and Others*). The Greek authorities had first failed to provide schooling for a number of Roma children, and the following year had placed them in special preparatory classes.

The instruction issued by the Greek Ministry of Education in August 2010 to all school institutions and local authorities that the right to education of Roma children must be enforced is more encouraging. The ministry stressed that education from the age of 5 was an imperative: lack of a permanent residence certificate could not be accepted as an excuse for failing to enrol Roma children; transportation for children living at a distance from the school should be provided; and that segregation from other pupils contravened the Greek constitution.

Quality education for Roma pupils requires material in their mother tongue. Although this is not easy, particularly considering the variations and dialects of the Romani language, efforts should be undertaken to meet this need.

Teachers may need formal training to handle diversity in the classroom. Currently, there are few Roma teachers, and their numbers should be increased. More could be done to ensure that staff who are Roma are recruited to work and teach in schools. Experiments with Roma class assistants in some schools have produced positive results.

It is also important for schools to establish closer contact with Roma parents. If education is to be promoted to Roma children, Roma parents must feel welcome in the school system. If they so wish, they should also be offered basic education themselves.

Employment

Roma adults do not get jobs – they are put in a "glass box": this was a conclusion of a survey published by the European Roma Rights Centre (ERRC) in 2006. Discrimination in employment was found to be endemic and blatant, especially in central and South-Eastern European countries.

This study was carried out in Bulgaria, the Czech Republic, Hungary, Romania and Slovakia, but the situation has not improved in recent years and there are similar problems in several other European countries. The unemployment rate for Roma is high throughout Europe. Even when Roma have jobs, they tend to be jobs related to service provision for the Roma community itself.

The study also showed that in cases where Roma are employed, they run the risk of discrimination. One in four of Roma in employment reported that their pay and other conditions were less favourable than for non-Roma in the same job.

However, the main problem is that Roma are discriminated against when they try to enter the job market. The study showed that a great number of applicants were rejected because they could be visibly identified as Roma. Indeed, many were openly told that the reason for their not getting the job was because they were Roma.

Another conclusion of the survey was that government-run employment offices were of limited help. The study exposed prejudice and even outright racism among officials in some of these public institutions.

This finding is all the more unfortunate as economic development in recent years has worked against the Roma. Their traditional occupations are no longer in demand and many suffer from low levels of formal education. This is the type of problem for which competent and non-discriminatory public employment services are needed.

While these social and socio-economic factors are real, educated Roma also meet discriminatory attitudes when seeking employment. There is no excuse for states passively accepting problems caused by prejudice.

Housing

In country after country across Europe, a large number of Roma families live in rudimentary habitats.

I have visited poor and overcrowded settlements in several countries, including Bulgaria, Greece, Italy and Serbia. Electricity, running water and sewage systems have been non-existent or inadequate, making hygiene a real problem. I have met mothers who asked how their children could be sent clean to school or could be expected to do their homework in such circumstances.

Families who live on land without permission face extreme difficulties. Roma families have been evicted by force from their homes. In most cases the decisions were taken by local authorities, and the families were not given adequate notice nor offered a real alternative. Even when such evictions have been approved by a court, it is clear that several of these actions violated both European and international human rights standards.

Several serious cases have been reported to me. One took place in Milan in April 2010 when local police "cleared" three Roma settlements, involving more than one hundred inhabitants. Those "cleared" included people who were sick, some with disabilities, pregnant women and children. Everyone was forced to leave but not offered any alternative accommodation. Their homes were then bulldozed.

In the last couple of years, I have received reports about similar police actions in Albania, Bulgaria, France, Greece, Serbia, Turkey and the United Kingdom. In several cases the destruction of homes and property was accompanied by violence and racist language.

An argument often put forward for these evictions has been the need to construct new, more modern buildings in the same area. However, Roma families are seldom offered places in such new housing developments. Instead, the Roma remain disproportionately represented among the homeless and those living in substandard housing. Roma ghettos and shanty towns can still be found today on our continent.

City regeneration plans sometimes require that people be moved from their places of residence. Such decisions can be justified. However, the manner in which such measures are planned and implemented should be in accordance with agreed human rights standards. Those standards state that forced evictions can only be carried out in exceptional cases and in a reasonable manner; everyone affected must be able to access courts to review the legality of evictions before they are carried out; alternatives to evictions should be sought by way of genuine consultation with the people affected; and compensation and adequate resettlement must be offered when forced evictions prove inevitable.

The monitoring mechanisms of the European Social Charter have found several countries at fault in their treaty obligations regarding the housing rights of Roma. Given some of the appalling housing conditions described above, the European Court of Human Rights has judged that poor housing conditions can amount to breaches of the European Convention's prohibition of torture and inhuman and degrading treatment. The UN Committee Against Torture has taken a similar position.

In a recommendation from 2005, the Committee of Ministers of the Council of Europe requested all member states to improve the housing conditions of Roma. The best way to stop forced evictions of Roma is to ensure that they are consulted to ensure that their right to adequate housing is respected and put into practice.

Mobilising political will

The marginalisation of Roma cannot be overcome solely with measures aiming at formal equality. The Roma must have effective equality of opportunity with others, and this requires positive measures to compensate for the treatment experienced in the past. Human rights principles recognise that such pro-active measures, when aimed at tackling discrimination or exclusion, are justified – subject only to them being in pursuit of a legitimate aim and being proportionate to the objective.

There is a shameful implementation deficit with regard to Roma rights. In spite of the many conferences and action plans, at both national and European level, progress has been extremely slow. Programmes have been allocated insufficient personnel and financial resources to be effective. When resources have been allocated, they have not been well used. Co-ordination between state agencies and local authorities has often functioned badly. Consultation with Roma and human rights organisations has often been organised as an afterthought, if at all.

Too often the Roma have been excluded from the discussion on how to improve their situation – instead "experts" *(gadze)* have dominated. This is not a human rights approach. Roma must participate fully in efforts to secure their rights.

There are now local, national and international Roma organisations, and they should be respected by the authorities. The Roma and Travellers Forum in the Council of Europe has faced problems but can be a crucial consultative and standard-setting body for Roma rights all over Europe.

Roma organisations are conducting important discussions about their own responsibilities – in particular how to make themselves truly representative of the community's diversity (including Roma women, and young Roma). Activists from within the community warn against allowing Roma vulnerability to result in attitudes of victimisation and dependency. The challenge is to transform this vulnerability into an opportunity for equality.

The Swedish writer and Roma rights campaigner Katarina Taikon stressed that these problems are human rights issues:

> *We are not asking for privileges, only the same human rights as others enjoy. We request the same right to education, the same chance to get a job and the same right to decent housing – not as Roma but as citizens.*
>
> *We request the same legal protection against assault which others would get. And we do request that generations of Roma who have grown up without housing and schooling and who have been suffering abuse and discrimination by the state and the local authorities receive recognition and compensation.*

Roma political representation

Roma populations are grossly under-represented in local and national assemblies and government administrations all over Europe. This is a violation of their right to political participation,

and perpetuates the exclusion and marginalisation of some 10 to 12 million people.

The political exclusion and alienation of Roma has many roots. An important root lies in the long history of discrimination and repression faced by the community. In several European countries, Roma families were chased from place to place, even in the wake of mass murders in the 1930s and 1940s. Roma found that they were not welcome anywhere. All efforts to encourage Roma participation in public life must recognise the impact of this historic experience, and the bitterness and feeling of exclusion which have developed as a consequence.

In many countries, Roma communities are still nowadays socially isolated and fragmented. As a result they are often less aware of political and electoral processes. They often lack vital information which means they are vulnerable to electoral malpractices. Many are disenfranchised because they are not included in civic and voter registers, or they lack the necessary identity documents required for voting. Informed and conscious political participation tends to come with higher educational attainment, so the dramatic educational gap between many Roma and non-Roma is yet another obstacle to participation.

Majority mainstream political parties have to be held to account for this state of affairs. By and large, they have shown very little interest in Roma communities. Not only have Roma representatives not been invited onto party electoral lists, but the views of the Roma have seldom been sought.

So, yet another vicious circle is created. A low voter turn-out among the Roma renders the community less interesting to politicians seeking support and votes at election time. This in turn means that, post-election, politicians may feel less responsibility towards these non-voters. Moreover, political parties are aware that campaigning for Roma might cause actual harm to their own election chances. Extremist parties have targeted the Roma with xenophobic statements in order to exploit reactionary tendencies among the general electorate. This is one reason why some of the poisonous clichéd lies about the Roma have spread so widely.

Unfortunately, some established political parties have not made it clear that such bigotry is unacceptable. I have noticed that even senior politicians have made prejudicial statements about the Roma. There is, of course, no simple and quick solution to these problems. Prejudicial attitudes are often deeply ingrained among both the Roma and the majority population. However, efforts in several countries can be analysed and some conclusions drawn.

Lessons and inspiration can be drawn from the efforts of the Organization for Security and Co-operation in Europe (OSCE); it has tried for many years to make a contribution to finding solutions. The OSCE has run campaigns such as Roma, Use Your Ballot Wisely! and convened meetings which have drafted standards such as the 1999 Lund recommendations and the Guidelines to Assist National Minority Participation in the Electoral Process in 2001. The Council of Europe's Advisory Committee on the Framework Convention for the Protection of National Minorities has adopted a commentary on the effective participation of persons belonging to national minorities in cultural, social and economic life and in public affairs.

One lesson, if we are to increase political representation by under-represented groups, is that pro-active measures are essential. It is not enough to remove obstacles; it is also necessary to institute positive action to compensate for a long history of exclusion and marginalisation.

By way of example, reserved seats for Roma representatives in national or local assemblies have been tried in Bosnia and Herzegovina, Croatia, Romania and Slovenia, with some positive results. When in Slovenia, I found that the practice of reserving one seat in local assemblies had created a channel in some municipalities between the Roma communities and the authorities. Another example of good practice is to have consultative bodies for Roma affairs at the governmental level (or include Roma in bodies working on general minority issues). This type of solution is particularly useful in countries with dispersed and numerically small Roma populations, such as Finland or Poland.

Another lesson is to focus on the local level. Roma participation will not be successful on the national level unless it is also encouraged at the municipal level. Efforts to encourage participation must of course be undertaken with Roma involvement. The Roma themselves should represent their community's interests and voice their concerns.

On the basis of these principles, there is a need for a comprehensive approach in order to empower Roma populations:

- governments should repeal laws and regulations which discriminate in terms of political representation against minorities, including the Roma and non-settled communities;
- non-governmental organisations should be encouraged to support programmes in civic education for Roma communities. These programmes should include human rights components and practical information about the electoral system. Such support programmes should reach women and young Roma. Written information should be available in the Romani language;
- more outreach efforts are needed to ensure voter registration. Again, it is important to reach women also. A high priority must be given to resolving the lack of personal identification documents; and effective measures must be taken to ensure the rights of those who are stateless;
- public life is not only about elections. Participation in public life includes the possibility to influence authorities on a more routine basis. More organised consultation is needed between the local authorities and the Roma population on housing and other policy and practical problems. Such consultation must be participative and meaningful; any tendency towards tokenism is wrong and will backfire;
- mechanisms for equal, direct and open communication are needed. Advisory bodies could be set up to give continuity to the consultative process and to promote the legitimacy of

Roma representatives. Authorities should support Roma cultural centres. Where such centres have been tried in the past, they have had a positive effect on inter-Roma communications;

– Roma should be recruited into public service positions at both the local and the national level. Again, a pro-active recruitment policy is justifiable and is required. It is particularly important that Roma join the police and teaching professions;

– the impact of such measures will depend on progress towards putting an end to discrimination. Comprehensive anti-discrimination legislation must be adopted and enforced, and the various Roma communities recognised as national minorities;

– further efforts to raise awareness among officials and the general public are necessary. Xenophobic discourse and attitudes must be rejected. In countering xenophobia, our elected politicians carry a particularly heavy responsibility.

Roma without citizenship

In several European countries, there are Roma with no nationality. They face a double danger: in addition to being stigmatised, and facing a plethora of serious, discrimination-related problems, their lives are made even harder by their statelessness. For those who are migrants as well, their situation is even worse.

Many Roma lack personal identity documents. This hinders their access to education and health services, and increases their susceptibility to continued statelessness. Thousands have no administrative existence at all. They have never obtained a birth certificate, and have not overcome the administrative obstacles placed in the way of being recognised by the state. They often live entirely outside any form of basic social protection or inclusion.

This is a hidden problem. It is difficult to establish the facts, but state authorities have made too little effort to collect relevant data about the scope and nature of this systematic marginalisation. As repeatedly noted by the European Committee of Social Rights, states have an obligation to identify the extent of the exclusion of vulnerable groups such as the Roma, including gathering relevant statistics.

Political developments in recent years have made Roma in Europe more vulnerable. The break-up of the former Czechoslovakia and the former Yugoslavia caused enormous difficulties for persons who were regarded by the new successor states as belonging somewhere else – even though they had been long-term residents.

The Czech Republic introduced a citizenship law which rendered stateless tens of thousands of Roma; the intention had been that they should move to Slovakia. After interventions by the Council of Europe and others, this law was amended in 1999, and the problem was in large part (but not entirely) resolved.

In Slovenia, several thousand persons, among them many Roma, became victims of a decision to erase non-Slovene residents from the Register of Permanent Residents. The residents, many of whom had moved to Slovenia from other parts of Yugoslavia before the dissolution of the federation, had missed a deadline and had not sought or obtained Slovenian citizenship in a timely manner after the country became independent. In 2010, the government managed to get the parliament to adopt a law addressing this issue.

The Kosovo[13] conflict led to a large displacement of Roma people primarily to Serbia, Bosnia and Herzegovina, Montenegro and "the former Yugoslav Republic of Macedonia" but also to other countries outside the region. In Pristina, I met with one NGO which was working on a large civil registration project, hoping to register the around 10 000 Roma who found themselves without papers.

It is not acceptable that Europeans are deprived of their basic human right to a nationality.

---

13. The Council of Europe is status-neutral in relation to Kosovo. In official documents it adds the following clarification when this territory is mentioned: "All reference to Kosovo, whether to the territory, institutions or population, in this text shall be understood in full compliance with United Nations Security Council Resolution 1244 (1999) and without prejudice to the status of Kosovo."

European host states where children of Roma migrants have been born and have lived for several years should provide a secure legal status to these children and their parents. Both the UN Convention on the Rights of the Child and the International Covenant on Civil and Political Rights stipulate that children shall have the right to acquire a nationality. In other words, the host country has an obligation to ensure that children do have a citizenship; the fact that their parents are stateless is no excuse for not respecting the rights of the children involved.[14]

When in Italy in January 2009, I was pleased to learn that the government was preparing draft legislation to provide Italian nationality to stateless minors whose parents had left war-torn former Yugoslavia, and where at least one of their parents was in Italy prior to January 1996. The government also announced that it would ratify the 1997 European Convention on Nationality without any reservation. When finalised, such legislative developments will benefit a number of stateless Roma children.

Problems relating to nationality affect many adult Roma too. During my visits to countries in South-Eastern Europe, I learned about the efforts of the UN High Commissioner for Refugees who is trying to break the vicious circle caused by the absence of identity documentation. Without such papers, individuals cannot assert their most basic rights. In Montenegro, the UNHCR programme has already helped many Roma, including some who had left Kosovo.

I also noticed positive steps when visiting "the former Yugoslav Republic of Macedonia", where progress has been made to ensure Roma can obtain basic personal documents including birth certificates, identity cards, passports and other documents related to the provision of health and social security benefits.

These are good examples, but we should note that such measures are an obligation upon states. The Strasbourg Court has stated that the

---

14. See United Nations Convention on the Rights of the Child (Article 7) and International Covenant on Civil and Political Rights (Article 24).

non-provision of personal documentation to facilitate employment, medical care or the provision of other crucial needs may contradict the right to private life, a human right protecting the individual's moral and physical integrity.[15]

The Council of Europe has been a pioneer in protecting Roma rights. The messages coming from its various bodies emphasise that host states should employ all possible means to end the de facto and de jure statelessness of Roma. The Roma must be provided with a nationality, in accordance with the standards of the 1997 European Convention on Nationality, and the 2006 Council of Europe Convention on the Avoidance of Statelessness in Relation to State Succession.

Both of these treaties contain general principles, rules and procedures of the utmost importance for the effective enjoyment in Europe of the human right to a nationality. Some core provisions include:

– respect for the overarching principle of non-discrimination in law and practice;
– an obligation on states to avoid statelessness, including in the context of state succession;
– special protection to be provided to children born on their territories and who do not acquire another nationality at birth;
– restrictive conditions on loss of nationality by law; and
– the duty on states to reason and provide their nationality-related decisions in writing.

The problem of the stateless Roma must be addressed with determination. Roma themselves often lack the means to speak out, and many do not have easy access to ombudsmen or other national human rights institutions.

National human rights action plans should pay attention to the urgent need to provide resources to facilitate legal work for stateless Roma.

---

15. See *Smirnova v. Russia*, judgment of 24 October 2003.

Discrimination against Roma migrants

European governments are not giving Roma migrants the same treatment as others in similar need of protection. Roma migrants are returned by force to places where they are at risk.

In Germany, Austria and "the former Yugoslav Republic of Macedonia", large numbers of Roma migrants have been given tolerated status, a form of temporary protection against expulsion. It does not confer residence or social rights. An example of this is the German *duldung* status.

There are credible allegations that Roma from outside the European Union are more likely to be provided with *duldung* (rather than a more durable status) when compared to non-Roma third-country nationals.

These concerns were examined in an April 2009 study – *Recent migration of Roma in Europe*, published jointly by Knut Vollebeck, the OSCE High Commissioner on National Minorities, and myself.

The study analyses human rights standards on migration in Europe and highlights the discriminatory practices that Roma migrants still face. It concludes with recommendations for action by member states to protect the human rights of Roma migrants in Europe.

I have had to deal with this issue with respect to the forced returns of Roma, Ashkali and Egyptians to Kosovo. After a visit there in March 2009, I published a report which concluded that there was not the infrastructure that would allow a sustainable reintegration of the returnees, especially Roma.

Another visit in mid-February 2010 convinced me that this continues to be the case. There are still about 20 000 internally displaced persons (all categories); these people have been there since 1999, unable to return to their original habitats. The unemployment rate is about 50%, and there is no capacity to provide humane living conditions for more returnees.

The reintegration strategy endorsed by the authorities in Pristina is not being implemented; the relevant actors at the municipal level are not aware of their responsibilities; and there is not even a budget allocated to implement the strategy.

Some forcibly returned Roma ended up in the lead-contaminated camps of Česmin Lug and Osterode in northern Mitrovica. These camps were inhabited for 10 years by whole Roma families, including children, and have had a terrible effect on people's health.[16]

Though steps are now, at long last, being taken to move the camp inhabitants to a less hazardous environment, the Roma and Ashkali families who lived there are in desperate need of intensive health care.[17]

It must also be recognised that those involved fear for their own safety: they have not forgotten how the Roma were chased away in 1999; houses were burnt and women raped. Another concern among the Roma is about schooling for their children in a language they understand, and the need for the adults to find employment.

The relationship between the local authorities and European governments is not one of equal partners: it is deeply asymmetric. The fate of refugees becomes secondary when the Pristina authorities' willingness to receive returnees is made a condition for talks about visa liberalisation or openings for other privileges.

This raises questions about the re-admission agreements now requested by European governments. My conclusion is that only voluntary returns – genuinely voluntary – should be pursued for the moment.

During 2009 more than 2 600 forcible returns took place. Of these, 429 related to Roma and Ashkali. The majority of returnees came from Germany, Sweden, Austria and Switzerland, and preparations are under way to increase the rate of returns.

---

16. In 2009 alone, credible information provided to me in Pristina suggests that no less than 18 returned families ended up in these camps.
17. Apart from the Roma, there are also two other minorities living there under very similar conditions – the Ashkali and the Egyptians.

Individual assessments of need should be applied in these cases. However, such testing must also consider the particularly vulnerable situation of the Roma and Ashkali in this area today.

European governments seem not to accept that Roma could have protection needs. In the European Union, the policy is that all EU member states shall be considered "safe countries of origin" in asylum matters. Consequently, a citizen of one EU member state may not be granted international protection in another EU member state.

Directives within the EU have not supported Roma rights. The "Free Movement Directive" impacts differently on Roma than on non-Roma. This directive provides that every EU citizen has the right to reside in any EU member state for three months without any requirement other than a valid passport. For longer periods of stay, however, the person concerned must prove that he or she is not a burden to the host state, through either employment or adequate financial resources.

A majority of Roma cannot fulfil these requirements, as also shown in a report published by the European Union Agency for Fundamental Rights in 2009.[18] So, the protective provisions of the "Free Movement Directive" are breached much more easily in respect of Roma than any other identifiable group.

Expulsions of Roma have been carried out in contravention of EU law. In other cases, the destruction of Roma dwellings has been used as a method to persuade Roma to leave "voluntarily".

Discrimination against Roma in migration policies has met with little or no opposition in almost every European country. It is high time to review the approach.

To push Roma families backwards and forwards between countries, as now happens, is inhumane. It victimises children – many of whom were born and grew up in the host countries before their deportation. A report published by UNICEF in June 2010 documents the stories of

---

18. EU Agency for Fundamental Rights, "The situation of Roma EU citizens moving to and settling in other EU Member States", November 2009.

many children caught up in this situation. Deported from Germany to Pristina – they have no links, do not speak the language, and often drop out of school.

The policy on return is also ineffective. Of those forcibly returned, 70-75% could not reintegrate there, and they moved to secondary placements, or went back – through illegal channels – to the countries they were deported from.

Expulsions between EU countries have also failed in many cases as the Roma have used their right as EU citizens to move freely within the European Union area.

European states now spend considerable amounts of money to return Roma to their countries of origin. Measures facilitating the inclusion of Roma into the wider society would be a much better use of such funds.

Chapter 3: Immigration and asylum policies

It is now more difficult for both refugees and economic migrants to reach our borders. Airlines are pressured to refuse passengers who may not be granted entry on arrival. Patrol boats along Europe's southern coasts are used to intercept and turn back migrants from African countries. Individuals whose freedom or lives are under threat have also been among those stopped in this way.

Photo © Council of Europe.

Rights for migrants

The demographic trend in Europe is clear: an ageing continent needs more immigration. However, anti-foreigner political parties have advanced or maintained their popular support in recent elections. At the same time, some mainstream parties – instead of explaining facts and defending the rights of immigrants – have copied the slogans of the extremists, and thereby legitimised xenophobic jargon. Expressions such as "if they do not love our country they can get out" have been widely canvassed.

Such an atmosphere victimises all foreigners, including refugees and even citizens of foreign origin. However, the main victims of such xenophobia are often irregular migrants who are in the country without permission. This atmosphere can ferment efforts to round up such migrants for deportation.

Each state has the right and duty to control its borders effectively, and to know who is within its jurisdiction. Irregular migration can pose problems and may also harm the many migrants who suffer exploitation, including those who have been trafficked. The challenge for the state is to strike a proper balance between protecting the rights of those who are inside or at its borders, while maintaining control of its frontiers.

This is not a small problem. For obvious reasons, precise statistics are unavailable, but it is estimated that there are some 5.5 million irregular migrants within the European Union, and more still in other parts of Europe. For the Russian Federation alone, it is estimated that there are no less than 8 million irregular migrants.

Irregular migrants may have entered the host country illegally without valid visas, either by avoiding border controls or with the aid of false documents. There are also those who enter legally, but overstay their visas; this is likely to account for most irregular migrants, including those who are trafficked. Migrants may also enter on a non-working visa but then take on employment.

A humane migration policy requires that we learn more about the present situation of irregular migrants and about alternative ways of protecting them. Some steps have been taken in national programmes to tackle trafficking. Victims of trafficking in several countries, when identifiable, are now treated with respect, given protection and sometimes even a permit to stay, at least for a limited time.

Irregular migrants, even if their right to stay is not protected, have human rights that must be respected. Indeed, most human rights standards apply without distinction between citizens and foreign aliens. The principle of equality and non-discrimination means that distinctions between groups are only permissible if they are prescribed by law, pursue a legitimate aim and are strictly proportionate to that aim.

The UN Convention on the Rights of the Child applies to migrant children, including those who have been denied a permit to stay. For instance, the state has an obligation to ensure a child's right to health care and education.

The Council of Europe's Parliamentary Assembly has spelled out the need to clarify the rights to be enjoyed by irregular migrants. On the basis of the European Convention on Human Rights and other relevant treaties, the Assembly highlighted rights such as the right to primary and secondary education for children, the right to emergency health care, the right to reasonable working conditions, the right to have one's private and family life respected, the right to equality, the right to seek and enjoy asylum and be protected from *refoulement* (enforced return to a place where the individual's life or freedom could be threatened), and the right to an effective remedy before any removal.[19]

However, although irregular migrants formally have such rights, their insecure status makes them vulnerable to abuse. In reality, they are often unable to claim their rights when these have been infringed by officials, employers or landlords. Exploitation is common. This is the

---

19. PACE Resolution 1509 (2006).

problem which governments in Europe still have not tackled with sufficient priority.

Another reality needs to be recognised: a large proportion of irregular migrants will remain in Europe and will not – or cannot – be returned to their country of origin. In some cases this is because removal would constitute *refoulement* and is therefore prohibited under international law.[20] In other cases, removal would not be realistic because nationality or identity is disputed, or because the country of presumed nationality refuses to co-operate. In other cases, the migrants are stateless and there is therefore no country to return them to.

This raises the issue of regularisation – government decisions to legalise the presence of certain irregular migrants. Such moves do not entail any diminution of national sovereignty, nor of a state's right to control its national borders. They are voluntary acts, similar to amnesties, in which the state intentionally decides to overlook the infringement of immigration controls in limited and specific cases.

Regularisation is a controversial issue but the Council of Europe's Parliamentary Assembly, to its credit, has raised the issue.[21] I recommend that member states respond positively to this initiative and consider such regularisation programmes as a means of safeguarding the dignity and human rights of a particularly vulnerable group of persons.

As in many other fields, the European Union itself is becoming a key player in the broad policy area of migration. The European Commission is working towards a comprehensive EU immigration policy which would improve border controls, and prevent illegal employment in EU countries, as well as developing common admission procedures and strengthening integration policy.

---

20. The principle of *non-refoulement* was first laid out in 1954 in the UN Convention Relating to the Status of Refugees, which in Article 33(1) provides that "No Contracting State shall expel or return ('*refouler*') a refugee in any manner whatsoever to the frontiers of territories where his life or freedom would be threatened on account of his race, religion, nationality, membership of a particular social group or political opinion."
21. See PACE Recommendation 1807 (2007) on regularisation programmes for irregular migrants.

Measures for stricter border control have included strengthening the Borders Agency and the establishment of the Rapid Border Intervention Teams. Co-operation between the European Union and the UN High Commissioner for Refugees has been initiated to ensure that border operations fully observe international standards, including the right to apply for asylum.

Of particular urgency is the need for all parties to recognise and respect the responsibility to rescue persons at sea, and to guarantee the principle of *non-refoulement* so that no one is forced back into a situation of persecution and torture.

Governments in Europe must be serious about co-operation: there is a need for a common European migration policy, and to co-ordinate its development with relevant countries outside the EU. The Council of Europe and its Parliamentary Assembly are important partners in these efforts and it is vital that policies relating to migrants are based on facts and respect for human rights – not on xenophobia.

The criminalisation of migration

There is a trend in today's Europe to criminalise the irregular entry and presence of migrants as part of a policy of "migration management". Such a method of controlling international movement corrodes established principles of international law. It also causes many human tragedies without achieving its purpose of genuine control.

There are binding international agreements about the right to seek asylum through fair, rights-based procedures. The principle of *non-refoulement* has been established in order to protect individuals from being sent back to situations which would threaten their lives or personal safety.

However, many migrants cannot claim refugee status, even if their enforced return would amount to personal tragedy and economic disaster. Many have not managed to regularise their presence in their new country and live an underground existence, in constant fear of being caught by the police and expelled from the country. A number have lived in the host country for long periods, and may have children at school.

Migrants are now finding themselves increasingly targeted, and some governments have even set quotas for numbers to be pursued and deported through fast-track procedures. It is necessary – and important – to remind everyone that irregular migrants also have human rights.

Proposals are being made to criminalise attempts to enter a country or to stay there without a permit. This may be popular among xenophobes but would be a retrogressive step.

For one thing, to put a criminal stamp on attempts to enter a country would undermine the right to seek asylum and adversely affect refugees (see next article). In addition, people who have been smuggled into a country should not be seen as having committed a crime. There are agreed international standards to protect victims of human trafficking from any criminal liability.

The 1990 International Convention on the Protection of the Rights of All Migrant Workers and Members of their Families expressly holds that if migrants are detained for violating provisions relating to migration, they should be held separately from convicted persons or persons detained pending trial; they should not be seen or treated as criminals (Article 17, paragraph 3).

Criminalisation is a disproportionate measure which exceeds a state's legitimate interest in controlling its borders. To criminalise irregular migrants would, in effect, equate them with the smugglers or employers who, in many cases, have exploited them. Such a policy would cause further stigmatisation and marginalisation, even though the majority of migrants contribute to the development of European states and their societies. Immigration offences should remain administrative in nature.

There are two side-effects which states should also bear in mind when they think about resorting to criminal law to control irregular immigration. When in Italy, I learned that judges were worried about the introduction into domestic legislation of new criminal offences aimed at migrants. Courts in several European countries already experience excessively lengthy proceedings – in violation of Article 6 of the European Convention on Human Rights. These very delays in turn give rise to a large number of the applications coming to the European Court of Human Rights. Any move towards criminalising irregular migration would further exacerbate this problem.

There is also the overcrowding in prisons and detention centres. Categorising irregular migrants as "criminals" under national law would entail their pre-trial and post-conviction detention. It is well known, and I have personally witnessed this in several countries, that a number of Council of Europe member states are already facing a serious problem of overcrowding. I comment in a separate chapter on the inhuman and degrading conditions in some detention centres and prisons. Foreign aliens in administrative detention are particularly vulnerable to abuse.

In this context, it is obvious that the possibility of detaining irregular migrants in EU member states for up to 18 months is highly unfortunate. Yet the "Returns Directive", adopted by the European Parliament in June 2008, allows for this possibility. This measure was improper in human rights terms and is an unfortunate response to an urgent need to harmonise European policies in this area.

Political decision makers should not lose the human rights perspective in this discussion and should try to formulate a rational long-term strategy. This has to include a recognition that migrant labour very often performs those jobs which nationals refuse to take. In other words, European states should face up to the reality that irregular migrants are working because migrant labour is in demand.

By way of example, the agricultural sector in southern European countries is one where irregular migrant workers have been extensively employed. Sadly, they often fall prey to substandard working and living conditions.

Migration is a social phenomenon which requires multilateral and intelligent action by states. Irregular migration has increased and thrived, and not only because of underdevelopment in migrants' countries of origin. Another root cause is the lack of clear immigration mechanisms and procedures which would allow regular migration channels to respond to labour demands effectively.

Immigration law in most European states remains one of the most complex areas of law and efforts to simplify it should be further promoted. I draw attention to the important guidelines adopted by the Council of Europe regarding irregular migrants. Member states should establish transparent and efficient legal immigration avenues if they wish to respond positively to this challenge and avoid irregular migration routes.[22]

Such efforts would benefit from accession to the 1977 European Convention on the Legal Status of Migrant Workers – an important treaty concerning regular migrant workers from Council of Europe member states. It covers the principal aspects of regular migration, such as migrant labour recruitment, working and living conditions, social and medical assistance. Regrettably, after more than 30 years, this treaty has still only been ratified by 11 member states and signed by another four.[23]

Member states should also accede to the 1990 international convention on migrant workers, the most comprehensive international treaty on migrant workers which reaffirms and establishes basic human rights standards for regular and irregular migrants. To date – that is, nearly 20 years later – the convention has been ratified by three Council of Europe member states, and signed by a further three, even though many European countries actively participated in drafting this important treaty. Its ratification and implementation will help protect

---

22. Council of Europe Parliamentary Assembly Recommendation 1618 (2003) and Resolution 1509 (2006).
23. The number of registered ratifications and signatures is based on the situation as at 1 December 2010.

the fundamental rights of all migrant workers, which should be the priority for the immigration policy and practice of every state.

The right to asylum

The right to seek and enjoy asylum is not fully protected in Europe today. In spite of a downward trend in asylum applications in several countries, policies have remained restrictive. Concerns about irregular migration and the threat from international terrorism have prevented a constructive discussion of asylum and refugee-protection issues and created a human rights deficit.

It is now more difficult for both refugees and economic migrants to reach our borders. Airlines are pressured to refuse passengers who may not be granted entry on arrival. Patrol boats along Europe's southern coasts are used to intercept and turn back migrants from African countries. Individuals whose freedom or lives are under threat have also been among those stopped in this way.

Asylum seekers who, in spite of these difficulties have managed to reach European countries, have as a rule been given no chance to file their claims – even when they have come together with others in "mixed flows". The Spanish Government has tried to secure this right for those arriving on the Canary Islands.

However, the proposals to have abbreviated procedures for sending back large groups of new arrivals may, if enforced, undermine the right to seek asylum – even for those who are in desperate need of protection. Asylum seekers must be identified within larger migratory flows at an early stage, and provided with fair and just procedures for adjudicating their claims.

The 2003 Dublin II Regulation allows for the return of an asylum seeker from one EU member state to another if the applicant had arrived there as their first destination within the EU. However, the UN High Commissioner for Refugees warns that this practice may in reality undermine the chances for refugees to obtain asylum because of the different standards applied in different EU countries. The High

Commissioner also recommends a liberal approach so that family connections and previous stays in the country can be fully considered before final decisions are taken.

The fragility of the Dublin regulation was exposed in January 2011 when the Strasbourg Court ruled that the European Convention had been violated in a case of the return from Belgium to Greece. The Court found that the applicant had been deprived of fair procedures as the Greek asylum system was dysfunctional.

There are several EU directives on refugee policies aimed at a common approach within the Union, and this is a laudable and necessary objective. However, the tendency in some EU countries has been to lower standards to the minimum extent possible. It would be deeply unfortunate if moves towards harmonisation were to lead to a lowest-common-denominator approach. Even more restrictive legislative and administrative provisions have been introduced during the transposition of the directives into national practice.

A major problem is that a great number of migrants come without documents. Smugglers and traffickers in many cases confiscate or destroy passengers' passports or other identity papers. Some migrants may also prefer not to give information about their identity or home country, hoping that this will improve their chances of staying or will protect family members left behind.

This, however, is no justification for treating such migrants as if they were criminals: fair procedures must be respected in all cases. There might be genuine refugees among them. A person who has fled severe persecution may not have been in a position to obtain a passport.

Non-governmental organisations have repeatedly reported the negative treatment sometimes accorded to asylum seekers by the police. Their criticism is that little consideration is given to the vulnerability of applicants and that they may have had traumatic experiences of previous contact with officials in uniform.

Talking to a stranger about deeply personal and humiliating experiences of torture or other ill-treatment may also be difficult.

Nevertheless, when some applicants do not give all relevant information in their very first interview, this is often used against them. The implied message – which many refugees understandably take as an insult – is that they have been deliberately hiding important facts and have not been honest.

Sometimes, of course, a person lies. But this should not taint the overall approach to interviewing asylum seekers. This first encounter with representatives of the host society must be as humane as possible, without sacrificing the need to obtain the necessary information.

Interpreters must be available, and trained appropriately so that applicants have no reason to worry that their accounts will be reported back to the home authorities. Interviews of children require special skills and yet it is very important that their experiences be heard independently.

Finally, governments should review the need for detention as well as the conditions of detention facilities. Asylum seekers who have done nothing wrong are kept in prison in several European countries while the host government tries to secure their reception in the country of origin. This sometimes takes a very long time, and possibilities for those in this situation to obtain legal assistance is often restricted or non-existent. We Europeans should do better.

Detention of asylum seekers

Solidarity with others requires, as a basic minimum, offering sanctuary to those who are fleeing from oppression. The "right to seek and to enjoy asylum from persecution" is a key provision in the Universal Declaration of Human Rights. Sadly, this right is not fully observed in parts of Europe today. Instead refugees are met with suspicion, and detained and imprisoned.

Some people seeking to enter Europe have a well-founded fear of persecution. They may be under threat because of their ethnicity, religion, nationality, political opinion or membership of a particular social group. Some have already suffered serious ill-treatment in their country of origin. They are refugees who have been forced to migrate.

This background distinguishes them clearly from other migrants and has meant that they are provided with a special protective status under international law. Unfortunately, that status is not always respected. Actions taken with the general intention of deterring migrants from arriving have also rendered it impossible for refugees to arrive and apply for asylum.

Refugees who have entered the country without permits should not be penalised and restriction of movement may take place only on exceptional grounds: these fundamental principles have been integral to international refugee law for 60 years.

The 1951 UN Convention Relating to the Status of Refugees (as amended by the 1967 Protocol) prescribes in Article 31 that "Contracting States shall not impose penalties, on account of their illegal entry or presence, on refugees who … enter or are present in their territory without authorization, provided they present themselves without delay to the authorities and show good cause for their illegal entry or presence".

States may only restrict refugees' freedom of movement if such restrictions are considered "necessary": that is, in clearly defined exceptional circumstances, and in full consideration of all possible alternatives. The United Nations High Commissioner for Refugees has consistently stressed this principle.

This well-established legal position was endorsed by the Council of Europe's Committee of Ministers in 2003 when it adopted Recommendation Rec(2003)5 to member states on measures of detention of asylum seekers. In 2005, the European Union expressly accepted this principle in Article 18 of Council Directive 2005/85/EC on minimum standards on procedures for granting and withdrawing refugee status.

These standards conclude that detention upon entry of asylum seekers should be allowed only on grounds defined by law, for the shortest possible time, and only for the following purposes:
- to verify the identity of the refugees;
- to determine the elements on which the claim to refugee status or asylum is based;
- to deal with cases where refugees have destroyed their travel or identity documents or have used fraudulent documents to mislead the authorities of the country of refuge; or
- to protect national security or public order.

As with all limitations to fundamental rights and freedoms, these exceptions should be applied restrictively. Some vulnerable categories – for instance unaccompanied children – must never be detained. Unfortunately, my own experience, and the information I receive from credible sources, show a very different reality.

The detention of persons who have claimed asylum, but whose claims have been refused, is also a matter of concern. Such deprivation of liberty can only be defended if there is an objective risk that the individuals would otherwise abscond, and that alternative measures such as regular reporting do not exist. Such detention, if necessary, should be limited in time, and open to challenge before a judicial authority.

I am concerned that, in the context of the Dublin II Regulation, some EU member states detain asylum seekers when their transfers are under way to the member state responsible for examining their application. This regulation should be revised to reflect the basic principle of the non-detention of asylum seekers. An effective EU-wide monitoring system is also necessary so that places used for detaining asylum seekers are effectively overseen by an independent body. Special attention should be paid to the widely used practice of detention in airport (transit) areas in revising the regulation, and in subsequent oversight.

The need for common European procedures in this area is obvious. I have met government representatives who have been worried that a rights-based policy would send 'signals' that would attract further refugees. That attitude tends in turn to feed an unfortunate chain reaction. Policies must be co-ordinated on the basis of the agreed human rights standards.

I sincerely hope that the judgment of the European Court of Human Rights' Grand Chamber in the case of *Saadi v. the United Kingdom* will not be understood as a justification for a general practice of detention. The Court accepted, in effect, that a state may detain an asylum seeker for seven days "in suitable conditions" for a fast-track procedure, if that state is confronted with an "escalating flow of huge numbers of asylum seekers" (paragraph 80 of the judgment).[24]

No doubt, an increase in asylum applications may cause administrative problems. This, however, should not be seen as a reason to allow the corrosion of a principle established in international law that proscribes the detention of asylum seekers upon entry. It is important that state interests do not prevail over the rule of law.

In view of the above, I think it would be useful to recall and stress some crucial principles that European states have already accepted – in law, if not always in practice:

- refugees are particularly vulnerable persons subject to persecution in their countries of origin; thus, they are in need of special protection by the states of refuge;
- the non-detention of asylum seekers upon entry remains a fundamental principle of international law;
- detention should be allowed restrictively only in the situations cited earlier and laid out in international law;
- detention, if it is to take place, should only occur in specialised detention facilities for refugees;
- alternatives to detention measures should be considered by states and provided for in domestic legislation;

---

24. Judgment of 29 January 2008.

- states should always provide special attention and care to particularly vulnerable refugees – such as victims of torture or other trauma; unaccompanied minors; pregnant women; single mothers; and elderly persons or persons with mental or physical disabilities;
- states should apply the procedural and substantive safeguards provided for by Article 5 (right to liberty and security) of the European Convention on Human Rights;
- state organs and agents dealing with asylum seekers in detention should be specially trained, and should be subject to ongoing, specialised training and oversight.

These are not just humanitarian principles. Under international human rights and refugee law they correspond to individual rights which engage state responsibility.

Family reunification

A restrictive refugee policy in European countries has affected the principle that separated families should be reunified. Where refugees already reside in a country, governments try to limit the arrival of their close relatives. The result is unnecessary human suffering especially in those cases where dependent family members have been kept apart. This policy violates the right to family reunification stipulated in international human rights standards.

In a number of declarations, the world community has agreed that the family is the fundamental group unit in society.[25] From this follows the right to family unity which in turn places certain obligations on

---

25. See Article 16 of the Universal Declaration of Human Rights; Article 8 of the European Convention on Human Rights (this right emphasises the importance of protecting the family circle, the social unit that nurtures most children to adulthood); Article 16 of the 1961 European Social Charter; Articles 17 and 23 of the International Covenant on Civil and Political Rights; Article 74 of the Additional Protocol of 1977 to the Fourth Geneva Convention Relative to the Protection of Civilians in Times of War; Articles 9, 10 and 22 of the United Nations Convention on the Rights of the Child; and Article 9 of the Charter of Fundamental Rights of the European Union.

state authorities. For refugees, this right is particularly crucial since they are often forced to leave family members behind when fleeing.

Prolonged separation from close family members can cause severe stress and prevent a normal life for both those who have left and those who remain at home. Indeed, many refugees and other migrants live isolated lives, cut off from normal social relationships and, as a consequence, they face even more difficulties in integrating into their new environment. Those left behind – often women and children – tend to be vulnerable emotionally, economically and often physically.

Though states must be able to retain their right to regulate and control the entry of non-nationals, there has been a progressive development in international law as regards the right to family reunification across borders. Nowadays, respect of the right to family life requires not only that states refrain from direct action which would split families, but also that measures be taken to reunite separated family members when they are unable to enjoy the right to family unity somewhere else.

This development started when the 1951 UN Convention Relating to the Status of Refugees was adopted. The diplomatic conference stated in a final act that the unity of the family was an "essential right" and recommended that governments take the necessary measures to protect the refugee's family especially to:

- ensure that the unity of the refugee's family is maintained, particularly in cases where the head of the family has fulfilled the necessary conditions for admission to a particular country; and

- protect refugees who are minors, in particular unaccompanied children and girls with special reference to guardianship and adoption.

The Executive Committee of the UN High Commissioner for Refugees has since adopted several authoritative statements promoting family reunification as both a human right and as a humanitarian principle. The agency has encouraged governments to adopt legislation to implement "a right to family unity for all refugees, taking into account the human rights of the refugees and their families".[26]

In the Council of Europe, both the Committee of Ministers and the Parliamentary Assembly have used similar language to the UNHCR in several recommendations and resolutions. Notions of "family" and "family reunification" also enjoy protection under the European Convention on Human Rights and the European Social Charter.

The UN Convention on the Rights of the Child stipulates that children should not be separated from their parents against their will (Article 9), and that governments should deal with cases of family reunification across borders "in a positive, humane and expeditious manner" (Article 10).

However, in practice, government policies have not always been positive, humane and expeditious – either for children or for adults. A number of governments have chosen to interpret their obligations narrowly, a stance that is reflected in the 2003 EU Council Directive on the Right to Family Reunification. Under this directive, only spouses and unmarried minors would benefit from favourable treatment while other family members would not. Only persons with full refugee status would be accepted as sponsors, while those with subsidiary protection or other migrants would not.

In practice, policies have varied, but many countries in Europe have defined "family" as including only parents and their immediate children. This ignores the obvious fact that the shape of the core family differs depending on different traditions and situations. In war-torn and HIV-affected areas, for instance, it is not unusual for orphaned children to be cared for by other relatives. Elsewhere, it is often grandparents, or other members of the extended family, who depend on younger family members. A positive and humane policy should consider the family pattern in each specific case.

---

26. UNHCR Executive Committee's Conclusions 1, 9, 24, 84, 85 and 88.

Some governments argue that family unity could be achieved if the newcomers would go back to their family members in the country of origin: the implied message is that the family separation is self-inflicted. However, many cannot go back home for the very same reasons which forced them to flee. This inability to return applies not only to those granted asylum, but also to those seeking such status, and indeed to many of those with temporary or subsidiary protection. Again, a positive and humane policy would allow for individual cases to be considered on their own merits.

Other obstacles are frequently placed in the way of family reunification. For example, reunification is sometimes refused because of strict requirements imposed on individuals to be financially self-supporting, and those receiving social assistance are often barred from acting as sponsors. Yet this policy ignores the reality in many cases. It certainly ignores the fact that – as family unification is a human right – the poverty of the resident family member should not hinder an application.

Official attitudes to requests for family reunification across borders have been strikingly negative. The response has often been marked by suspicion – as if applicants want to deceive the authorities and to obtain undeserved favours. There have, of course, been cases where people have provided inaccurate information in order to secure entry for others, but it is a great mistake to allow such cases to dictate overall policy.

Significantly, DNA testing has been introduced in several countries as a key means of assisting government decision-making. The purpose is to verify whether the applicant really is either the child or the parent of the resident family member. By definition, this method excludes consideration being given to any other relations, for instance adopted children. Nor is this procedure adjusted to reflect the actual family pattern in those cultures from which many refugees fleeing to Europe come.

The UN High Commissioner for Refugees has also rightly warned that DNA testing can have serious implications for the right to privacy. Though voluntary testing can be acceptable in certain circumstances in order to prevent fraud, this should be carefully regulated, and the sharing of any data thus obtained should be bound by principles of confidentiality. When testing is considered necessary, the costs should be borne by the requesting authorities.

Some governments have adopted even more restrictive rules in response to the popular public perception that foreigners constitute a danger. Very often, these measures are discriminatory. For example, in my follow-up "Memorandum to the Danish Government", I took issue with the requirement that a person must be a citizen of the country for 28 years before obtaining the right for his or her foreign partner to secure a residence permit. This clearly discriminates against those who have not lived in the country since childhood.

I was also concerned that the right to family reunification of children ends when the child turns 15. The government has responded to the fact that this rule violates the UN Convention on the Rights of the Child by declaring that exceptions could be considered, which is hardly a satisfactory answer.[27] In late 2010 the Danish Government introduced a "points system" to the effect that less educated relatives would be further disadvantaged when seeking family reunification. Several regulations similar to those in Denmark have also been introduced in the Netherlands.

The administrative processing of applications is far from "expeditious" in many countries. In fact, the process is often both extremely slow and unnecessarily bureaucratic. Some countries require that applications be made at the embassies or consulates in the country of origin which is not always easy or even possible. In other cases, the authorities request documents or information offering hard proof of various facts which can be very difficult for applicants to obtain from the authorities in their countries of origin. Requirements to provide evidentiary proof of family relationships for the purpose of reunification have therefore to be realistic.

---

27. Commissioner for Human Rights' "Memorandum to the Danish Government", CommDH(2007)11.

Those who have seen the pain suffered by separated families realise how much of a mistake it is to deny the right to family unity – for the refugees, for the family members left behind, and indeed for the host country. Facilitating family reunification helps to ensure the physical care, protection, emotional well-being and often also the economic self-sufficiency of refugee communities. This is in the interests of everyone.

Traffioking

There has been much talk about trafficking in human beings – but not enough action. UNICEF and the non-governmental organisation Terre des Hommes have reported failures to protect children from falling prey to traffickers in South-Eastern Europe. They have requested stronger action to address the root causes and the patterns of supply and demand that govern this shady business.

They are right: the campaign against the trafficking of both children and adults must become more effective. The Council of Europe Convention on Action against Trafficking in Human Beings is a key instrument for that purpose, and should be ratified by all European states without further delay.

Trafficking is a serious criminal offence and yet one that is difficult to uncover. The shadowy nature of the trade, the code of silence applied by the criminal networks in this dirty business and the victim's fear of retaliation if they report their condition, all make it particularly difficult to estimate the precise nature and scope of this crime. The degree of force and deceit involved in the exploitation also varies greatly.

What we know, however, is that trafficking in human beings is a major source of income for organised criminal groups, and that the number of victims is incredibly high. We also know which are the most common countries and regions of origin, transit and destination.

Some trafficking is connected to sexual exploitation, but not all. Many victims end up in begging, domestic work or manual labour (in the latter instance, often in agriculture or construction).

What these victims have in common is that they easily develop a dependency relationship with the criminals trafficking them, and that they are frequently exploited by local employers or clients. A large number are undocumented migrants and therefore particularly vulnerable. Many live in slave-like conditions.

Therefore, human rights standards must be at the core of all counter-trafficking strategies. Police action is essential but insufficient. It must be supplemented by preventive measures and by effective protection of the rights of the victim. This also goes, of course, for victims without permits.

Undocumented trafficked migrants have the right to safety and protection and to be treated as victims, not as criminals. They should be granted a fair hearing with due process. They should be granted a residence permit in the country if they co-operate with law enforcement, or if the humanitarian situation so warrants.

Many trafficked victims hesitate to seek help from the authorities because they fear either that they will not be heard, or that they themselves will be treated as criminals and hastily deported. Governments both in transit and in destination countries must find humane and effective ways of contacting and helping these individuals.

Criminal traffickers must be caught and punished; the conduct of employers and clients who knowingly exploit those who have been trafficked should be pursued in the courts; and the victims should be effectively protected and assisted. However, much more must also be done to break the trafficking chain at its very source.

The root causes are known: poverty, unemployment, abuse and marginalisation. These human rights problems must be addressed. People are lured by the traffickers because they are desperate and public information about the risks involved is inadequate. The usual transit and destination countries would do well to support countries of origin in their efforts to tackle these root causes. After all, the consequences of not doing so affect us all.

The Council of Europe convention is a comprehensive treaty and aims to prevent trafficking, protect the victims and prosecute the criminal organisers. The convention calls for information and education for persons at risk of being trafficked and actions to discourage consumers in destination countries from contributing to the exploitation.

The convention is not perfect. Negotiations and compromises have, in my opinion, weakened the rules for protecting victims and reduced its specificity about the means to stem their exploitation. However, the convention is still the most advanced and ambitious treaty targeting the trafficking in human beings, and member states should sign, ratify and implement its provisions.

The convention has a clear human rights dimension and provides for multiple measures of physical, psychological and legal assistance to the victims, including compensation for the damage suffered. Its implementation is monitored by a group of independent experts to ensure the effectiveness of the system.

Statelessness

Everyone has the right to a nationality. Also, no one shall be arbitrarily deprived of his or her nationality or denied the right to change nationality. These rights are spelled out in the 1948 Universal Declaration of Human Rights – but still not respected in a number of European countries. The victims are stateless.

A stateless person is an individual who is not considered as a national by any state. Some stateless people are refugees or migrants, having left their country of origin. Others live in their home country but are not recognised as citizens.

The plight of the stateless has received limited attention in recent years and seems to be little understood. The UN High Commissioner for Refugees believes that there are about 12 million stateless persons worldwide but recognises that this figure is uncertain, and there may be even more. The number in Europe is estimated to be 640 000.

Europe's shameful history of producing and repressing stateless people contributed to the elaboration of agreed international standards to protect the right to a nationality and to be well treated when without citizenship. The 1954 UN Convention Relating to the Status of Stateless Persons contains provisions to enable stateless persons to access fundamental human rights. Host states are also encouraged to facilitate their integration and naturalisation.

The convention is complemented by the 1961 Convention on the Reduction of Statelessness, which includes provisions to prevent the emergence of new cases of stateless persons. The UNHCR has been charged with the task of helping to eliminate statelessness globally.

Both the UN Convention on the Rights of the Child and the International Covenant on Civil and Political Rights stipulate that children shall have the right to acquire a nationality.[28] The host country has an obligation to ensure that children have citizenship. The statelessness of a child's parents is no excuse to deny children this basic right to a nationality.

These rights are not respected in practice. The exclusion of stateless persons from participation in the political process undermines the reciprocal relationship between duties and rights. Non-citizens tend to be marginalised. Many face gross discrimination in their daily lives: they may be denied employment, housing or access to education and health care because they do not have personal identification documents that are valid. When travelling across borders they are particularly vulnerable – that is, if they can travel at all.

Political developments in Europe after 1989 led to increasing numbers of stateless persons, especially those belonging to national minorities. The break-up of the Soviet Union, Yugoslavia and Czechoslovakia caused enormous difficulties for people who were regarded by the new governments as belonging somewhere else – even when they had resided in their current location for many years.

---

28. Article 7 of the UN Convention on the Rights of the Child, and Article 24 of the International Covenant on Civil and Political Rights.

Large numbers of residents in Latvia and Estonia, including children, remain non-citizens. I have recommended that steps be taken to grant citizenship automatically to children and to relieve older people from the requirement to go through the tests for naturalisation.[29] The European Court of Human Rights has highlighted the obligation of states to effectively protect personal and family life in such situations.[30]

Several thousand people, among them many Roma, became victims of the decision in Slovenia in 1992 to erase non-Slovene residents from the Register of Permanent Residents. Many had moved to Slovenia from other parts of Yugoslavia before the dissolution of the federation. It was only in 2010 that this unjust regulation was changed through amendments to the law.

In other states in the Balkans, there are Roma who are without citizenship or even basic identity papers. Those who have moved from the former Yugoslav Federation to other parts of Europe – for instance Italy – often lack personal documents and live in legal uncertainty. They are de facto stateless. Their newborn children are frequently not registered and risk losing their right to apply one day for citizenship as they cannot prove legal residence in the country.

In Greece, a nationality code caused the de-nationalisation of a large number of members of the Muslim minority in Thrace – many of them of Turkish origin. This provision was withdrawn in 1998, but the change did not apply retroactively, which meant that Muslims who had lost their citizenship did not get it back. These people had to start a naturalisation process as if they were newcomers. The Greek authorities should give priority to addressing this unjust situation.[31]

In Bosnia and Herzegovina the authorities initiated a review of the citizenship granted since 1992 to a significant number of foreign

---

29. See the Commissioner for Human Rights' memoranda to the Latvian Government, CommDH(2007)9, and the Estonian Government, CommDH(2007)12.
30. See *Slivenko v. Latvia*, judgment of 9 October 2003; and *Sisojeva v. Latvia*, judgments of 16 June 2005 and of 15 January 2007.
31. See the Commissioner for Human Rights' "Follow-up report on the Hellenic Republic (2002-2005)", CommDH(2006)13.

nationals. It was argued that they had obtained their status through improper procedures during the chaotic wartime situation and several hundred citizenships have been revoked.

In France, the National Assembly adopted an immigration law in October 2010 which increased the possibility of withdrawing citizenship of those who had obtained this status within the last 10 years and had committed a serious crime.

There were some strong arguments in these cases, but revoking citizenship, when already granted, must certainly be regarded as a very serious action and should only be possible in extreme circumstances of deliberate deceit in the original application.

A case which must be brought to a positive conclusion is the fate of the Meskhetians who were deported in 1944 by the Stalinist regime from Georgia to other parts of the Soviet Union. Very few have been able to return to Georgia, and many of those who now are in, for instance, Krasnodar Krai in Russia are stateless. There are hopes that the Georgian authorities will now implement their pledge to ensure the return of this minority.

The Council of Europe has adopted two highly relevant treaties to guide a rights-based approach, especially to those problems which flow from the state dissolutions and successions of 1989 onwards. One is the 1997 European Convention on Nationality, and the other is the 2006 Convention on the Avoidance of Statelessness in Relation to State Succession.

Both treaties contain general principles, rules and procedures of utmost importance for the effective enjoyment in Europe of the human right to a nationality. Some core provisions are:

- the overarching principle of non-discrimination in law and practice;
- the special protection that must be provided by states to children born on their territories and who do not acquire another nationality at birth;

- restrictive conditions by which someone may lose nationality *ex lege*;
- the duty of the states to reason and provide in writing their decisions regarding nationality.

I am concerned that only 20 Council of Europe member states have ratified the 1997 European Convention on Nationality. This is in spite of Recommendation No. R (99)18 of the Committee of Ministers (on the avoidance and reduction of statelessness), which encouraged ratification. Moreover, only five states have ratified the 2006 Convention on the Avoidance of Statelessness in Relation to State Succession.[32]

The problem of statelessness in Europe should be given priority. The victims have in most cases little possibility themselves to be heard, and are in many cases silenced by their fear of further discrimination. Governments, ombudsmen, national human rights institutions, and non-governmental organisations must all take action for the rights of stateless persons.

The persistence of "legal ghosts" in today's Europe is unacceptable. Council of Europe member states should protect the rights of stateless persons on their own or other states' territories and adopt a pro-active policy. Governments should realise that measures aimed at reducing and eliminating statelessness can prevent, as well as resolve, conflicts. This is one way of promoting social cohesion and harmony in our societies.

Displaced persons

Armed conflict and inter-ethnic violence continue to force people to flee from their homes and seek refuge in safer places. The outbreak of the war in South Ossetia in August 2008 created a new wave of displaced persons, some of whom may have to wait a long time before being able to return home. In Georgia, as in other parts of the Caucasus, and in the former Yugoslavia, there are still many

---

32. The registered number of ratifications is based on the situation as at 1 December 2010.

who have had to wait for more than a decade following earlier conflicts and have therefore been doubly victimised.

When I visited North Ossetia and Georgia soon after the war in August 2008, I saw the huge humanitarian challenge caused by forced displacement, compounded by a polarised political environment. A large number of the victims with whom I met were deeply traumatised, and some in Georgia lacked the most basic necessities, such as beds, mattresses, blankets, adequate nutrition and medical assistance. Parents were worried about their children missing school.

It was also very sad to see that these experiences have given rise to strong negative feelings about the neighbouring community – Ossetians towards Georgians, and vice versa. An unfortunate mix of fear and hatred has taken root which may make it more difficult for those in the minority position to return in the future.

The principle of the right to return must be defended even in such situations, and this right must be assured by the responsible authorities. This obligation on the authorities requires guaranteeing security to potential returnees; it also underlines the importance of bringing to justice those who caused the displacement. It is essential that other living conditions be adequate, for instance, that damaged houses are repaired or rebuilt, and occupied property is returned to lawful owners.

In reality, the return of displaced persons may be very complicated, even when the political and material obstacles have been removed. A hostile atmosphere is not easily overcome – as was seen in Bosnia and Herzegovina where displaced people have sold their houses rather than move back. Though this tendency may indicate failure, it is important to underline that return must always be voluntary – it cannot be made obligatory.

It is estimated that there are about 2.5 million internally displaced persons (IDPs) in Europe today. The majority fled or were chased away from their homes in situations of inter-community conflict, and their safety was in danger.

Those who have crossed international borders for similar reasons are seen as refugees and have a different legal status since the protection owed them by host states is clearly provided for by the 1951 Convention Relating to the Status of Refugees. IDPs have not been the subject of a special international treaty. This does not, however, mean that they are in a legal vacuum. The European Convention on Human Rights is applicable to them if they are on a contracting state's territory, and the European Court of Human Rights has on many occasions provided relief to IDP applicants.

The Representative of the UN Secretary-General on the Human Rights of IDPs has promoted three alternative durable solutions, which as a matter of principle should be sought by the competent authorities. He has made clear that states have the duty to establish conditions and provide the means to allow displaced persons to enjoy one of the following options:

- voluntary return: that the IDPs return to their homes or places of habitual residence in safety and with dignity;

- voluntary resettlement: that they resettle in another part of the country; or

- integration locally: that they obtain support for their choice to stay in the community where they are and integrate there.

In the course of any of these three possible processes, all of which necessitate strenuous efforts and determination on the part of the state, the competent authorities should not forget to ensure the full participation of the displaced persons in the planning and management of the required measures.

These state obligations are part of the United Nations Guiding Principles on Internal Displacement, which restate the relevant international human rights and humanitarian law standards. The Council of Europe's Committee of Ministers has recognised the importance of these principles in their recommendation on internally displaced persons which develops some of the principles further on the basis of the existing Council of Europe standards.[33]

I recommend that relevant states carry out a systematic review of national legislation and practice in order to bring them into line with the UN guiding principles and other relevant international instruments of human rights or humanitarian law. These principles are particularly relevant to member states which are directly or indirectly involved in the South Ossetian crisis.

There are examples from recent history where large groups of displaced persons have been kept in unacceptable conditions and even in tented camps. Their suffering has been used as a propaganda tool in order to illustrate that the political problems remain unresolved. Tactics like this are not acceptable; such a policy amounts to keeping people who have already been victimised as hostages for political purposes.

For obvious reasons, displaced persons tend to flee to areas where they would not be in a minority position and where people from the same ethnic, religious or national community live. However, there are IDPs who either choose not to do this, or for whom this is not an option – the Roma, for example. Action plans on IDPs therefore need to pay particular attention to the needs and rights of minority groups in order to avoid a further cycle of violations. Many persons from minority groups may need special protective measures given that they may lack proof of identity or of their residence before displacement.

Children are particularly at risk in these crisis situations. Their rights must be protected. The UN Convention on the Rights of the Child continues to apply, even in the abnormal situation of forced internal or external displacement. Children, especially those who become "unaccompanied minors" during armed conflicts, should be given particular attention and assistance. Only in this way will it be possible to guarantee their basic needs and rights, including housing and

---

33. Recommendation Rec(2006)6 of the Committee of Ministers to member states on internally displaced persons, adopted on 5 April 2006.

access to education. Women and girls are also at heightened risk of abuse and gender-based violence. Survivors of violence and torture require specialised support.

We also must not forget that states have the duty to prevent displacement disasters from taking place in the first place. The UN guiding principles state that, "all authorities and international actors shall respect and ensure respect for their obligations under international law, including human rights and humanitarian law, in all circumstances, so as to prevent and avoid conditions that might lead to displacement of persons" (Principle 5).

In modern Europe, the root causes of forced displacement are found primarily in the sometimes violent emergence of nation states, and in the lack of broad-minded and tolerant policies towards national minorities, although these virtues are considered integral to European democratic values.

European history continues to teach us, bitterly but clearly, that the protection and promotion of the rights of national minorities are essential for stability, democratic security and peace on our continent. Governments have still to realise that the creation of a climate of tolerance and dialogue is necessary to encourage and enable ethnic and cultural diversity as a factor, not of division, but of enrichment and cohesion for European societies.

Chapter 4: Protection against homophobia and transphobia

The dehumanisation of lesbians, gays, bisexuals and transgender persons (LGBT) did not disappear with the Nazi rule which had some 100 000 people arrested because of their sexual orientation, and more than 10 000 sent to concentration camps. Extreme right-wing groups still incite hatred and violence against LGBT persons. Some of the old Nazi arguments against homosexuals are again being voiced in public debates.

Photo © ILGA-Europe.

Yogyakarta Principles

A number of people around the world, including Europe, continue to be stigmatised because of their actual or perceived sexual orientation and gender identity. In some cases these individuals are still being denied their rights to education, health care, housing or work. Some are harassed by the police; are left unprotected when attacked by extremists; or are deported to countries where they risk torture or execution. Also, some of their representative organisations are denied registration or are refused a permit to organise peaceful meetings and demonstrations.

It is sometimes said that the protection of the human rights of lesbians, gays, bisexuals and transgender (LGBT) people amounts to introducing new rights. That is a misunderstanding. The Universal Declaration of Human Rights and the agreed treaties establish that human rights apply to everyone and that no one should be excluded.

What is new is that there is now a stronger quest for this universal principle to be applied consistently. When grounds for unacceptable discrimination are listed in human rights treaties, or when previous such lists are interpreted, there are clear references to sexual orientation. For instance, the prohibition of discrimination on the grounds of "sex" in the 1966 International Covenant on Civil and Political Rights is understood to include a ban on discrimination based on sexual orientation. The European Union's Charter of Fundamental Rights explicitly includes discrimination based on sexual orientation.

The idea is to make clear the obvious – that lesbians, gays, bisexuals and transgender people have the same rights as others. International standards therefore apply to them as well. In other words, discrimination against anyone on the grounds of sexual orientation or gender identity is a human rights violation.

This is the main message of the Yogyakarta Principles on the Application of Human Rights Law in Relation to Sexual Orientation and Gender Identity.[34] These principles, which were adopted after an expert meeting in Yogyakarta in Indonesia in 2006, identify the obligations of states to respect, protect and fulfil the human rights of all persons, regardless of their sexual orientation[35] or gender identity.[36]

The principles are the unanimous result of discussions between 29 independent international human rights experts from different parts of the world, of whom almost half have served on United Nations treaty committees or as special rapporteurs. One of the experts was the former United Nations High Commissioner Mary Robinson.[37]

In the introduction to the principles, the experts make clear that they do not ask for new standards, only that the existing standards should be properly respected. The experts state that it is critical to clarify state obligations under agreed international human rights law so that the human rights of all persons are promoted and protected on the basis of equality and without discrimination.

Therefore, the Yogyakarta document goes further than just defining the principles: it also spells out the state's obligations. It asks for legislative and other measures to prohibit and eliminate discrimination against individuals because of their sexual orientation or gender identity. Legislation and action plans against discrimination should

---

34. The full text of the principles is published at www.yogyakartaprinciples.org.
35. The Yogyakarta document states that the term "sexual orientation" refers to: "each person's capacity for profound emotional, affection and sexual attraction to, and intimate and sexual relations with, individuals of a different gender or the same gender or more than one gender."
36. The document defines "gender identity" with reference to "each person's deeply felt internal and individual experience of gender which may or may not correspond with the sex assigned at birth, including the personal sense of the body (which may involve, if freely chosen, modification of bodily appearance or function by medical, surgical or other means) and other expressions of gender, including dress, speech and mannerisms."
37. Other Europeans among the experts are Maxim Anmeghichean (Moldova), Yakin Erturk (Turkey), Judith Mesquita (United Kingdom), Manfred Nowak (Austria), Michael O'Flaherty (Ireland), Dimitrina Petrova (Bulgaria), Nevena Vuckovic Sahovic (Serbia), Martin Scheinin (Finland), Stephen Whittle (United Kingdom) and Roman Wieruszewski (Poland).

address this form as discrimination as well, and laws which criminalise consensual sexual acts between people of the same sex should be repealed.[38]

The document also requests that governments take concrete action to counter prejudices through education and training. Steps should be taken to dispel discriminatory attitudes or behaviours which are founded on the idea that any one sexual orientation or gender identity is superior/inferior.

One particularly important chapter in the document relates to the principle of the right to security of persons. In this chapter it is recommended that governments do the following:

- take all necessary policing, or other, measures to prevent, and provide protection from, all forms of violence and harassment related to sexual orientation and gender identity;

- take all necessary legislative measures to impose appropriate criminal penalties for violence, threats of violence, incitement to violence and related harassment, when based on the sexual orientation and gender identity of any person or group of persons; such measures should cover all spheres of life, including that of the family;

- take all necessary legislative, administrative or other necessary measures to ensure that the sexual orientation and gender identity of the victim may not be advanced to justify, excuse or mitigate such violence;

- ensure that such violence is vigorously investigated, and that, where appropriate, when evidence is found, those responsible are prosecuted, tried and duly punished. Victims must also be provided with appropriate remedies and redress, including compensation;

---

38. More than 80 countries still criminalise consensual same-sex acts and at least seven maintain the death penalty for such "crimes".

- undertake campaigns of awareness-raising, directed at the general public as well as actual and potential perpetrators of violence, in order to combat the prejudice that underlies violence related to sexual orientation and gender identity.

Such steps are necessary. During my missions I have been confronted with some of the realities behind the aggressive intolerance that is exhibited towards those who are perceived as different. I have met individuals who live in fear of being exposed and others who have "come out" but suffer serious consequences.

Transgender persons are humiliated. Some have been denied necessary health care and have been confronted with medical practitioners who refuse to provide gender reassignment therapy. Others have been prevented from changing their name in their passports or identification documents (see separate article).

Prejudice in this area is indeed very deep, not least in countries with a recent past of dictatorship and an absence of open public debate. Some religious preaching has also been tendentious and has not been helpful in the defence of the human rights of LGBT persons. Advocacy against homophobia is clearly not considered acceptable in a number of countries. This underlines the importance of broader and more systematic education and awareness-raising efforts, and of leading politicians taking clear principled positions. I believe that the Yogyakarta Principles are important in this endeavour.

For my part, I fully endorse the principles. Some governments have already made them an integral part of their human rights policies, and I recommend that all governments study the document and take the actions it recommends.

Homophobia

The European Court of Human Rights took a significant decision against homophobia in 2007. A non-governmental group in Poland, the Foundation for Equality, had been denied permission to organise a demonstration in Warsaw on their "Equality Days"

two years earlier. The Court found that the local authorities had violated three provisions of the European Convention – relating to freedom of assembly, the right to an effective remedy and the prohibition of discrimination. **This ruling sends a message to authorities all across Europe.**[39]

The lesbian and gay movements are more and more organised and they often urge their members to "come out" in public: this is a logical response to centuries of systematic discrimination in country after country.

The real problem is not the sexual orientation of individuals, but the reaction of others. Whatever the psychological roots, many people still react aggressively against homosexuals. Sadly, some religious teachers have also given direct or indirect support to homophobia, which has delayed the necessary attitudinal change in a number of countries.

Gay Pride Parades are banned or disrupted by the authorities in some European countries. This has been the case in Chișinău, Moscow, Tallinn, Riga and other cities. In some cases, the demonstrators took the risk of marching even when denied permission – for example, in Warsaw 2005 – and these parades have generally been peaceful. When there have been problems, this has been due to mob attacks against the marchers and lack of police protection.

It is a sad fact that discrimination against individuals because of their sexual orientation is still widespread on our continent. During my visits to member states, I have repeatedly seen the signs and consequences of such prejudice. Individuals are victimised in their daily lives. Some live in constant fear of being exposed while others, who have "come out" in public, face discrimination or even harassment. Their representative organisations have been made targets of hate speech.

Few politicians have fully stood up to this challenge. Instead, some have themselves contributed to popular prejudice through stereotypical descriptions of homosexuals as dangerous propagandists who

---

39. *Bączkowski and Others v. Poland*, judgment of 3 May 2007.

should not be allowed to be teachers or even show their "lifestyle choice" to others. In discussions about demonstrations, some mayors and other politicians have made intolerant and homophobic public statements. This kind of populism is most unfortunate and tends to "legitimise" discrimination.

The dehumanisation of lesbians, gays, bisexuals and transgender persons (LGBT) did not disappear with the Nazi rule which had some 100 000 people arrested because of their sexual orientation, and more than 10 000 sent to concentration camps. Extreme right-wing groups still incite hatred and violence against LGBT persons. Some of the old Nazi arguments against homosexuals are again being voiced in public debates. Therefore, it is particularly important that politicians, religious leaders and other opinion makers stand up for the principle that all people have human rights – irrespective of their sexual orientation.

The Council of Europe Congress of Local and Regional Authorities has adopted recommendations on the need to protect the freedom of assembly and expression of LGBT persons. These ought to be studied carefully by local and regional politicians.

The Committee of Ministers has recommended that member states act to combat discrimination on grounds of sexual orientation or gender identity. The proposed measures include action against hate crimes and hate speech; protection for freedom of expression, association and peaceful assembly; the right to seek asylum; the right to non-discrimination in employment, education and health; as well as the right to respect for private and family life.[40]

The legal standards are absolutely clear. The European Convention on Human Rights – which is part of the national law in all Council of Europe countries – does not allow discrimination against persons because of their sexual orientation or gender identification. Guarantees against discrimination on any grounds are provided in Article 14 of the Convention and in its Protocol No. 12. The protocol, which is now in force in 14 countries, prohibits discrimination in the

---

40. Recommendation CM/Rec(2010)5, adopted on 31 March 2010.

enjoyment of any right set forth by law as well as any discrimination by public authorities.

In significant rulings, the Strasbourg Court has decided that consensual sexual relations in private between adults of the same sex must not be criminalised; that there should be no discrimination when setting the age of consent for sexual acts; that homosexuals should have the right to be admitted into the armed forces; and that same-sex partners should have the same right of succession of tenancy as other couples. On the issue of parenting rights, the jurisprudence of the Court has developed and it has ruled against discrimination on grounds of sexual orientation for granting parental responsibility.

The Court has been more cautious on the question of adoption and largely left it to member states to strike a reasonable balance. Of course, no one has the right to adopt – the best interest of the child must be the decisive consideration. However, the obvious human rights approach is that homosexuals should have the same rights as other adults to be considered as candidates when decisions are taken about who would be the best adoptive parent for a child in such need.

This is now the approach in several European countries, including Belgium, Denmark, Germany, Iceland, the Netherlands, Norway, Spain, Sweden and the United Kingdom. Some of these states also grant access to joint adoption by a homosexual couple. As for individual adoption by unmarried individuals, laws in most European countries do not discriminate on the grounds of sexual orientation.

The number of European countries that legally recognise same-sex partnerships is increasing and already includes Andorra, the Czech Republic, Denmark, Finland, France, Germany, Iceland, Luxembourg, Norway, Slovenia, Sweden, Switzerland and the United Kingdom. In other countries, this debate is still under way. Same-sex marriage is already possible in Belgium, the Netherlands and Spain; other countries, like Sweden, are likely to follow shortly.

In other words, homophobic policies are on the retreat. However, there is no room for complacency. Remaining prejudice does not disappear

by itself – further measures should be taken for the protection of the human rights of lesbians, gays, bisexuals and transgender persons:
- the legislation in several European countries needs to be reformed in order to ensure that LGBT people have the same rights as others;
- there should be a stronger reaction against officials who take unlawful decisions – for instance by banning peaceful demonstrations – or who use their influential position to spread prejudice against people because of their sexual orientation;
- the teaching of history should be reviewed, with the purpose of ensuring that the Nazi crimes against LGBT persons – as well as other aspects of their victimisation – be objectively taught;
- schools should give objective information about homosexuality, and encourage respect for diversity and minority rights;
- authorities should treat organisations advocating for the rights of LGBT persons with the same respect as they are expected to show to other non-governmental human rights organisations;
- hate crimes against LGBT persons should be seen as serious crimes;
- courts as well as ombudsmen and other independent national human rights institutions need, as a priority, to address discrimination based on sexual orientation.

Transphobia

During missions to member states of the Council of Europe I have been reminded of the continued discrimination against certain individuals on account of their gender identity. Transgender persons still encounter severe problems in their daily lives as their identity is met with bureaucratic insensitivity, suspicion or outright rejection.

There have been some extremely brutal hate crimes against transgender persons. My discussions with non-governmental organisations defending their rights indicate that a number of hate crimes (even very serious ones) go unreported. One of the reasons appears to be a lack of trust among transgender people towards the police.

Some people seem to have problems with the mere existence of human beings whose inner identity is not the same as their appearance or as the one determined at birth. The aggression directed against transgender people cannot, however, be dismissed only as a psychological problem of those who do not know better. These attitudes victimise a number of innocent and vulnerable persons and must therefore be countered.

I have been struck by the lack of knowledge about the human rights issues at stake for transgender persons, even among political decision makers. This is probably the reason why more has not been done to address transphobia and discrimination on grounds of gender identity and gender expression. The result is that, in all countries, individuals are discriminated against, including in such crucial areas as housing, employment and health care.

In a number of cases, problems start already at the stage of the state recognising a person's gender identity when issuing birth certificates, passports and other documents. Most transgender persons who want to state that they no longer identify with their gender as registered at birth have difficulties in processing those changes in official records. This in turn has caused a number of practical problems when showing identification papers: in the bank or the post office, when using a credit card, crossing a border or in other similar situations.

One well-publicised case related to Dr Lydia Foy in Ireland who had been trying to obtain a birth certificate to reflect her female gender since April 1997. Some 10 years later the Irish High Court delivered a landmark judgment ruling that the state was in breach of Article 8 of the European Convention on Human Rights. On 21 June 2010, the Irish Government confirmed that it has withdrawn its appeal: Lydia Foy will now be legally recognised as a woman, and the government will introduce legislation to recognise transgender persons in their new gender, and allow them to obtain new birth certificates.

In fact, these problems have now been addressed in most European countries, where it has become possible to obtain corrections of such records and also obtain new forenames. However, in some countries a change of birth certificate is still not allowed and, in others, such changes are permitted only upon proof that a person is sterilised, declared infertile, or has gone through other medical procedures such as gender reassignment surgery or hormone treatment. The medical obstacles thereby created for the individual are ignored, and the opinion of the individual is seen as insufficient.

Additionally, many countries require that a person divorce before the new gender can be recognised – regardless of whether or not the partners actually want to divorce. This in turn has a negative impact on the position of children, both in terms of their rights, as well as in terms of their relationships with their parents. In fact, in several countries, the parent who has undergone gender change will lose custody rights. Such legislation needs to be reformed in the spirit of the best interests of the child.

To require surgery as a condition for enjoying the right to one's gender identity ignores the fact that only about 10% of the transgender persons in Europe undergo gender reassignment operations.

While the official policy in some situations makes surgery a condition for the gender change to be accepted, such operations are not always a practical option for those who want them. A study by ILGA-Europe and TransGender Europe showed that a large proportion of transgender respondents in the European Union are refused state funding to alter their sex.

Even access to ordinary health care can be a problem for people with a "non-standard" gender identity. The lack of trained staff and the lack of familiarity with the specific health care needs of transgender persons – or simply the absence of prejudice towards transgender people – render this group of people very vulnerable to unpredictable and sometimes hostile responses when they use medical services.

In the United Kingdom, some 4 000 male-to-female transgender persons have been struggling to get their gender status accepted, including for the purpose of accessing pension benefits. In spite of overwhelming legal arguments, they have so far been denied the pension rights that all other women in the country have.

Other obstacles stand in the way of living a normal life like everyone else. A major problem for transgender persons is the harassment and discrimination many of them face in workplaces. The effect is that some just leave their jobs, while others avoid undergoing gender reassignment surgery as they fear being stigmatised.

Data presented by the Agency for Fundamental Rights[41] has shown that some jobless transgender persons have been unable to find other employment and have then ended up in prostitution. A report from Human Rights Watch on the situation in Turkey[42] drew attention to the situation of transgender prostitutes in that country – victimised by violence, drug addiction, sexual abuse, lack of health insurance, homelessness, police attacks and a high risk of HIV/Aids.

To date, very little factual information has been gathered on the situation of transgender people in Council of Europe member states. This information is needed to determine where the rights of transgender persons to recognition of their identity are infringed, and the extent of their problems in terms of discrimination and violence, and when accessing health care or other public services.

The European Court of Human Rights has ruled that states are required to recognise the gender change in post-operative transsexuals. A case was raised by Christine Goodwin from the United Kingdom who herself was a post-operative male-to-female transsexual. She complained of sexual harassment in the workplace, discrimination in relation to

---

41. European Union Agency for Fundamental Rights, "Homophobia and discrimination on grounds of sexual orientation and gender identity in the EU Member States Part II: the social situation", March 2009.
42. Human Rights Watch, "We need a law for liberation. Gender, sexuality and human rights in changing Turkey", May 2008.

contributions to the National Insurance system, and denial of her right to marry.

The Court stated that:

> *the very essence of the Convention was respect for human dignity and human freedom. Under Article 8 of the Convention in particular, where the notion of personal autonomy was an important principle underlying the interpretation of its guarantees, protection was given to the personal sphere of each individual, including the right to establish details of their identity as human beings.*
>
> ...
>
> *In the twenty-first century the right of transsexuals to personal development and to physical and moral security in the full sense enjoyed by others in society could no longer be regarded as a matter of controversy requiring the lapse of time to cast clear light on the issues involved.*[43]

There is no excuse now for not granting this minority their full and unconditional human rights. This message from the Court has to be followed through in all Council of Europe member states. States must take all necessary actions to ensure that transphobia is stopped and to end any discrimination against transgender persons.

---

43. *Christine Goodwin v. the United Kingdom*, judgment of 11 July 2002; see also *Grant v. the United Kingdom,* judgment of 23 May 2006.

Chapter 5: Rights of people with disabilities

For far too long policies concerning persons with disabilities have focused exclusively on institutional care, medical rehabilitation and welfare benefits. The policies build on the premise that persons with disabilities are just victims, rather than subjects able and entitled to be active citizens. The result has been that men, women and children with disabilities have had their civil, cultural, economic, political and social rights violated.

Photo © Shutterstock.

Making society inclusive

There are more than 80 million people with disabilities in Europe. Their rights are recognised in several international human rights treaties, in particular the 2006 UN Convention on the Rights of Persons with Disabilities. However, these rights are still far from realised. Moving from rhetoric to implementation has been slow, and requires a change of attitude – from a charity approach to rights-based action.

For far too long policies concerning persons with disabilities have focused exclusively on institutional care, medical rehabilitation and welfare benefits. The policies build on the premise that persons with disabilities are victims, rather than subjects able and entitled to be active citizens. The result has been that men, women and children with disabilities have had their civil, cultural, economic, political and social rights violated.

However, a gradual shift in thinking has started as a result of pressure from the disability movements and other civil society groups. These groups played an important and active role in the development of the UN convention and the Council of Europe Disability Action Plan 2006-15.

These two instruments confirm clearly that the rights of persons with disabilities are human rights. States have an obligation to respect, ensure and fulfil these rights. The participation of persons with disabilities in all decisions affecting their lives is recognised as a fundamental principle in both.

However, persons with disabilities still face a number of barriers when seeking to participate in society. Children with physical disabilities cannot play with other children in public playgrounds because of their inaccessible design. TV programmes without subtitles exclude persons with hearing impairments from much shared culture.

Persons placed under guardianship on grounds of disability are excluded from almost all areas of life. They cannot, for example, vote, buy or sell things, or decide where to live, work, travel or marry.

Making societies inclusive requires planning and systematic work. It is therefore encouraging that several European states have now formally adopted disability plans and strategies. Every country will need to tailor such plans to its own circumstances. Those who have tried to set priorities, define time limits and allocate budget resources and responsibility for implementation have generally been rewarded with positive results.

These plans must also address the situation of children with disabilities, many of whom are still not accepted in ordinary schools because the schools are not equipped to meet their needs. This is also true of day-care centres, sometimes forcing parents to choose between leaving their children in institutional care or giving up their jobs in order to care for their child.

The situation of children without parental care is particularly serious. Life in an institution, separating children from their family and their social context, almost inevitably leads to exclusion. More resources are needed to support families – especially families living in poverty and single-parent households – to enable children to grow up within their own family environment.

Childcare centres and schools should be open to all children and equipped to meet their different needs. Social services and community health care providers must be accessible and competent to care for persons with different disabilities. Such reforms are challenging and require commitment and a reallocation of resources.

The right to education is equally important for all children. Even though every child's ability to learn is undisputed, there are still children in Europe of school age who are considered to be "uneducable" and denied any form of education.

Such practices limit not only children's options to support themselves later as adults, but also their possibility to become independent and participate in society. The obvious principle is that persons with disabilities have the right to receive quality education and no one should be excluded from ordinary schools because of their disability.

Another group not to be forgotten in such action plans is elderly people with disabilities. As a consequence of getting older, many of us will develop reduced vision, reduced hearing or reduced mobility.

Innovative approaches are required to meet these challenges across a wide range of service areas. Co-ordinated action to enable elderly people with disabilities to remain in their community to the greatest extent possible is essential. This requires an assessment of individual needs and forward planning so that the required services are available.

An aspect which must be taken account of in action plans is the situation of persons with mental disabilities. The situation in psychiatric institutions in several European countries is shockingly bad. I have seen institutions where the conditions are so inhumane and degrading that they should be closed down immediately.

Unfortunately, medication is too often used as the only form of treatment. There is an urgent need to apply alternatives, such as different forms of therapy, rehabilitation and other activities. Unclear admission and discharge procedures constitute another problem resulting in what, in reality, is arbitrary detention.

There are, however, also positive examples of measures which empower patients with mental disabilities by facilitating their active involvement in their own treatment plans, and providing complaints procedures for those who feel that their rights have been violated.

As with all closed institutional settings where the liberty of individuals is restricted, effective complaints procedures as well as independent monitoring visits are of crucial importance. The Optional Protocol to the UN Convention Against Torture requires states to establish national inspection systems to monitor all places of detention, including mental health and social care institutions.

Persons with disabilities are also victims of hate crimes and hate-motivated incidents. Violence, harassment and negative stereotyping have a significant negative impact on their security and well-being, and also on their ability to participate both socially and economically in the wider community. Research conducted by Mencap[44] in the United Kingdom demonstrated that 90% of people with a learning disability had experienced bullying and harassment. In addition to general awareness-raising measures, hate crime against persons with disabilities should be tackled through pro-active policing and prompt prosecutions.

Full removal of social, legal and physical barriers to the inclusion of persons with disabilities will take time and require resources. But it has to be done. We cannot afford to have barriers that prevent 80 million people from fully participating in, and contributing to, society as voters, politicians, employees, consumers, parents and taxpayers like everybody else.

Governments should take action in order to more fully realise the human rights of persons with disabilities; they should:

– ratify the UN Convention on the Rights of Persons with Disabilities and the Optional Protocol and start implementing it. Use the European action plan to make the convention standards a reality;

– develop national and local action plans to remove physical, legal, social and other barriers that prevent persons with disabilities from participating fully in society. Persons with disabilities and their organisations should be consulted and included in the planning and monitoring of laws and policies affecting them;

– adopt wide-ranging anti-discrimination legislation;

– set up independent ombudsmen or other equality bodies to ensure that persons with disabilities can fully exercise their rights;

– develop programmes to enable persons with disabilities to live in the community;

---

44. *Living in fear. The need to combat bullying of people with a learning disability*, published by Mencap, 2000 (www.mencap.org.uk).

- cease new admissions to unsuitable social care institutions and allocate sufficient resources to provide adequate health care, rehabilitation and social services in the community instead;
- review the laws and procedures for involuntary hospitalisation to ensure that both law and practice comply with international human rights standards;
- set up independent mechanisms equipped to make regular, unannounced and effective visits to social care homes and psychiatric hospitals in accordance with the Optional Protocol to the UN Convention Against Torture;
- tackle hate crime against persons with disabilities through legislation, pro-active policing and prompt prosecutions.

Rights for persons with mental disabilities

Individuals with mental health or intellectual disabilities continue to face discrimination, stigmatisation and even repression. They find that their mere existence is seen as a problem, and they have sometimes been hidden away in remote institutions, or in the back-rooms of family homes. They have been treated as non-persons whose autonomy is negotiable and whose decisions are meaningless.

Though attitudes to disabilities have changed with the human rights advances made more generally, persons with mental health or intellectual disabilities still face problems relating to their right to take decisions for themselves. Their legal capacity is often restricted or non-existent and they are often placed under the guardianship of someone else who is entitled to take all decisions on their behalf.

Some persons with mental health or intellectual disabilities may have objective problems in representing themselves and their concerns to authorities, banks, landlords and other such institutions as a consequence of their actual or perceived impairments. They may also be manipulated into making decisions which they would otherwise not make.

A basic principle of human rights is that the agreed standards apply to every human being, without distinction. However, international human rights standards have been denied to persons with disabilities. It was this failure which prompted the UN Convention on the Rights of Persons with Disabilities, which emphasises that people with all types of disabilities are entitled to the full range of human rights on an equal basis with others.

The aim of the standards is to promote the inclusion and full participation in society of people with disabilities. When we deprive individuals of their right to represent themselves, we contradict these standards.

How then should concrete difficulties be handled?

The UN convention addresses this issue in its Article 12, which starts by stating that governments shall "recognize that persons with disabilities enjoy legal capacity on an equal basis with others in all aspects of life".

The convention goes on to recognise the reality that some people – because of their impairments or external barriers – are unable by themselves to take important decisions. The convention requests that governments provide such individuals with access to the support they may require to exercise their legal capacity.

The nature of this support is crucial. Supported decision-making is a developing field in some Council of Europe member states, but the practice has been embedded for several years in many provincial laws. What happens in those jurisdictions is that a network of supporters is recognised – but not imposed on the adult – and these supporters provide information and options to help the adult to make a decision.

The convention states that there should be appropriate and effective safeguards in order to prevent abuse. The rights, will and preferences of the person concerned should be respected and care should be taken to ensure that there is no conflict of interest involved or undue influence being exercised.

The support arrangements should also last for the shortest time possible, and be subject to regular review by a competent, independent and impartial authority or judicial body.

These formulations allow for the provision of a range of alternatives to guardianship to adults with disabilities. The starting point for the reforms is full legal capacity combined with the right of the individual to seek support. The exercise of this support should always be regulated with safeguards to avoid the misuse of trust.

This is not the reality in the majority of European countries, where there has been a tendency almost routinely to declare people with mental health and intellectual disabilities legally incapable, and to place them under legal guardianship.

However, the UN Convention – as well as the Council of Europe 2006-15 action plan to promote the rights and full participation of people with disabilities in society – may have had a positive effect in some countries. A European Union high-level group on the implementation of the convention reported in 2009 that it had obtained assurances about a review process on this issue from the Czech Republic, France, Hungary, Ireland, Latvia, Portugal and Slovakia.

The report also referred to the fact that these countries and others "had all expressed an interest in sharing information by organising conferences, expert working groups and seminars on the topic, involving civil society and all relevant players, including the judiciary, and discussing legal terms with a view to developing legislation, policy and practice in this area".

Such discussions are necessary in order to make real the reform of laws and policies agreed in principle when the UN convention and the Council of Europe action plan were drafted and agreed. Obviously, the case law of the Strasbourg Court will be studied in detail during this process, and more litigation before that Court is needed in order to better integrate the UN convention's approach into European jurisprudence.

In a case in 2008 the Court had to deal with the deprivation of legal capacity and enforced hospitalisation and treatment without consent. Mr Shtukaturov, an adult who was diagnosed with schizophrenia, had been deprived of his legal capacity in a decision made without his knowledge at the request of his mother, who had become his guardian. He was legally prohibited from challenging the decision in Russian courts, and had subsequently been detained in a psychiatric hospital.[45]

After reviewing his case, the European Court of Human Rights stated that "the existence of a mental disorder, even a serious one, cannot be the sole reason to justify full incapacitation". The Court stated that domestic legislation must provide for a "tailor-made response". The Court found that the decision-making process depriving Mr Shtukaturov of his legal capacity constituted a disproportionate interference with his private life, and found various violations of the European Convention on Human Rights.

This judgment must be interpreted as promoting a Europe-wide approach in line with the UN convention. Any restrictions of the rights of the individual must be tailor-made to the individual's needs, be genuinely justified, be the result of rights-based procedures and be combined with effective safeguards.

The UN convention also underlines the particular importance of protecting the right of persons with disabilities to own property, control their own financial affairs and to have equal access to bank loans and mortgages. This emphasis appears to derive from the experience that decisions on incapacitation in this area have often been taken in violation of human rights standards.

Obviously, persons with mental health and intellectual disabilities should also have the right to vote in elections and stand for election. Although this is stated clearly in the UN convention (Article 29), certain individuals in a number of European countries are excluded by law. Being deprived of one's legal capacity, or having that capacity restricted, denies these basic democratic rights as well. This has further

---

45. *Shtukaturov v. Russia*, judgment of 27 March 2008.

exacerbated the political invisibility of people with mental health or intellectual disabilities.

We should remember that there is a great difference between taking away the right to take decisions about one's life and providing "access to support". The first views people with disabilities as objects of treatment, charity and fear. The second places the person with disabilities at the centre of decision-making, respecting their autonomy and treating them as subjects entitled to the full range of human rights.

Discrimination against people with intellectual disabilities

People with intellectual disabilities tend to be among the most marginalised of all. Even today their treatment is clearly inhuman in country after country. They have limited possibilities to make themselves heard and this has contributed to making their situation one of a hidden human rights crisis. It is time for political decision makers to stop ignoring these vulnerable citizens.

Before policies are designed, it is necessary to be clear about different kinds of disabilities and to apply the relevant terminology. A distinction should be made between persons with mental health or psychiatric problems (for example, schizophrenia and bipolar disorder), and those with intellectual disabilities (for example, limitations caused by, among others, Down's syndrome).

Though there are some persons with intellectual disabilities who also have mental health problems, the two kinds of impairment are different: they have different causes and effects – and create therefore different needs.

Though persons with any of these disabilities suffer human rights abuses, I am here focusing on those with intellectual disabilities.

Experts on disability and health rightly stress that there are great differences among individuals regarding the degree of intellectual impairment, and that generalisation should be avoided. They all agree that the needs and responses to need have to be individualised. At the same time, despite these individual variations, there is a shared commonality which lies in a person's reduced level of intellectual functioning, which may affect learning and language capacity as well as social skills.

The key point here is that persons with intellectual disabilities are entitled to basic human rights and fundamental freedoms. This was also the uncomplicated demand formulated at a remarkable World Health Organization (WHO) conference in Montreal some years ago. Among the participants were persons with intellectual disabilities, their representatives, families, service providers and other specialists.[46] The conference adopted the Montreal Declaration on Intellectual Disabilities and made points which should not have had to be raised. Yet these self-evident assertions had remained largely ignored until then and are still not taken seriously enough.

The declaration called upon governments to implement agreed human rights standards for persons with intellectual disabilities; to consult with them on relevant laws, policies and plans; and to take steps to ensure their full inclusion and their right to participate in society.

The declaration also asked governments to allocate sufficient resources; to provide the necessary support to them and their families; to strengthen their organisations; and to develop education, training and information programmes for them.

These proposals have only been realised to a limited extent. During missions to member states, I have had to conclude that persons with intellectual disabilities are still stigmatised and marginalised; that they are rarely consulted or even listened to; that a great number of them continue to be kept in old-style, inhuman institutions; and that moves to provide housing and other services in community-based settings have met obstacles and been delayed.

---

46. The meeting was organised by the World Health Organization and the Pan-American Health Organization on 5 and 6 October 2004. The declaration can be found at www.declaracionmontreal.com.

In many countries across Europe, the conditions in some of the so-called "social care homes" are appalling. In these segregated institutions very little, if any, rehabilitation is provided. Often, persons with intellectual disabilities are housed with persons having psychiatric problems, and unnecessarily given sedatives against their will. They are in some cases deprived of their liberty and treated as if they were dangerous. Many are cut off from the outside world. Intellectual disabilities – like other disabilities – carry a stigma, and many people have been abandoned by their families through shame and a lack of alternative options.

The staff at these institutions is almost always underpaid. Yet, I have met many dedicated and caring employees who try to do their very best with extremely limited budgets. Almost without exception they stress the need for more political support and more resources. Though many governments have adopted action plans in this field, these have not been sufficiently funded. Many have also not been monitored appropriately, so that plans often fall off of political agendas, and there is no follow through.

The call for deinstitutionalisation has, however, not gone entirely unheard. In Albania, for instance, I noticed that the process of moving persons to community and family-based housing had already yielded some satisfactory results. In "the former Yugoslav Republic of Macedonia" an ambitious strategy was adopted, and concerted efforts were also made in Serbia (though in the latter case, some families were unable to take their relatives back home).

More effort is obviously needed to properly prepare such community placements and to develop adequate services at the local level. This can only be done effectively in consultation with organisations protecting persons with disabilities. It has to be recognised that life in the wider community may not be easy, even for those who have not been overly institutionalised. Prejudice against persons with intellectual disabilities is widespread.

Greater progress has been made in the case of children. The infamous collective homes for disadvantaged children are being slowly phased out, including in eastern European countries where they used to be common. Every European government has recognised that such institutions are not good for children.

However, their closure must be done with care so as to avoid further damaging long-institutionalised children. Furthermore, there is a need to create practical alternatives, including support for families, a child-friendly foster care system, and proper monitoring.

In spite of some progress over recent years regarding children's rights in general, too little is done to ensure that children who show symptoms of intellectual disability are given sufficient attention, care and support. Efforts to diagnose problems at an early stage, in order to facilitate early intervention, are given insufficient priority.

Schooling is another problem. Very few children with intellectual disabilities are offered specialist assistance tailored to the individual child in ordinary schools while "special schools" – a segregated system which fuels adult institutions and begins a lifetime of social exclusion – remain the norm. Many children are not accorded their right to education at all. For instance, the European Committee of Social Rights concluded that children with intellectual disabilities and living in homes for mentally disabled children in Bulgaria were deprived of an effective right to education.

Health care for both children and adults with intellectual disabilities is another serious problem. Persons with intellectual disabilities may have greater health needs than others. At the same time, they are often confronted with discrimination by systems whose staff neglect to provide them with health care on an equal basis with others. Often there is a failure to appropriately communicate with persons with intellectual disabilities.

The result is that the care they receive tends to be of poor quality, and health problems go undetected. There are indications that people with intellectual disabilities have a shorter life expectancy and higher mortality rate than the average population. The conclusion must be that the medical system is failing to meet their needs.

Adults with even minor intellectual disabilities are discriminated against in the labour market, even for jobs where they have all the necessary qualifications and skills. Efforts to accommodate the reasonable needs of persons with disabilities have been half-hearted, and the sheltered employment opportunities sometimes on offer have, in some cases, contributed to the further unfortunate isolation of individuals.

Little is also being done to develop a wise and rights-based approach to the problem of the legal capacity of those with intellectual disabilities. It may be in the nature of this impairment that problems occur in relation to how one represents oneself towards authorities, banks and other such institutions. As pointed out in the previous article, this is, however, no justification for a policy to routinely incapacitate people with mental disabilities by putting them under legal guardianship where they have no say in important decisions affecting their lives.

Families with members having intellectual disabilities are often left to cope on their own – in spite of their important role as caregivers and as the people sometimes best placed to understand and communicate with the person with intellectual disabilities.

A sad consequence of this isolation is that parents and other family members sometimes fail to cope well and the individual with a disability comes to be seen as a burden. In some countries, and often with the best of intentions, families seek to place adult children under guardianship and send them to an institution. Relatives may see this as the only option if they want to ensure that an adult child survives when the parents are no longer able to look after them.

There is one area where there has been considerable progress since the Montreal meeting in 2004 because of the UN Convention on the Rights of Persons with Disabilities and the Council of Europe Disability Action Plan 2006-15.[47]

---

47. According to information from the United Nations in April 2010 the following 22 European countries had so far ratified the UN Convention on the Rights of Persons with Disabilities: Austria, Azerbaijan, Belgium, Bosnia and Herzegovina, Croatia, Czech Republic, Denmark, France, Germany, Hungary, Italy, Latvia, Montenegro,

It is urgent to move from words to action and to ensure that effective steps are indeed taken. The UN convention requires states to set up a mechanism to co-ordinate government action; to establish an effective system of independent monitoring; and to invite civil society – and in particular persons with disabilities themselves and their organisations – to take part in the process of monitoring (Article 33).

Such measures would help address the stigmatisation and marginalisation of persons with intellectual disabilities and encourage instead their greater participation and integration into society. This change would make all our societies more humane.

Portugal, San Marino, Serbia, Slovenia, Spain, Sweden, Turkey, Ukraine and the United Kingdom. Another 21 states in Europe had signed though not yet ratified.

Chapter 6: Gender rights

Sexual assault should be seen as a serious human rights violation. The fact that such abuses are largely hidden is not an excuse for ignoring their existence. On the contrary, it should be a political priority to protect women, children and men from this threat. The very first step should be to investigate why there are so few convictions in cases brought to court – and to remedy this failure.

Photo: Poster used for the Council of Europe Campaign to Combat Violence against Women, including Domestic Violence (© Council of Europe).

Gender representation in politics

Across Europe, the distribution of power between men and women is still unequal. This was the underlying motivation for a milestone recommendation by the Council of Europe in 2003. The Committee of Ministers agreed on action for "balanced participation of women and men in political and public decision-making". The idea was to open the door for women into positions of power.[48]

Interestingly, the Committee defined a precise benchmark. It stated that balanced participation in decision-making bodies meant that the representation of either women or men should not fall below 40%. How far have European states moved towards that goal?

Progress has been very slow. Only four countries have passed the 40% threshold in their parliaments: Sweden, Iceland, the Netherlands and Finland. More than 30% female representation was reported from another seven states: Norway, Belgium, Denmark, Spain, Andorra, Germany and "the former Yugoslav Republic of Macedonia".[49]

Though the average level is 22%, almost half of the European parliaments have not even reached the level of 20%, and five countries have less than 10% women in the national parliamentary body, that is Armenia, Turkey, Malta, Ukraine and Georgia.

The average female representation in European governments is well below one third, and several governments have no female ministers at all. Female ministers also tend to be given portfolios considered less central and important. The exceptions are Denmark, Finland, Iceland, Norway, Spain and Sweden, where an almost complete gender balance has been established over the years, but even there key ministries tend to be run by male ministers.

What ought to be done?

---

48. Recommendation Rec(2003)3, 12 March 2003.
49. The data (correct as of 30 September 2010) is provided by the Inter-Parliamentary Union (IPU) and based on reports from national parliaments (references here are only made to the lower house if there are two chambers).

In its 2003 recommendation, the Committee of Ministers asked for special measures to stimulate and support women's participation in political and public decision-making. Such efforts are needed, especially in regions where patriarchal attitudes remain and where women are kept on the sidelines. Social and family policies which help women to return to work after having children ensure that women remain in active employment, and also ensure that they feel able to engage in the political life of their country.

There has been some progress in this regard. For instance, recent reports from Turkey show encouraging signs of more women seeking political positions.

However, the Committee of Ministers went further and raised the issue of quotas. It recommended that member states "consider setting targets linked to a time scale with a view to reaching balanced participation of women and men in political and public decision making."

This approach is controversial. It has been argued that quotas imply a form of discrimination against those who are thereby excluded from consideration. Another argument against quotas has been that those favoured through such target-setting might not be fully respected or might be characterised as having failed to get their position on their own merits. It has also been proposed that a target, if it is not sufficiently ambitious, may merely preserve the *status quo*.

Admittedly, positive action can have negative consequences and should therefore only be used when there is an objective and reasonable justification for such measures. The underlying idea of such action is, however, important – it is aimed at compensating for and rooting out persistent discrimination and at breaking the habits and perceptions which perpetuate inequality. Indeed, gender quotas can, in my opinion, contribute to attitudinal change, and thereby ensure political progress.

Obligatory legal quotas are still unusual in Europe; it is more common for countries to try various forms of voluntary targets. In some cases, the mere threat of a binding regulation has spurred political parties to rethink their nomination procedures.

In Spain and other countries, the breakthrough started inside political parties. Some parties, for instance, decided that every second candidate on the electoral party list should be a woman.

In these countries it has now become an electoral disadvantage for parties not to propose a gender-balanced list to the electorate. In fact, gender targets are no longer necessary; the nomination process has become self-correcting – this is what should become the normal situation.

Is this issue of female political representation important? Yes, it is for the following reasons:

- it is a matter of the full enjoyment of human rights and social justice for everyone;
- it is about genuine democracy. A society where half of the population is by and large excluded from political participation is not truly democratic;
- it is a necessity in order to avoid the wasting of intellectual and other human resources;
- it would – as the Committee of Ministers put it – "lead to better and more efficient policy making through the redefinition of political priorities and the placing of new issues on the political agenda, as well as to the improvement of quality of life for all".

The pay gap

Equal pay for equal work is a fundamental principle of justice. This is one of the core standards of the International Labour Office and a central provision in the agreed treaties on economic and social rights, including the European Social Charter. However, surveys demonstrate that women's salaries continue to be considerably lower than those of men and that the trend towards closing the gap

is slow. This pay gap is a symptom of structural injustice that should be tackled much more forcefully than has been the case so far.

According to reports from the European Commission, women in European Union countries earn on average 15% less than men. In some countries the gap is reportedly even wider, for instance in Cyprus, Slovakia, Estonia, Germany and the United Kingdom. There is less statistical data available for other parts of Europe, but it seems clear that the pattern in many states is more or less the same.

There are still cases of blatant injustice where women are paid less than men even when performing identical jobs. Such gaps are often "disguised" through different job titles or job classifications though the actual work is the same.

Job sectors that are dominated by women are also typically paid less than those professions where men tend to predominate. This is a major and enduring problem. Although some of these stereotypical dividing lines are now being overturned – not least through advances in the education system – there is still a need to reassess the inherent importance of some professions, for example, in the health, childcare and education sectors. The skills, competences and responsibilities required for these jobs must be better recognised and rewarded.

Other forms of indirect or hidden discrimination permeate personnel policies in too many work places: we regularly see gender biases operating in methods of job evaluation, as well as in the setting of pay grades and pay rates.

The well-known phenomenon of the "glass ceiling" is based on outdated attitudes, but persists nevertheless. Though there has been an important breakthrough in some countries, women continue to be grossly under-represented in senior positions. It is still relatively rare that women are welcomed into managerial jobs. This is not only unfair, but also a tremendous waste. Great competences are being lost today, not least in the private sector.

The other side of this coin is that, in general, men still take limited responsibility for household obligations and the support of their children. One European Union report showed that while men on average spent seven hours a week on such unpaid work, women invested much more time – 35 hours (for those working part-time outside the home) and 24 hours (for those in full-time employment).

Another negative tendency, though often more difficult to identify, is that women are denied promotion or employment opportunities because male managers or employers fear that they may become pregnant or have to stay at home sometimes with sick children. Such discrimination is unacceptable.

It is in fact largely a reflection of the gender difference in terms of childcare responsibilities that explains why many more women than men work part-time. This in turn creates gender differentials in terms of career choices, wage levels and, later on, pension entitlements. The availability of day-care services for children is therefore of direct relevance when seeking to ensure greater gender equity on the labour market.

It ought to be feasible to combine paid work and childcare, both for men and for women.

Women who take leave for child-bearing and childcare must not be disadvantaged professionally. Provisions for paternity leave, where they exist, have had a positive effect in encouraging parents to share responsibility for their children's upbringing. They should be extended. In many countries, paternity leave for fathers is restricted to two weeks: this sends a negative signal regarding paternal duties in the raising of children.

In other words, the gender pay gap is an injustice in itself and a symptom of other injustices towards women. These phenomena of discrimination rest to a large extent on deep-rooted societal attitudes, and therefore good laws are insufficient. There is a need for a comprehensive, political approach, led clearly and publicly from the executive.

The authorities can also use their role as large employers to set an example to others in terms of gender equality. Governments should fully implement the principle of equal pay for work of equal value within their administration at all levels; they should tackle the problem of the "glass ceiling" experienced by women; and promote labour market reforms to ensure a childcare-friendly profile.

Private employers and their collective bargaining partners in the trade unions and elsewhere should be called upon to develop gender-neutral salary scales and set up procedures to detect gender discrimination in pay-scales.

Tackling the gender pay-gap problem is urgent for society as a whole – for women, men and children.

Domestic violence

Domestic violence still plagues European society. In spite of all the international conferences and declarations, women continue to be battered in their own homes. It is apparent that it will take a long time before an end is put to such abuse and ill-treatment. That is why it is even more necessary than ever that further efforts are made now – by both central and local governments. This requires more than mere lip service.

During my country visits, I often discuss this question of domestic violence with leading politicians, who are mostly men (see separate article on the paucity of women in political leadership roles). Some have grasped the importance of the issue while others display an unfortunate complacency. They have argued that "there is no need to discuss this in our country". Not only have they been dismissive about the problem as such – some of them have even volunteered chauvinistic jokes which should belong long in the past.

Domestic violence is a problem in every country. Where there are shelters for women who must seek refuge, they have proved necessary to prevent even worse tragedies. I have visited shelters in, for instance, Cork in Ireland, Vlora in Albania and Graz in Austria and been convinced of their value. Residents, both past and present, have explained that the protection and care in these homes provided a turning point in their lives.

Although such shelters are often run by committed non-governmental groups, the authorities have a responsibility to assist and co-operate. Shelters must also be complemented with other protective and social measures, and can only be seen as an emergency and temporary solution. Moreover, the very existence of a shelter should not be taken as a justification for the victim being the one who has to leave the family home, rather than the perpetrator.

In many cases it is a difficult step for a woman, sometimes accompanied by her children, to turn to a shelter; it is very often seen as a measure of last resort. Hotlines and telephone help services can provide help and useful advice. Health clinics are often the first service to come into contact with the victims of domestic violence. It is important that personnel there be well trained, gender sensitive and with clear referral systems in place to link to other support sectors. Health-care providers should be able to refer the victim to temporary safe housing, or counselling and, if need be, to the police.

Aftercare following a crisis period is essential to avoid any risk of repetition. There have been cases of women leaving a protected shelter only to be assaulted again. Decisions on whether or not to restrain the perpetrator are necessary. There should be legal measures in place to exclude offenders from the family home and to prevent further harassment where necessary.

Another weak link in the chain of protection has been the pursuit of judicial proceedings in those cases where a trial is necessary. Women are frequently forced to confront their aggressor in the courtroom and are subjected to cross-examinations of the most traumatising nature. Too little has been done to avoid the judicial procedure itself becoming part of a continuum of abuse.

Special attention has to be paid to those women most at risk. Staff at the shelters have stressed to me the particular vulnerability of migrants. A migrant woman who is subjected to domestic violence is unlikely to report the incident to the police for fear of losing her residence status – particularly, as is often the case, when her residence is dependent on her husband's status. Some countries have addressed this concern by allowing victims of domestic violence to apply for permanent residence status, irrespective of their spouses' support for the application. This is a responsible approach.

Sensitivity to the needs of the victims also calls for comprehensive and accessible services. Victims must be able to overcome all the various difficulties and consequences that violence has caused, and support services must take into account and respond to both the immediate and long-term needs of the victim.

Intervention centres which combine comprehensive police, judicial, social and health support should be developed so that victims can avoid the burden of having to go from one institution to the next. This is being experimented with in Austria, with positive results.

Services must be provided in a non-judgmental way. We know that women often avoid seeking assistance because they fear being stigmatised or blamed for the abuse they suffer. Others have suffered years of abuse and lack the confidence to start a new life on their own.

A broad policy framework for reform is needed. What ought to be done is known. Some governments have indeed already started to develop programmes which ought to inspire others; there should be:

- a precise and strict legal framework providing a broad definition of violence against women;
- legal provisions or guidelines to enforce the law;
- a well-thought-out strategy and an action plan (at both national and local levels) which would include preventive and educational measures;
- a programme for the training of police, social workers, health workers, teachers and the judiciary which would include information about how to recognise and deal with violence against women; and
- support services which would contribute to rehabilitation and the rebuilding of victims' lives.

Such a policy framework could be enhanced by a comprehensive, international treaty on violence against women. A convention or a protocol with binding standards should of course include measures against domestic violence. The purpose would be to encourage national reforms and the necessary attitudinal change. A discussion should start on the most effective format of such a treaty, European or international. The aim is clear: zero tolerance.

Rape

Sexual assault crimes must be taken more seriously by governments and parliaments. The injuries inflicted by rape are deep and long-lasting, in many cases gravely damaging the psychological as well as the physical integrity of victims. These crimes are largely hidden and their precise scale is difficult to determine, but we know that they are widespread and that many, many women live in constant fear of being assaulted. They have the right to be protected: more needs to be done both to prevent and to punish these crimes.

In fact, most rape is never reported. This is particularly true when the women raped are migrants. A high number of women migrants who reach Europe have suffered abuse on the way; others are in a particularly vulnerable situation if their status is not regularised upon arrival.

Other women do not report rapes because the perpetrator is a family member or close acquaintance, for example a husband, a partner or ex-partner, a father or a step-father, or another relative. This makes it more difficult for the victim to go to the police, because this may lead to retaliation or other serious consequences for her or for others near to her.

Those who do report abuse are not always taken seriously at the police station or during the trial. Too often victims are interrogated in a most insensitive manner by (male) officials who have little understanding of the traumatic aspects of such crimes. This is another disincentive when bringing charges.

Though the legislation on sexual assault has improved considerably across Europe, court proceedings are generally insufficiently adapted to the seriousness of this crime, and to recognising the psychological impact upon the victims. The trial itself may mean having to relive a deeply agonising experience, and any confrontation with the perpetrator may prove extremely traumatic.

Moreover, in those cases which actually do reach the courts in spite of all the many obstacles, the number of convictions continues to be very low. In most cases, the perpetrators go unpunished, which can be a very hard blow to those women who have risked reporting a crime, and it deters other victims from initiating proceedings. There is a need to investigate why so few convictions are secured in cases brought before the courts – and to remedy this failure.

There have been too many trials during which the credibility of the woman has been questioned in an inappropriate manner. In many cases, the woman's own behaviour or even her style of dress have been given undue attention during the proceedings. The suspicion is aired that she herself might have provoked the assault. That she has "asked for it". In such cases the blame, or at least part of the blame, is shifted from the attacker to the victim.

This is unacceptable. It must be made clear that free consent is necessary every time for sexual intercourse. This principle must dominate not only the law but also the practical procedures followed throughout the justice system. Marriage or partnership shall not be construed as an excuse for sexual abuse; no type of relationship makes the principle of free consent a redundant one.

Consent should be real. There should be a genuine freedom of choice so that the participation in the act is truly voluntary. Absence of violence is not a sufficient criterion as a proof of consent. Sexual intercourse engaged in due to the threat of violence, or other coercive circumstances, must also be regarded as rape. It should not be necessary to prove that the woman physically resisted the attacker – she may be physically unable to do so, be paralysed by fear or drugs, or she might be being blackmailed.

The European Court of Human Rights has analysed these issues in a case relating to the judicial response to a rape charge:

> [T]he Court is persuaded that any rigid approach to the prosecution of sexual offences, such as requiring proof of physical resistance in all circumstances, risks leaving certain types of rape unpunished and thus jeopardising the effective protection of the individual's sexual autonomy. In accordance with contemporary standards and trends in that area, the member States' positive obligations under Articles 3 and 8 of the Convention must be seen as requiring the penalisation and effective prosecution of any non-consensual sexual act, including in the absence of physical resistance by the victim.[50]

The same point was made in decisions taken by the Council of Europe Parliamentary Assembly. It recommended that member states define consent as "agreement by choice when having the freedom and capacity to make that choice". It also suggested that rape by a spouse, partner or ex-partner might be regarded as an aggravating circumstance in the judicial process.[51]

The German parliamentarian Marlene Rupprecht, who acted as the rapporteur for the Parliamentary Assembly on this issue, stressed the need to empower girls and women not to be victims – instead, their self-esteem and their capacity for self-defence should be promoted. She also emphasised the need to teach boys and men to respect women and any decision to say "no".

An obvious element to be addressed within a comprehensive strategy giving better protection to women against sexual assault is the need to ensure that all relevant professionals fully understand the principle of free consent and its implications. Police, judicial staff and forensic personnel must all be sensitised to the question. In addition, the competence of social workers and health professionals in assisting

---

50. *M.C. v. Bulgaria*, judgment of 4 March 2004.
51. Parliamentary Assembly Resolution 1691 (2009) and Recommendation 1887 (2009), adopted on 2 October 2009.

victims is of great importance. Education and training to these ends should be further promoted.

Such training should make clear, as Marlene Rupprecht noted in her report, that rape should not be understood as a "sexual" activity since it is usually motivated by a desire to control, harm and humiliate a woman. Typically, marital rape is more common at the end of a relationship.

Rape is not solely a private issue between two individuals: it must be seen as a human rights concern. Governments have not provided sufficient protection for individuals against this great harm inflicted by others. The Strasbourg Court is right to refer both to Article 3 about protection against ill-treatment, and to Article 8 about respect for one's private life.

Sexual assault is also committed against men and boys, not least in closed institutions such as prisons or orphanages. The unacceptable and widespread sexual abuse by staff against inmates in US prisons has been exposed. The shocking scale of rapes and other abusive humiliation in religious institutions – including those perpetrated against persons who have disabilities – both in the US and in several European countries is finally coming into the public domain. These reports must be followed by strong corrective action.

Sexual assault should be seen as a serious human rights problem. Its scale appears to be widespread. The fact that it is largely hidden is no excuse for ignoring its existence – indeed, the hidden nature of sexual abuse renders it all the more insidious and damaging in its impact. So, it should be a political priority to protect women, children and men from this threat.

This is a question of respecting the physical and psychological integrity of the person, one of the most crucial aspects of human rights.

Chapter 7: Rights of the child

Although children make up a large section of the population and constitute the future of society (in more ways than one), their concerns are seldom given top priority in politics. Ministers responsible for children's affairs tend to be junior and are kept outside the inner circle of power. When political issues are divided into "soft" and "hard", those relating to children are dealt with as "soft-soft". Often these issues are seen as non-political and sometimes simply trivial.

Photo: Dr Janusz Korczak – the first campaigner for the rights of the child (© Ghetto Fighters' Museum Archives, Israel).

The UN Convention on the Rights of the Child

The UN Convention on the Rights of the Child has become one of the most well-known and broadly supported international human rights treaties. All the states in the world – except the United States and war-torn Somalia – have ratified it and thereby legally bound themselves to implement its provisions. As a result, the situation of children has been placed higher on the political agenda. Yet, the actual implementation of the convention has been less effective than we anticipated. The main reason for this failure is the absence of a systematic, comprehensive approach to children's rights as a political priority.

Although children make up a large section of the population and constitute the future of society (in more ways than one), their concerns are seldom given top priority in politics. Ministers responsible for children's affairs tend to be junior and are kept outside the inner circle of power. Children's concerns are often seen as non-political, and sometimes trivial. The image of politicians on the campaign trail kissing babies has become symbolic of this trivialisation.

Gestures are not enough to meet the requirements of the convention – what is needed is serious political discussion and real change. Improvement in the status of, and conditions for, children are of course the very purpose of the convention. With ratification, a state commits itself to respecting the principles and provisions of the convention, and transforming that commitment into a reality for all children.

One possible reason for the delay in implementing the convention could be the decision makers' lack of understanding or acceptance of the obligations arising from it. They appear not always to have made the distinction between charity and a rights-based approach.

Children in need, just like persons with disabilities, have long been the favoured "objects" of charity. They have been given support, not as a matter of right, but because people have felt sympathy for them. This is one of the attitudes that the convention challenges.

The convention sees the child as a subject. He or she has the right to schooling, health care and an adequate standard of living, as well as the right to be heard and to have his or her views respected. This goes as much for the cute toddler as for the problematic teenager.

The very notion that children have rights is a radical one, totally alien to the old-fashioned belief that children are only entitled to rights on their 18th birthday, and that their parents hold these rights until that date.

That children and their interests should be given priority is another important message in the convention. It states as an overarching principle that "the best interests of the child shall be a primary consideration" in all actions concerning them, whether those actions were taken by local or national authorities, parliaments, courts, or social welfare institutions, and including those run on a private basis (Article 3).

The convention also requires concrete steps to be taken to guarantee genuine implementation. It prescribes that governments must take legal, administrative and other measures and use "the maximum extent of their available resources" to ensure that children can enjoy their rights (Article 4).

Many of us who took part in the drafting of the convention were aware of the risk that the final text would be seen by some as an idealistic wish list rather than as a definition of the human rights of children. The challenge was to give substance to the obligations which would follow from a rights approach.

The UN Committee on the Rights of the Child, the elected body which monitors the application of the convention, has attached a great deal of importance to the methods and means used for its implementation. Based on that experience, and suggestions from UNICEF, non-governmental organisations and governments, one could develop a checklist for systematic measures that governments should take if they are serious about their obligations to children. These measures include the need to:

- develop a comprehensive national agenda for children;

- ensure that all legislation is fully compatible with children's rights, which requires incorporating the convention into domestic law and practice, as well as ensuring that its principles and provisions take precedence in cases of conflict with any national legislation;
- make children visible in the process of governmental policy development by introducing child-impact assessments;
- carry out adequate budget analysis to determine the proportion of public funds spent on children, and to ensure the effective use of all such resources;
- establish permanent bodies or mechanisms throughout all sectors of government (including local authorities) to promote co-ordination, monitoring and evaluation of activities in furtherance of the convention;
- ensure that adequate data is collected and used to constantly improve the situation of all children in each jurisdiction;
- raise awareness and disseminate information on children's rights and what they mean in reality, including through training for all those in government – especially, but not exclusively, for those whose work relates to children or who work directly with children;
- involve children themselves, as well as civil society, in the process of implementation and awareness-raising;
- develop independent statutory offices for children – a children's ombudsman, commissioner or other similar institution – to promote children's rights; and
- give children's rights priority in all forms of international co-operation, including programmes for technical assistance.

These 10 recommendations are mutually reinforcing and have several characteristics in common. Each relies on public debate and transparent procedures. Each advocates a "first call" for children, while recognising the need for co-ordinated efforts to ensure that children's rights are incorporated into the existing administrative structures, and they require children themselves to take part in the process.

The basic idea is that children's issues be moved from the exclusive realm of charity on to the political agenda – and placed high thereon.

Several European governments have taken action on these recommendations, for instance, through adopting a national strategy, improving their internal co-ordination around children's issues, developing good data collection systems and appointing an ombudsman for children (either within the office of the general ombudsman or as a separate body).

Yet, there are glaring gaps which appear to indicate that governments are still not being sufficiently serious. This is particularly reflected in the continued lack of child protection.

Too little is being done to give children with disabilities an opportunity for good schooling; children within minorities, not least the Roma, are disadvantaged in most spheres of life; children in conflict with the law are too often detained; children among irregular migrants are vulnerable and suffer exploitation; and refugee children are not well treated. Corporal punishment is retained in about half of the countries in Europe and some children also face violence at school. Justice systems, schools and cities are not yet child-friendly.

One reason why powerful politicians tend to issue rhetorical statements rather than develop concrete children's programmes is probably because many of them lead a life which isolates them from a child's everyday reality. Yet the opinions of children themselves are not taken seriously, and their parents or guardians are also accorded little time or opportunity to present their views.

In fact, the genuineness of political commitment is most clearly tested in budget discussions. In the current austerity programmes there have been budget cuts in several countries which have affected children and services directed at them – either directly in the state budget, or via reduced support to local authorities.

Funds for education, health care and social benefits for vulnerable groups have been significantly reduced in a number of countries, and this is before governments start paying back the debts incurred when public money was used to meet the financial crisis and rescue the banking system.

This has provoked a widespread discussion on the meaning to be accorded to the UN convention's commitment that "the maximum extent" of available resources go to children. Inevitably, children's interests will also suffer when society as a whole is forced to tighten its belt. However, it is clearly against the very spirit of the convention if decisions are made which would penalise those who are already vulnerable, and so increase existing inequalities. In a time of economic stringency, the human rights principle of non-regression is an important one for the authorities to bear in mind as they choose which government programmes to maintain or to abandon.

It is now particularly urgent that the short- and long-term economic impact on children be analysed before budgets are finalised. In Europe we already have a serious problem of child poverty – it is appallingly widespread in some countries, and a large number of children are disadvantaged from the outset. An economic crisis is hardly an argument for not addressing child poverty – on the contrary, it this is when it is even more urgent to do so.

Resource limitations cannot be seen as an excuse by states for ignoring their obligations to protect children's rights or for delaying the implementation of measures. The greater the difficulty, the more reason there is to act with a clear political strategy so as to address the problems in a systematic fashion.

Indeed, it is particularly in times of crisis that the state has to reaffirm its commitment and to fully respect the rights of children – all children.

Views of children

More needs to be done in several fields to grant children their full rights. One right which has not been ensured in reality is the right of children to have their views taken into account.

The importance of respecting children and their opinions was the main message of the Polish writer, doctor and educationalist Janusz Korczak, whose teaching came to inspire the drafting of the UN Convention on the Rights of the Child.

In an orphanage in the Warsaw Ghetto during the Second World War, Dr Korczak, his colleagues and some 190 children put the rights of the child directly into practice. In the midst of the horrible brutality outside, they developed a small democracy. They all formed an assembly when taking important decisions; they agreed upon rules of behaviour; and a court was established to deal with offenders. In most cases the "sentence" was to apologise. There was a billboard for messages, and a newspaper for news and discussion.

This experiment of child democracy came to a terrible end on 6 August 1942 when the German Nazi troops marched them all – staff and children – to a train which would bring them to the gas chamber in Treblinka.

Korczak's example and writings have, however, never been forgotten. His books are reprinted in different languages and still influence many. However, nearly 70 years later, some of his ideas are seen as either unrealistic or something purely aspirational.

Unfortunately, some people – despite all advice to the contrary – seem to think that that this is also true of the provisions in the UN convention relating to the views of children and the following provision is probably the least implemented aspect of the convention: "States Parties shall assure to the child who is capable of forming his or her own views the right to express those views freely in all matters affecting the child, the views of the child being given due weight in accordance with the age and maturity of the child."

It seems not to be fully understood that this specific provision – Article 12 of the convention – places an obligation on governments to ensure that children's views are sought and considered on all matters that affect their lives.

It is time to confront this challenge more directly. There is currently no clear vision of the content and the consequences of giving effect to a child's right to be heard, and to participate in decision-making.

Therefore, as a first step, goals and standards for the realisation of this right need to be spelled out by states in more concrete and substantive terms.

Implementing this right requires the elaboration of long- and short-term objectives and strategies to address questions of social attitudes and behaviour, and to develop viable models for children and adolescents to participate in political and societal decision-making. Mechanisms need to be developed within all political bodies to ensure systematic consultation with children and the serious consideration of their views.

The objective should be to create a culture of greater receptivity to, and respect for, children's views. Unfortunately, many adults seem to feel threatened by this prospect. The issue of children's influence is seen as a "zero-sum game" – that is, a situation in which one side wins only if the other side loses. In other words, if children get more power, adults believe they will lose some of theirs, and be less able to manage the family or uphold discipline in the classroom.

In some countries, adults in the name of parents' rights or even religious principles have aggressively opposed children's participation. To change such entrenched patriarchal attitudes towards children may take some time.

How can this issue be raised in a meaningful way? How can it be shown that there is no contradiction between giving children the possibility of influencing their lives and society on the one hand, and safeguarding the role of adults to care for, guide and protect children, on the other? How can it be made obvious that this is not a win–lose game, but that all sides stand to gain if adults learn to support children in the exercise of their rights?

Here are some suggested first steps:
- children's primary arena is in the home. Raising awareness among parents and caregivers about children's right to be heard, and helping them cope with their parenting roles in this respect, must be a priority;

- the other key arena in children's lives is the school and kindergarten. Interactive learning, relevant curricula, democratic attitudes and procedures are all essential. Such measures should focus on strengthening children's ability to express themselves, to handle democratic processes, and to understand society and its problems better. A huge task ahead is that of building capacity among teachers and other school staff. They need to learn how to listen better to children, enhance dialogue and promote conflict resolution in a democratic manner;
- children's organisations advocating the realisation of children's rights should be promoted, and other NGOs working with or for children, such as sports clubs or charity groups, should be encouraged to listen routinely to children and to respect their views;
- political parties should be encouraged to develop their capacity to consider children's views and enhance children's influence in political affairs;
- television, radio and the press should have "child-friendly" news presentations and make sure that children's views on matters of special concern to them are presented. More child-focused correspondents and young journalists should be welcomed;
- steps should be taken to make the justice system child-friendly. Court procedures must be adjusted to meet the needs of children, be they perpetrators, victims or witnesses. Children should have an influence on administrative or judicial decisions relating to them, for instance on care and adoption;
- governments should define issues which have a great impact on children's lives and on which they should therefore have a say. This is true, for instance, of family policies, the planning of community facilities, school policies, children's health care and recreational services. Channels of expression and communication, adequate for different age-groups (including young children), should be explored. Examples that have worked well on occasion include: dialogues with preschoolers, school councils, opinion polls,

and representative bodies. Special measures should be taken to enhance the voice of groups of children with disabilities or other disadvantaged groups and explore how to overcome possible constraints.

These steps would be in line with the vision of Janusz Korczak. Enabling children to express themselves and have their views heard and respected in the home, in school and in the community from an early age, will enhance their sense of belonging – and their readiness to take responsibility.

Children and violence

A majority of member states have now committed themselves to putting an end to all corporal punishment for children. A full prohibition in law has so far been adopted by 22 member states and at least seven others have publicly pledged to do the same within the near future. If these governments fulfil their commitment, Europe will be more than halfway to universal prohibition. This is welcome progress.

Some positive steps have also been taken in other parts of the world. In 2007, New Zealand became the first English-speaking country to prohibit all corporal punishment, including within the family; and during 2007-08 three Latin American countries (Uruguay, Venezuela and Chile) did the same.

These governments were responding to recommendations in the report of the UN Secretary-General's study on violence against children, submitted to the General Assembly in October 2006. Its main message was that no violence against children is justifiable; all violence against children is preventable. It recommended that all states move quickly to prohibit all forms of violence against children, including all corporal punishment, before the end of 2009.

This was another strong and vital challenge to the still fairly widespread opinion that relations inside the family are no matter for outsiders. Already, the 1989 UN Convention on the Rights of the Child had made clear that there are situations in which authorities have to protect a child from all forms of violence, even or especially those which occur within the family home.

This is not a zero-sum game between children and parents. The convention is very family-friendly; it stresses the absolute importance of a good family environment and the need, in some cases, for community support to parents in crisis. Violence against children is a reflection of family breakdown and requires responses aimed at the protection of the life, well-being and dignity of the child. This is a major reason why the prevention of domestic violence against children is nowadays recognised as a human rights concern.

The purpose of prohibiting the corporal punishment of children is one of prevention. The idea is to encourage a change of attitudes and practice and to promote non-violent methods of child-rearing. An unambiguous message of what is unacceptable is very important. Adults responsible for children are sometimes confused about how to handle difficult situations. The line should simply be drawn between physical or psychological violence on the one hand, and non-violence on the other.

The problem of violence against children is deep and serious. As part of their daily lives, children across Europe and the world continue to be spanked, slapped, hit, smacked, shaken, kicked, pinched, punched, caned, flogged, belted, beaten and battered in the name of "discipline", mainly by adults on whom they depend.

This violence may be a deliberate act of punishment or just the impulsive reaction of an irritated parent or teacher. Both cases constitute a breach of human rights. Respect for human dignity and the right to physical integrity are universal principles. But despite this, the social and legal acceptance of adults hitting children and inflicting other humiliating treatment on them persists.

Corporal punishment of children is often inhuman or degrading, and it invariably violates their physical integrity, demonstrates disrespect for their human dignity and undermines their self-esteem. This sense of deeper damage was described by the Polish doctor, writer and educationalist Janusz Korczak who once said: "There are many terrible things in the world, but the worst is when a child is afraid of his father, mother or teacher."

Special exceptions allowing for some level of violence against children in defiance of otherwise universally applicable laws against assault are therefore particularly unfortunate. They also breach the basic human rights principle of equal protection under the law. The invention of concepts such as "reasonable punishment" and "lawful correction" arises from the perception of children as the property of their parents. Such "rights" are based on the power of the stronger over the weaker and are upheld by means of violence and humiliation.

The Parliamentary Assembly of the Council of Europe called already in 2004 for a Europe-wide ban of corporal punishment. It stated that "any corporal punishment of children is in breach of their fundamental right to human dignity and physical integrity. The fact that such corporal punishment is still lawful in certain member states violates their equally fundamental right to the same legal protection as adults. Striking a human being is prohibited in European society and children are human beings. The social and legal acceptance of corporal punishment of children must be ended."

In 2008 in Zagreb, Croatia, the Council of Europe launched a Europe-wide campaign for universal prohibition of violence against children. Progress is being made, but some member states have not as yet responded. In order to encourage further discussion, I have been in correspondence with the governments of those member states that have yet to reform their laws adequately, and I will continue to follow up these exchanges, hoping that they will move quickly to fulfil their obligations to children.

Of course, eliminating corporal punishment requires more than legal reform. Sustained public education and awareness-raising around the law and with regard to a child's right to protection is required, together with promotion of positive, non-violent relationships with children. The Council of Europe programme Building a Europe For and With

Children is promoting the abolition of corporal punishment through law reform, the promotion of positive parenting, and awareness-raising efforts likely to change public attitudes and behaviour.

Children have had to wait the longest to be given equal legal protection from deliberate assaults – a protection the rest of us take for granted. It is extraordinary that children (whose developmental state and small size is acknowledged to make them particularly vulnerable to physical and psychological harm) have been singled out for less protection than adults from assaults on their fragile bodies, minds and dignity.

Challenging the legal and social acceptance of violence has been a fundamental component of women's struggle for equal status. The same applies to children: there could not be a more symbolic reflection of the persistently low status accorded to children than the assumption made by adults that they have the "right" and even the "duty" to hit children.

Sexual abuse of children

The media reports on the scandals involving Catholic clergy in the sexual abuse of children have highlighted an urgent child rights issue. Such incidents are not isolated: they have been widespread in all kinds of childcare institutions, including those run by private foundations and state or municipal authorities. Among the victims are children with disabilities, orphans and those coming from dysfunctional families. The number of cases brought to justice is steadily rising in several European countries.

Sexual violence against children does not take place only in such institutions. Even more frequent are the cases of abuse perpetrated behind closed doors, by persons in the immediate family or social circle of the victim. Very often the abuser is someone on whom the victim depends in one way or another. There are also cases of other young people violating a child. It is assumed that children in poor and disadvantaged circumstances are more likely to be victims of sexual abuse, but there is evidence that this problem is present in all social classes and in all types of communities.

Children are also made victims of trafficking for the purpose of sexual exploitation. Barnardo's, a prestigious charity in the United Kingdom, recently published a report entitled "Puppet on a String", about the enforced prostitution of minors, some of them as young as 10 years of age. The trend is such that the victims are increasingly younger and the predators more organised. Mobile phones, text and picture messages, bluetooth technology and the Internet are regularly used to snare the children targeted.

One of the cases in the report is about Aaliyah who became estranged from her parents when she was 14. She began to go out a lot and met men older than her. She said afterwards that she was desperate for love and attention, and became fooled by the attention they pretended to show her. Things soon turned nasty and she was physically and mentally abused. Her so-called boyfriend brought her to a hotel room "to have his friends come over and do what they wanted with me".

We do not know the extent of these different kinds of sexual violations of children. One reason is that the victims themselves hesitate to report the violations. They may be afraid of the consequences, especially when they are still dependent on the perpetrator(s). Another obstacle may be a feeling of shame and guilt, which is a known psychological reaction among victims of sexual violence.

Children who have been abused in private, without any witnesses, may also fear that they are unable to prove what actually happened. Social workers, the police and the judicial authorities are not always prepared to deal with complaints from molested children. A child victim who speaks up without being believed, or even listened to, will hesitate to try to do so again.

Victims who after many years have mustered the strength to talk about their experience have testified about the pain and humiliation of not being heard and therefore being forced to keep the trauma inside. An abused child is extremely lonely and needs considerable courage to break the silence.

The truth tends, in many cases, to come out a long time after the abuse took place, if at all. Statistics in this area will therefore always be uncertain. However, we know enough to be able to conclude that such types of abuse have been alarmingly widespread. This is confirmed by different academic and other studies.

It is also clear that the problem remains. Many of the present generation of children have also been abused. Barnardo's reported that the organisation presently works with more than one thousand child trafficking cases like Aaliyah's in the United Kingdom alone – and believes they are only the tip of the iceberg.

Studies in several European countries, based on answers from children themselves, show that about 10 per cent or more have suffered from sexual abuse. Experts believe that the true figure might be even higher.

The Council of Europe has adopted a treaty to address this pattern of serious child rights violations: the Convention on the Protection of Children against Sexual Exploitation and Sexual Abuse (CETS No. 201). It establishes standards for the effective protection of children, the prevention of abusive acts and the punishment of its perpetrators.

The convention builds on the widely ratified UN Convention on the Rights of the Child and treats sexual abuse of children as a crime, irrespective of where and by whom it is committed – at home, in a childcare institution, through organised crime networks or the Internet. It requires states to extend the statutory limitation for bringing child sexual abuse cases to trial.

The convention stresses the need to establish services to which children can safely report abuse. Judicial procedures must be adjusted to take into account the traumatic impact of violations and the necessity of protecting the privacy and security of the victim.

The emphasis on punishment is crucial, even if this in a concrete case might make it more difficult for the victim to testify. There should be no impunity for these crimes. Abusers tend to go from one child to the next if not stopped. Church leaders who fail to report abusive colleagues to the police thereby facilitate further violations. An attitude of zero tolerance is crucial, and will hopefully contribute to fewer such crimes in the future.

As abusers in many cases have tended to target insecure and otherwise vulnerable children, more efforts should be made to create safe spaces in which children can talk with confidence about what is happening to them, with people who will believe them and respond in an appropriate manner.

Other prevention measures must of course be tried. Appropriate sex education in schools is vitally important. When children are informed about the realities of sex abuse they will be more equipped to avoid putting themselves at risk and escape dangerous situations. Advisory information is also needed for parents and other adults on how they can protect their children, how they might detect signs relating to such problems and how they should best react when harm has been done.

One of the most important steps is to organise regular, continuous training for professionals working for and with children. They have to be aware of the risks of abuse and recognise the signs of abusive relationships. They must know how to respond to suspicions of violations in a way that keeps children safe and ensures that their rights are respected.

It is indeed positive that sexual abuse and exploitation are now seen as a serious problem. Politicians are challenged to develop effective programs for the prevention, care and support of victims and appropriate criminal action against the perpetrators.

Children in unsuitable care institutions

Notorious large-scale institutions for orphans and children with disabilities are being phased out, including in the former communist countries of central and eastern Europe. This process of deinstitutionalisation must continue, but it has to be pursued

with care and always in the best interests of the child. Suitable alternatives must be developed and supported by the authorities – also in periods of economic crisis.

An extreme example of distorted attitudes towards children was exposed after the fall of the Ceauşescu regime in Romania some 20 years ago. Steps had been taken under the dictatorship to prevent people from using contraceptives and, as a result, many unwanted children were born. Parents who could not care for their children were asked to hand them over to state institutions.

These collectives functioned badly. Contacts between the parents and the children were actively discouraged or even prevented. There were too few staff to cope with the numbers of children involved. They were untrained for their task, badly paid, and their job carried little status. I visited some of these homes at the time and was struck by the difficult material conditions and the depressed atmosphere.

Some of the institutions, especially those for children with disabilities, were hidden far away from population centres and were rarely provided with even the bare minimum of staff and material resources. No efforts were made to encourage the development of these children – no schooling, no organised play, no love. Some of the children were kept tied to their beds, day and night.

The situation in Romania was extreme, but large, inhumane institutions also existed in countries such as Bulgaria, Estonia, Hungary, Latvia, Lithuania, Moldova, Poland and Russia. It became a major task for the new leaders to start the process of deinstitutionalisation. Progress has been made during the past two decades, though major problems remain and require further efforts.

It has become widely recognised that a family environment is generally much better for children than institutional care. The adoption of the 1989 UN Convention on the Rights of the Child – and the discussion of its consequences – strengthened this understanding. Recommendations from Council of Europe bodies have contributed

further to a child-friendly approach which could be summarised as follows:
- placement of children in institutions should as far as possible be avoided. In particular the old-style, large institutions have a negative effect on children and their development. They tend to neglect children's need both for affection and to be recognised as individuals. In such institutions, cases of abuse tend to be common – both perpetrated by adults and by other children;
- a first line of defence would be to give strong, sustained support to parents so that the rights of the child can be fully protected in the home environment;
- unfortunately, there are situations in which it is in the best interests of the child for them to be moved somewhere else. The aim in such circumstances should be to seek a good alternative family environment, and foster care might be the best option;
- for each child in this situation there should be an individual plan based on his or her needs and the family circumstances. The principle of the best interests of the child should guide all decisions, and children themselves should be able to influence these;
- if an institutional placement is necessary, it should be as family-like as possible. Staff should be well trained and professional;
- the spirit in such child centres should be clearly child-friendly and education should be seen as a right for everyone. There should be clear and effective complaints procedures;
- if at all possible, the child should be able to communicate with and see the parents – reintegration into the family should normally be the objective;
- monitoring of the situation of each child is of key importance. All forms of alternative care should be regularly reviewed. There should also be a serious follow-up review of the situation after a period of alternative care.

The fact that these principles have been recognised does not mean that they are automatically applied. Some of the old-style institutions are still there, and suitable alternatives have not been sufficiently developed. In addition, too little is being done to strengthen families and thereby prevent the risk that children are abandoned.

It is of paramount importance that the current economic crisis does not undermine the process of supporting children at risk. Unfortunately, budget cuts which will inevitably damage the best interests of children have been made.

There is an obvious risk that the number of abandoned children will increase as the social support for troubled families is reduced. It is a proven fact that families break down under the pressure of poverty and unemployment. Too many children are forced to grow up in families where alcoholism and other drug abuse is part of daily life. These factors are root causes which place children at risk.

Most of the children in orphanages have at least one living parent. In her Korczak lecture, the Russian social policy expert Marina Gordeeva called them "social orphans" and explained some of the background:

> *Traditional family ties between generations are disrupted, the number of divorces is growing, the level of material support of families with children is lowering, many parents lead an asocial life and avoid their parental duties.*[52]

She argued for a policy which would combine determined efforts to support vulnerable families, step-by-step closure of old residential care institutions and creation of support services to substitute guardians, such as foster families. She stressed that the main aim is not to close down the residential institutions per se but rather to achieve a successful family placement for each child in need.

These steps would require strong political backing and sufficient budgetary resources. In addition, local authorities must take their share of responsibility for providing support services for children. I have

---

52. Marina Gordeeva, Janusz Korczak Lecture: "Children in out-of-home care: more prevention, fewer institutions", Moscow, April 2009. Published in *Janusz Korczak: The child's right to respect*, Council of Europe, 2009.

noticed that there are shortcomings in this regard in several countries, including in Russia and Bulgaria. Co-ordination between ministries also tends to be insufficient in family policy matters. Marina Gordeeva spoke about "a gap in managerial decision making".

Financial and managerial gaps cannot be filled by reliance solely on the work undertaken by civil society groups. Non-governmental initiatives should in general be welcomed, but charity at the hands of volunteers is not the solution; this task of caring for vulnerable children is primarily a government obligation.

We know now what to do to protect children in need. The programmes are not controversial and they are grounded in extensive expertise. What is needed is the political will to turn these programmes into a practical reality.

Children in prison

There is a disturbing trend in Europe today – we are detaining and locking up more children and at an earlier age. The age of criminal responsibility is already very low in some countries such as the United Kingdom. Suggestions to lower the age limit to 12 years old have also been made for instance in France. In my opinion, the time has come to move the argument away from fixing some arbitrary age for criminal responsibility for minors and to find a more child-friendly approach to juvenile justice.

A caring society responds promptly, resolutely and fairly to juvenile offenders. Juveniles are certainly not helped by a *laissez-faire* response if they violate the law: in such instances, it is imperative that young persons be taught to take responsibility for their actions. However, experience has shown that criminalisation, and in particular imprisonment, tends to undermine efforts to assist juveniles reintegrate positively into the community.

Criminalisation and periods spent in juvenile detention centres often have exactly the opposite effect of turning these juvenile offenders into adult criminals.

Young offenders are children first and foremost, and should be able to rely on all the agreed human rights protections as they apply to children. This is one of the messages of the United Nations Convention on the Rights of the Child in its call for a distinct system of justice for children. Under the convention, children are defined as those under 18 years old.

This need for a re-think of youth justice has been stressed by the European Network of Ombudspersons for Children (ENOC) in a position statement issued in 2003. These experts urged states "to review their juvenile justice systems against the requirements of the UN convention and European human rights instruments".

Let us first separate the concepts of "responsibility" and "criminalisation". Human rights law allows for – indeed requires – that responsibility for conduct contravening the law should be established. Where responsibility is disputed, there has to be a formal process to determine responsibility. Where a child is involved, this formal process must be pursued in a manner which respects the age and the capacity of the child. No one is suggesting that wrongdoing go unchallenged; however, the challenge does not have to be by way of a criminal process nor involve the criminalisation of children.

Once the facts of an offence are established, there needs to be a multidisciplinary assessment of what is required to ensure awareness of the offence by the child. Such an assessment would also determine how best both to respond to the needs of the victim and to prevent the child from re-offending. Such measures would, where necessary, be compulsory. The proceedings would not identify the child publicly and would not be the same as in the adult criminal justice system.

International standards make the arrest, detention and imprisonment of minors possible in principle (subject to the minimum age of criminal responsibility). However, these responses should be used "only as a measure of last resort and for the shortest appropriate period of time", as the UN convention states. This approach is within the spirit of a state's commitment to children's rights. Moreover, we also know that it makes practical sense: depriving children of their liberty tends to increase the rate of re-offending.

The only legitimate reason for locking up children is that there are no other alternative ways to deal with what is thought to be an immediate serious risk to others. Frequent periodic reviews of the necessity of detention on a case-by-case basis are required and the conditions of any detention must be humane. Any detention must take into account the special needs of an individual of that age and must be aimed at rehabilitation.

Full-time education is particularly essential. Each young offender should be given an individual programme of rehabilitation – a plan that should continue after the detention period and engage the support of guardians, teachers and social workers. In all this, the child him- or herself should have a say. This is both a right and is also a more effective way of preventing recidivism.

In many of my country reports, I underline the importance of keeping juveniles separate from adult offenders and, in particular, from hard-core criminals. Such detentions should take place in specific and children-friendly establishments. A judgment of the European Court of Human Rights against Turkey highlights the possible dire consequences of not respecting that important principle.[53]

Guidelines on child-friendly justice have been developed within the Council of Europe. They recommend reforms of the juvenile justice system to avoid criminalisation of children and to put their best interests at the centre of the policy.[54]

Promoting policies and procedures aimed at respecting the human rights of young offenders does not contradict the rights and concerns of victims, as is sometimes claimed. Victims must receive appropriate reparation and support from the state. But victims' interests – and those of the wider society – are not served by a system which

---

53. *Guvec v. Turkey*, judgment of 20 January 2009.
54. Guidelines of the Committee of Ministers of the Council of Europe on Child Friendly Justice, 17 November 2010.

insists solely on punishment at the expense of seeking to rehabilitate offenders.

During visits to European countries, I have met many juvenile inmates in prisons and detention centres. Many of them have suffered neglect and violent abuse within their own families, and have received little support from society at large. Understanding the origins of violence and serious offending in children does not mean condoning or accepting it.

An effective and humane policy would put a strong emphasis on prevention. Social workers are more important than prison guards in this context. Certainly, broader reforms aimed at genuine social justice have to be part of a strategy to tackle the problem of youth offending.

Unfortunately, in many countries, this has not been the focus of the public debate. Instead, people's justified concerns about juvenile misbehaviour have been exploited for populist political purposes: children and young persons have been demonised and described as major threats to society.

The UN convention encourages a minimum age to be set for criminal responsibility. Below such an age, it is presumed that a child does not have the capacity to infringe the penal law. Children in Scotland can be held criminally responsible at the age of 8 years old. In England, Wales and Northern Ireland the minimum age is 10. In several of the Nordic countries the age for criminal responsibility is set at 15, and in Belgium it is 18 years old. The European Committee of Social Rights (which monitors state compliance with the European Social Charter), the UN's Committee on the Rights of the Child and other UN treaty bodies have all recommended to different states a substantial increase in the age of criminal responsibility.

I would like, however, to move the debate on from that of fixing some arbitrary age for criminal responsibility. Governments should seek rather a more holistic solution to juvenile offending and one which does not criminalise children for their conduct.

The United Nations Guidelines for the Prevention of Juvenile Delinquency, while adopted two decades ago, still provide the right benchmark. "Labelling a young person as 'deviant' or 'delinquent' or 'pre-delinquent' often contributes to the development of a consistent pattern of undesirable behaviour by young people."

Yes, it is in all our interests to stop treating children as criminals. We should therefore treat them as children while they are still children and save the criminal justice system for adults.

Child migrants

Migrant children are one of the most vulnerable groups in Europe today. Some of them have fled persecution or war; others have run away from poverty and destitution. There are also those who are victims of trafficking. At particular risk are those who are separated from their families and have no – or only temporary – residence permits. Many of these children suffer exploitation and abuse. Their situation is a major challenge to the humanitarian principles we advocate.

Typically, there is little data on the reality of Europe's migrant population, and still less on migrant children. Yet, in order to formulate a wise and comprehensive policy on this issue, we need more facts. Statistics and other relevant data are missing on almost all aspects of the migration cycle: about those coming to the borders, who they are and what happens to them; about those who are in the country without a permit, whether they are in school or work and with whom they live; and about those who have residence permits and their social situation.

Though the scope and nature of the problem is partly hidden, we know enough to realise that the situation is serious. The lack of precise statistics and facts is therefore no excuse for political passivity. While efforts should be made to collect more data, this should not be an excuse for inaction and a more energetic policy should be developed to protect the rights of migrant children.

There are international standards in this area. Both the UN Convention on the Rights of the Child and the UN Convention on the Protection of the Rights of All Migrant Workers and Members of Their Families give clear guidance on how the rights of migrant children should be protected.

The Parliamentary Assembly of the Council of Europe has also adopted recommendations on refugee children and separated migrant minors. The UN High Commissioner for Refugees has issued guidelines to governments and also launched a joint project together with Save the Children, the Separated Children in Europe Programme.

Such efforts are needed as the agreed rules and guidelines are not always enforced. One reason for these shortcomings in several European countries today is obviously xenophobia. There are extremist political parties and groups promoting prejudice and fear. Some of them have even got a foothold in parliaments or local assemblies. Unfortunately, some of the bigger political parties have adapted their message to reflect such tendencies instead of exposing them as unacceptable. Populist media have also played a negative role in disseminating stereotypes.

The consequences have also been negative for those migrants, not least the younger ones, who already live in Europe. It is therefore particularly unfortunate that so few politicians highlight the value of diversity and multiculturalism in today's world.

What should be done in concrete terms to protect and promote the rights of migrant children? How should the standards and guidelines be implemented?

The starting point must be that migrant children are children. They are vulnerable and have the same rights as others. The principle of the best interest of the child means that each child must be seen as an individual and special consideration must be given to his or her particular circumstances. All children should be listened to with respect.

Many migrant children have already been uprooted once or several times. Separation from earlier homes, relatives and friends can cause trauma. This makes it even more crucial that adult support be provided. Save the Children and the UNHCR have proposed that a legal guardian or representative be appointed for each arriving separated child. These children have the right to be met with respect and by personnel who have the training and capacity to understand children and their needs.

Family reunification is an urgent need for many migrant children. Tracing of other family members should be undertaken as a matter of priority and on a confidential basis. No child should, however, be sent back to their country of origin if adequate reception and care cannot be guaranteed.

The Council of Europe Parliamentary Assembly has recommended that member states "facilitate the family reunification of separated children with their parents in other member states even when parents do not have permanent residence status or are asylum seekers, in compliance with the principle of the best interest of the child".[55]

This may be seen as controversial by some, but is fully in line with the agreed standards on children's rights. The right to family reunification applies to all children. Those governments which have limited this right only to younger children – for instance, only to those below 15 years of age – should be reminded of their obligations concerning the rights of all children.

The right to health should be given priority. Poverty and poor housing conditions undermine health in general. Also, many migrant children have a difficult background and may require psychological support. This is an area where schools have a key role to play – not least in the detection of problems, but also in providing supportive treatment and in monitoring follow-up.

Considerations of health are also a strong argument against the detention of children at any stage of the migration process. It is shameful

---

55. Parliamentary Assembly Recommendation 1596 (2003) on the situation of young migrants in Europe.

that, even in Europe, unaccompanied children are still locked up while waiting for decisions about their fate or before being deported.

Whatever the child's background, the right to education is absolutely central. Migrant children should be ensured access to compulsory education – irrespective of their or their parents' legal status. It is crucial that the quality of the schooling be guaranteed and that pupils have the possibility to learn the majority language (while also developing their mother tongue). One of the problems in some countries has been a lack of trained teachers who can care ably for migrant children.

Europe cannot afford to fail our young newcomers; their fate is ours and they have much to contribute – if given a chance. The first step is to recognise that they have human rights.

Child poverty

New energy must be given to the fight against child poverty all over Europe. The first step is to recognise that this is a profound problem, affecting a great number of individuals, and with negative consequences reaching far into the future.

Statistics from South-Eastern Europe and the former Soviet countries in the Commonwealth of Independent States show that about 25% of children still live in absolute poverty. These children have not benefited from the earlier economic recovery to the same extent as other groups in society, and they are discriminated against again during the current recession.

In the richer parts of Europe, child poverty also exists. Few children are living in extreme poverty, but the percentage of children in households with incomes below half of the national median is still above 15% in relatively rich countries such as the UK, Ireland, Italy, Spain and Portugal.

These figures from UNICEF give an indication of the scope of the problem. Unfortunately, more precise measurement is not possible as it has not been possible to obtain all relevant data. Even if basic statistics about incomes and social benefits are reliable, it is difficult to assess their full impact on living standards. Also, poverty is not only about purchasing power – other additional indicators are necessary when measuring the quality of life.

That is why the UNICEF studies on poverty in Europe have focused on issues such as unemployment, health and safety, educational well-being, the family and the risk of violence.

These studies show that children who grow up in poverty are much more vulnerable than others. They are more likely to be in poor health, underachieve in school, get into trouble with the police, fail to develop vocational skills, be unemployed or badly paid, and be dependent on social welfare.

This does not mean that all poor children are failing in their development. However, they run the risk of being seriously disadvantaged.

Child poverty is usually closely correlated with the poverty experienced by the adults who care for them. It should, however, be understood that poverty has an even more profound impact on children than on adults. It affects them not only in their immediate present, but also in the long term. Moreover, children themselves can do little to improve their situation. As a consequence, they greatly depend on public policy to grow out of poverty. This is particularly true when it comes to accessing educational and health services.

The UNICEF studies on child poverty also show that there are large differences between the countries of Europe, and even between countries facing a similar general economic situation. This seems to suggest that levels of child poverty reflect political choices. Child poverty can and should be reduced through explicit policy measures.

An action plan against child poverty should of course seek to define vulnerable groups and situations of particular risk. Single-parent families and children with special needs may belong to this latter category. We know, for example, that children in rural areas and children of migrants and Roma communities are deeply affected by poverty.

Direct subsidies to these at-risk categories are necessary and are in fact the rationale for many social and family benefits. Such support has to be appropriately targeted and must be sufficient to lift children – and their parents – out of poverty.

However, it is equally important to ensure that schools, health services, day-care centres and other public welfare institutions function in a fair way which benefits the most marginalised or otherwise disadvantaged. A policy of privatisation of such services cannot be allowed to block or limit access to essential services by the poor.

One of the first steps towards reducing child poverty is to guarantee free access to education. Even when schools are free of tuition fees, education sometimes has hidden costs such as uniforms or books which have to be bought. In some countries, parents have even to pay for the heating of the school. Education policies should particularly target school drop-out rates and youth unemployment by providing appropriate training and employment-related education.

Access to basic health services often remains impossible for many children living in poverty. Due to a lack of health insurance on the part of their parents, or proper registration in the national system, or insufficient resources more generally, children can find themselves excluded from health care. Experiences of free-of-charge medical and dental check-ups at schools have been very positive.

One attitude has to be rejected strongly, and that is that poverty is the fault of the poor. This "argument" is ill-conceived, as far as adults are concerned, and clearly totally invalid in relation to children.

Instead, we need to acknowledge that the reality of poverty is deprivation of a broad spectrum of human rights. Anti-poverty policies should promote access to human rights, including the right to education, training and employment, decent housing, social services and health care.

Chapter 8: Social and economic rights

There are large groups of people who are poor and marginalised in Europe. They lack influence and opportunities for making their voices heard. They often feel ignored by political parties and have little confidence in the authorities. They suffer from crime more than other groups but lack a trusting relationship with the police. In courts they are disadvantaged in comparison to those who can hire senior lawyers and they are over-represented in prisons.

Photo © Council of Europe.

Poverty and marginalisation

Europe is a rich continent in comparison to other parts of the globe. However, of the about 800 million people in greater Europe more than 150 million are estimated to be living in poverty, that is, households with less than half the country's median income.

Many elderly people and persons with disabilities live in extremely poor circumstances which have become worse during the economic crisis. Women still suffer from pay inequalities and job discrimination, and even in the richest countries children live in acute poverty in many disadvantaged communities.

The poor and the marginalised tend to lack influence and opportunities to make their voices heard. Surveys have shown that they feel ignored by political parties and they often have little confidence in the authorities.

When they are victims of crime, they hesitate to report this to the police – because of mistrust. In courts, they are at a disadvantage in comparison to those who can hire senior lawyers and in prisons they are over-represented.

Children living in poverty often have little support to cope with problems in school. Some do not speak the majority language and are therefore doubly excluded. Social exclusion is passed on from one generation to the next. Inequalities prevent social mobility.

These problems are not new. The gap between rich and poor has been on the increase in most European countries during the past two to three decades. The current economic crisis – with continued high unemployment rates and decreasing resources for social welfare – puts a further burden on those who are already disadvantaged.

The poor and deprived within society – particularly the younger ones – are more aware of these injustices and inequalities than earlier generations were. The contrasts have become starkly highlighted through modern information media. It is not difficult to see the risk that this awareness of great social disparities poses to the social cohesion on which our societies – and security – are based.

The obvious conclusion is that the inequalities must not be allowed to grow further; social justice has to be restored. We need to remember that the Universal Declaration of Human Rights provides that "all human beings have the right to a standard of living adequate for their health and well-being, including food, clothing, housing and medical care" (Article 25).

The UN Covenant on Economic, Social and Cultural Rights and the European Social Charter have given further substance to these rights and highlight the necessity of implementing them without discrimination.

Another key human rights instrument to address injustice in Europe is Protocol No. 12 to the European Convention on Human Rights, which sets out a general prohibition against discrimination. This prohibition also covers discriminatory treatment in the provision of social rights. When ratified by a member state, the standard set out in Protocol No. 12 becomes the basis for applications to the European Court of Human Rights in Strasbourg. So far, 18 of the 47 Council of Europe member states have ratified this protocol and another 19 have signed and thereby signalled their intention to consider ratification.[56]

However, we have to realise that social justice cannot be established only by way of traditional human rights instruments, even if they are updated and modernised. The enormous gap between the haves and have-nots is a major ethical, ideological and political challenge – the resolution of which will require change in many aspects of our societies.

It is necessary to analyse in more depth how these gaps in human rights protection have emerged and grown: the link between the extreme wealth of some and the extreme poverty of others has to be analysed. The reckless speculation that caused the banking

---

56. The number of ratifications and signatures as at 1 December 2010.

crisis – leading to untold tragedies for many people – has illustrated the need for regulation and accountability.

Corruption is widespread, almost endemic, in several European countries. Too many politicians have allowed themselves to exchange favours with big business interests. When corrupt practices are tolerated in local and central government administration, it is the poor who suffer the consequences. Occasionally, people are forced to pay bribes for services which they should receive for free and as of right.

The unequal status of women is another reflection of continued discrimination and, at the same time, a source of injustice on a broad scale. It is estimated that about two thirds of those who live in absolute poverty are women. They are often in weak negotiating positions, in poor communities, and face almost insurmountable barriers preventing them from effectively asserting their rights (see gender rights chapter also). This is a tremendous loss for the whole of society.

The marginalisation of the poor also owes a lot to society's attitudes. When political leaders and opinion formers engage in rhetoric implying, for instance, that the poor have only themselves to blame, they justify political inaction in the face of poverty. There has also been a tendency to see marginalised groups as security threats rather than as people in need.

We are facing several inter-related gaps. One disjunction is the distance between the agreed standards on human rights on the one hand, and continuing violations on the other – the implementation gap. Another gap lies in the striking difference between the promises made by politicians (not least during election campaigns), and what is actually delivered when they are in office.

These gaps are really different sides of the same problem and they tend to undermine public trust in the possibility of social justice. I have become increasingly worried about this credibility gap and its consequences more generally for democracy and, thereby, the protection of human rights.

In the current atmosphere of xenophobia and reduced empathy, extremist political groups have been given an increased possibility to spread their message of fear and hatred. This is a threat against democracy itself – calling for reflection and action. The challenge is to build a society in which every one is included and no one is left behind.

The global economic crisis and human rights

Enormous sums of tax payers' money were poured into the banking system in order to prevent a global financial meltdown. Ordinary people have been forced to pay for the reckless practices of a few. On top of this, there are clear signs that it is the less wealthy who will suffer most from the continuing recession that the world is facing.

Increased unemployment has placed a further burden on state budgets and there is less space for social assistance just at the very time when needs will inevitably grow. This is likely to cause tensions and perhaps even social unrest. There is a risk that xenophobia and other intolerance will spread further and that minorities and migrants may become the targets of a general sense of malaise or unrest. Extremists might seek to exploit and provoke such tendencies.

This is an extraordinary challenge for governments today – requiring wise leadership. It is obvious that no country can resolve these problems alone. Multilateral co-operation is a must and inter-state institutions should demonstrate political determination and solidarity beyond narrow national interests. Rules to regulate the financial markets are a necessary first step, but insufficient on their own. It is also necessary to develop concrete programmes which promote social cohesion and prevent any watering down of already agreed human rights standards.

When I talk of the importance of human rights standards, I am obviously referring also to economic and social rights, several of which are included in the key modern foundational human rights document – the 1948 Universal Declaration of Human Rights. One of the sources of inspiration for the declaration was the experience of US President Franklin D. Roosevelt who had had to deal with the aftermath of the financial crises at the end of the 1920s. One of the four freedoms defined in the State of the Union speech delivered in January 1941 was "freedom from want". Not only should human beings be able to express their opinions and to practise a religion freely, they should also be protected against repression and social misery.

The Universal Declaration of Human Rights establishes that human rights include the right to social security, the right to an adequate standard of living, the right to food, the right to education, the right to housing, the right to health, the right to work and the right to rest and leisure.

Such rights have since been legally guaranteed in United Nations and Council of Europe treaties – the latter through the European Social Charter of 1961, revised in 1996. These rights are furthermore covered by core conventions of the International Labour Organization core conventions. The latter protections cover, for example, trade union rights, protection against forced labour and rules against the exploitation of child labour.

While economic and social rights must be regarded as an integral part of international human rights law, they have still not been fully recognised as justiciable rights in some European countries. This was obviously one reason why these rights were not incorporated into the 1950 European Convention on Human Rights but only later codified in the separate European Social Charter. Some countries have been slow in ratifying the revised European Social Charter.

There may well also be an ideological basis for the delay in embracing socio-economic rights on a par with the European Convention on Human Rights. Some European governments believe that their administrations should not take full responsibility for securing education, health care and a decent standard of living for all citizens. Some appear to regard these rights as merely political aspirations to be addressed only as and when government chooses to do so.

However, the fact that the full implementation of economic and social rights could be demanding is no rational basis for treating these rights as less important or as radically different from others. These rights deal with some of the most crucial issues on today's political agenda: the right to a job and acceptable working conditions, the right to go to school and have a meaningful education, the right to protection and care in situations of personal crisis.

These rights were agreed to by governments when they signed up to any number of international human rights treaties. It is quite wrong to portray socio-economic rights as the "poor cousins" of civil and political rights. All human rights are inter-related and interdependent; there is no hierarchy.

There are governments that accept this approach in principle but state that they just do not have the resources to meet these obligations. What is the answer to them?

The implementation of most human rights has a financial cost. It is true though that some economic and social rights tend to be expensive, for instance, the right for everyone to education or to health care. But this potential problem was foreseen by the drafters of the text, and the standards that governments agreed to be bound by allow for a gradual implementation of rights. Governments should establish minimum acceptable standards or core entitlements and at the same time strive to attain full implementation as soon as possible. They cannot postpone the realisation of these standards indefinitely.

To help achieve this goal, the definition of socio-economic indicators is particularly important. Such benchmarks have been developed in certain areas – for instance, by UNICEF in the field of children's rights, and the World Health Organization in the field of health care. It will be helpful when similar work is completed in other areas as well.

It is obvious that if we do not put our commitment to economic and social rights into practice, large numbers of the poor will remain marginalised. Ultimately, political and civil rights will become devoid of all meaning as well. The notion of human dignity is key here since it is the unifying concept that links civil and political rights on the one hand and social and economic rights on the other. The European

Court of Human Rights, for example, has lent its weight to this interrelationship by commenting that a wholly insufficient amount of social benefit or pension may, in principle, raise an issue under Article 3 of the European Convention on Human Rights. Article 3 prohibits inhuman or degrading treatment and, whilst it is most often thought of in terms of combating the physical or psychological torture of detainees, the Court used a wider (and popularly understood) interpretation of the concept of human dignity to apply it to the provision of social services.

Economic and social rights have not been defined in a vacuum; they are based on the experience of past crises and in the knowledge that ignoring social justice comes at an enormous cost. They also serve as vital guiding principles for political decision makers at a time when difficult choices have to be made.

Equality, discrimination and poverty

Governments all over Europe are introducing austerity programmes. Inadequate provision is being made for social assistance to respond to the needs caused by growing unemployment. If that attitude gains ground there is a risk that the continued economic crisis will turn into a political one as well. People may not accept a lowering of their standards – especially while financial institutions, widely regarded as having acted irresponsibly, are subsidised.

When speaking in Strasbourg in April 2009 the Spanish Prime Minister, José Luis Rodriguez Zapatero, recognised the necessity of meeting the needs of those who will suffer the most from the adverse consequences of the economic crisis.

Pleading for solidarity with the poor, the prime minister described poverty as the main reason for social backwardness and for the breach of human rights, not least the rights of women. "The only way to guarantee our welfare is fighting poverty. This is not only a moral must. This is not only a matter of image. This is a political responsibility", the prime minister said. Towards the end of his speech he added that the economic crisis should be seen as a positive opportunity for change.

Positive change requires that protectionist tendencies are resisted by governments. Fortunately, there seems to be a widespread recognition that solutions to the crisis must be sought across borders, through multilateral agreements and inter-state initiatives that go beyond narrow national interests. Another positive trend is the increasing view that governments must begin to play a more active role in preventing unethical business practices and in correcting structural market deficiencies. There is a clear link between this trend and human rights – not least social rights. It is of great importance that human rights principles are emphasised in the ongoing discussions about the lessons learned.

The time is long overdue for a serious attempt to address the enormous gaps between the wealthy and the destitute; between those who have the means and the contacts, and those who are marginalised and powerless. In a globalised and inter-connected world, such injustices will not be accepted or even possible.

In his inauguration speech in January 2009, US President Barack Obama made the point that the crisis is not only the result of reckless risk-taking by some bank officials or the "greed and irresponsibility on the part of some". It was also, he said, the result of "our collective failure to make hard choices and prepare the nation for a new age".

That new age will not arrive if we continue to ignore the deep inequalities and injustices in our societies. These inequalities undermine social cohesion and thereby undermine the security of all; they clearly violate the principles of human rights which, over and over again, we have pledged to respect.

Instead of allowing these inequalities to grow even further, the current global crisis ought to be a turning point for concrete measures to restore social justice. The crisis goes deeper than its obvious economic aspects; it touches on questions of public confidence and ethical values. It is time to start building a cohesive society which excludes no one and leaves no one behind.

It has been shown that an equal, rights-respecting society is better for everyone, not only for the most vulnerable. Equal communities have less illness and a longer life expectancy than unequal communities. Facts about social problems and crime rates demonstrate that inequalities, even in the most affluent societies, create insecurity which harms everyone.

This is a human rights challenge. The Universal Declaration of Human Rights says that all human beings have the right to a standard of living adequate for their health and well-being, including food, clothing, housing and medical care (Article 25).

There has been some resistance in the United States to recognising these rights (and the right to education) as full human rights. Also in Europe there have been voices arguing that an adequate standard of living cannot be more than an ambition. But this is not what the treaties say. An overwhelming majority of states have ratified the UN Covenant on Economic, Social and Cultural Rights and many European states have endorsed the European Social Charter and the revised European Social Charter. A majority of Council of Europe member states have now ratified the Charter in its original or revised form.

Another key instrument to address injustices in Europe is Protocol No. 12 to the European Convention on Human Rights, which stipulates a general prohibition of discrimination. When ratified by member states this standard can be the basis for applications to the Court of Human Rights in Strasbourg, and I hope that more member states will make ratification an early priority.

In fact, many countries have now adopted a comprehensive legal approach outlawing all forms of discrimination, on whatever grounds. Ombudsmen or other offices have also been established to promote equal opportunities and anti-discrimination. However, major aspects of social injustices are often not tackled in the context of these efforts against discrimination. The focus has instead been on status-based equality, such as gender or race.

A distinction between these two forms of injustices is artificial. They are in many real-life cases totally intertwined as is demonstrated, for instance, through the phenomenon of female poverty. Both these types of injustices must be tackled with a comprehensive approach, argues the Equal Rights Trust, a non-governmental body based in London which has presented a Declaration of Principles on Equality. The text was drafted by human rights and equality law specialists and although it has no formal status, it has been endorsed by a great number of international human rights experts.[57]

One of the major points in the declaration is that positive or affirmative action is necessary to overcome past disadvantage and to accelerate progress towards equality for particular groups. It also makes clear that equal treatment is not the same as identical treatment. To realise full and effective equality, it is necessary to assert the equal worth of people by treating them differently according to their different circumstances and enhancing their capabilities to participate in society as equals.

Perhaps this link between the individual and society as a whole was what the drafters of the universal declaration had in mind when they wrote (Article 28): "Everyone is entitled to a social and international order in which the rights and freedoms set forth in this Declaration can be fully realized."

The right to housing

States must guarantee the right to adequate housing. The revised European Social Charter and the International Covenant on Economic, Social and Cultural Rights are clear on this point. Yet there is a tendency today not to recognise housing rights; housing is often viewed merely as a market commodity.

Access to adequate housing is not simply a concern which affects certain vulnerable groups or minorities, even though special protection measures for them are required. Insecurity on the housing market can have profound consequences on the majority population too. Housing

---

57. See www.equalrightstrust.org.

conditions also often affect access to other basic services. Inadequate housing can put at risk the right to education, to health care and to employment. In addition, poor housing conditions can perpetuate a pattern of social and spatial segregation: this could well result in long-term inequalities which are especially difficult to remedy.

The scope of housing rights is quite wide. According to the revised European Social Charter they cover:
- access to adequate and affordable housing;
- reduction of homelessness and housing policies targeted at all disadvantaged groups;
- procedures to limit forced eviction and ensure security of tenure;
- equal access for migrants to social housing and housing benefits;
- housing construction and housing benefits related to family needs.

The enjoyment of the right to adequate housing must, moreover, be ensured without discrimination on any grounds. The collective complaints mechanism of the Social Charter has been used several times for cases concerning housing rights.

Homelessness should be defined in sufficiently wide terms. The European Federation of National Associations Working with the Homeless has proposed a European typology on homelessness and housing exclusion. This typology includes rooflessness, houselessness and living in insecure or inadequate housing.

Among the vulnerable groups concerned, the Roma and Travellers are usually mentioned first – for obvious reasons. They are still disproportionately represented among the homeless and those living in substandard housing. Migrants, refugees and asylum seekers often live in housing well below average standards in terms of space, quality and access to basic facilities. Non-documented migrants are particularly vulnerable as their irregular status with authorities can be exploited on the housing market. Furthermore, in central and eastern Europe there are still millions of families whose currently insecure leaseholds have not yet been transformed into full property rights. This problem stems from the complexity of the property restitution schemes carried out during the transitional period, but it results in human tragedy.

Persons with disabilities have particular requirements as regards housing. Deinstitutionalisation and the shift to community living have augmented the need to provide accessible and secure housing at an affordable cost. Victims of domestic violence, especially women with their children, often need accommodation outside their homes to get away from an abusive relationship. Yet we should not forget that there are many socially marginalised men among the homeless as well.

The positive obligation of states to uphold housing rights should be matched by robust national legislation. Constitutional provisions should be coupled with laws and statutes which clearly spell out the duties of national and local authorities. The right to adequate housing has to be made justiciable before the courts so that individuals can seek remedies if they cannot access adequate housing.

Legal developments in Scotland and France stand as good examples to follow in the field of housing rights. The Scottish Homelessness Act 2003 obliges local authorities to provide permanent accommodation to people who have priority needs, and temporary accommodation to people without priority needs. Priority needs will cease to be used as a rationing criterion in 2012. Individuals can complain to courts if their housing needs are not met.

The French legislation in 2007 on the right to housing renders the state responsible for housing rights. Priority needs are identified in the act while a two-tier system of complaints is envisaged. Regional mediation commissions are the forums of first instance, after which cases can go before administrative courts.

Governments should also recognise that their economic and social policies impact on the right to housing. With the necessary political will, national housing policies could be applied to control land and property speculation when such behaviour prevents the enjoyment of housing rights. The availability of several housing models in addition to home ownership is also necessary to meet the needs of labour mobility. Positive measures in favour of vulnerable groups are justified when they are proportionate to a legitimate aim.

A minimum programme for a rights-based housing policy ought to include these points:

– national laws should spell out housing rights and who is responsible for their implementation at different levels;

– minimum standards for adequate housing and emergency accommodation should be clearly defined;

– anti-discrimination legislation should include housing rights both in the public and private markets;

– positive measures are needed to support disadvantaged groups;

– effective remedies to violations of housing rights and discrimination should be available to everyone. The right to adequate housing should be justiciable before the courts.

The realisation of housing rights should be monitored at national and international level. Ombudspersons and human rights institutions have a role to play in this process.

The rights of older people

Older people have the same rights as others. However, they may be vulnerable and need special protection so the Universal Declaration of Human Rights states specifically that elderly persons have the right to security. However, the rights of elderly persons are still often ignored and sometimes totally denied. They suffer from a widespread perception that they are non-productive and therefore worthless to modern society. It is time for a more constructive debate on how human rights for the older generation can be ensured.

Older people often do not have a strong say in politics. Organisations defending their interests are – with few exceptions – weak and political parties often focus on younger generations. The fact that a clear majority of the elderly are women may also have contributed to a lack of attention to this constituency of interest on the part of politicians.

The revised European Social Charter contains the first binding human rights provision for the protection of the rights of the elderly. The main objective is to enable older persons to lead a decent life and participate in society. To put this into practice, states should ensure that their social protection systems, health care and housing policies are suitable for older people. They should also enact anti-discrimination legislation in certain areas, including the labour market.

A growing number of those who reach retirement age are fit and healthy, and would prefer to continue with their professional activities. This has not, however, provoked the necessary rethink about how the professional skills, experience and dedication of these individuals could be utilised for the common good.

Special attention should be paid to ensuring that older people who so wish have the possibility to continue their working life. Age on its own is not a valid reason to ignore someone in the recruitment process or to sack them. More flexibility on retirement ages on the basis of personal preferences and capabilities would be logical. With some adjustments in working conditions, including hours of work, many more would like to continue long after the present pension age. A UN conference stated some years ago that "older persons should have the opportunity to work as long as they wish and are able to, in satisfying and productive work".

Many people now aged 60 will live for two or three decades beyond retirement, and in some cases even longer. The number of very old persons is growing rapidly in countries all over Europe.

This is a category which in many cases will require special care, as some of them are clearly dependent and suffer from dementia or other disabilities.

Protection measures should be flexible so as to fit individual needs and they should only be put in place in those fields of the individual's life where they are indispensable. It should also be possible for an individual, at a time when he or she is still capable, to make decisions on what should happen in the future, and about who should act as his or her representative in case of any eventual incapacity. Such measures of self-determination respect the dignity of each person as a human being.

The increasing number of elderly people will inevitably put a strain on social and health-care systems. Even with a more flexible pension policy, there will in economic terms be a less favourable relationship in future between the proportion of the population that is working and those who are dependent. However, a humane and just society must accept that responsibility and must ensure proper respect for the human dignity and rights of the very oldest in society. Health-care systems should implement age-friendly policies and practices and consider how to promote healthy ageing.

Many older people are poor and their right to an adequate standard of living is not respected. In the transition countries in Europe, older people have suffered from major political and economic changes and have had little chance to compensate for significant price increases by working more or securing higher salaries. A great number have had to accept a dramatic downturn in housing (and general living) standards. The term "lost generation" is sadly appropriate.

New social security strategies are required so that older people have adequate protection in the future. Even in countries where social security is adequately protected, there is a need to review some aspects of the treatment of older people. There have been too many reports of bad treatment and even abuse in institutions for the elderly, some of which are privately run. In every case, this is an unacceptable failure. It is made worse by the fact that the residents in these homes are often unable to claim their rights and even less able to defend themselves against abuse.

During my travels throughout Europe, I have seen the extremes. I have visited modern and homely institutions with a democratic atmosphere and excellent medical care. Unfortunately, I have also seen centres in which the residents were treated more like numbers than human beings, and the staff were untrained, overstretched and acquiescent. There is clearly a need in some countries to monitor the conditions in institutions for elderly persons more thoroughly.

Persons living in institutions should of course get appropriate care and services. Their right to privacy and dignity should be fully respected. They also have the right to participate in decisions concerning their treatment as well as the conditions of the institution. Independent complaints and inspection systems should be set up to prevent ill-treatment and promote quality care. Rules on minimum standards for elderly persons in institutional care should be drawn up.

Even in countries with age-friendly institutions, many elderly people prefer to stay at home as long as possible. This requires a different care response from the social authorities. Such reforms have indeed taken place in many countries. However, it is my impression that more could be done to offer older people more choices and more influence over what care they would prefer, both now and later.

One policy option is to give greater priority to supporting, and sometimes providing respite care for, family members who provide regular assistance for their elderly relatives. The well-being of caregivers has a significant impact on the quality of care, and on the dignity and quality of life of the dependent person. Among the very old there are those who are particularly vulnerable. We know for example that elderly women suffer discrimination in some cases and that they often receive a reduced pension allowance because they have had to care for family members rather than be professionally active.

Persons with disabilities face particular difficulties which may increase as a consequence of the ageing process: for instance, reduced vision, reduced hearing or reduced mobility. The needs of older people must be taken into account when designing policies and programmes aimed at people with disabilities. The ratification of the UN Convention on the Rights of Persons with Disabilities, which creates a number of safeguards for such persons, should be given a high priority. The same is true in Europe regarding the importance of implementing the Council of Europe Disability Action Plan 2006-15.

Older migrants are also vulnerable; some have language difficulties. With a growing immigrant population, European countries are faced with a challenge for which the authorities seem to be grossly unprepared. The result is that individuals are discriminated against on several grounds.

European political leaders should review their policies regarding the rights of older people – ideally, well before they themselves have to face the consequences of their present-day policies, or lack thereof.

HIV, Aids and the right to health

Further action is needed against the HIV/Aids pandemic in Europe. The international focus has been on the apocalyptic situation in some African and Asian countries, but the infection is also spreading fast in certain European states, notably in the Russian Federation, Ukraine, Estonia, Latvia and Moldova. The disease has generated a severe public health crisis as well as urgent human rights problems.

It is estimated that more than one million persons are living with the HIV/Aids infection in Russia, and about half a million in Ukraine. This is more than 1% of the population and the epidemic continues to spread more rapidly. High figures are also registered in Estonia, Latvia and Moldova. In western Europe, the highest rates have been recorded in Spain, Italy, France, Switzerland and Portugal.

HIV/Aids is changing the demographics in all affected countries. Given that the hardest-hit section of society is the 15 to 30 age-group, HIV/Aids has a disproportionate impact on the young and those of child-bearing age, and therefore in turn on birth-rates. In Russia and Ukraine the disease is likely to become an obstacle to economic growth.

Many of those affected have had their human rights undermined. Ignorance about how the disease spreads has bred prejudice and discrimination which, in turn, has stigmatised or marginalised those who carry the virus.

Such discrimination must be combated and governments should work closely with non-governmental support groups, not least with those that have been organised by HIV carriers themselves and their relatives.

A large section of the infected population does not receive the necessary anti-retroviral treatment or psychological support. Also, carriers are often discriminated against in areas of medical assistance, education and labour-market opportunities.

Particularly vulnerable are the growing number of children born to HIV-positive mothers. Some may be infected themselves; some risk becoming orphans; they all have the right to special support.

Prevention is certainly a key priority. Research aiming at an effective vaccine may not produce results for many years though governments that have invested in available methods of prevention have had some encouraging results.

First, and most important of all, governments must openly recognise the full scale of the problem. Until recently, HIV/Aids was not high on the governmental agenda. Indeed, in Russia and Ukraine, for instance, funds allocated to both prevention and treatment were meagre. Attitudes are now changing, and the Russian authorities have acknowledged that the actual infection rate might be four times higher than the official figures.

Systematic information campaigns about safe sex, combined with making condoms available, have had a positive impact where tried. Unfortunately, religious leaders have not in all cases been supportive of these important endeavours.

Part of the strategy has to be directed towards the groups that are particularly at risk:
- drug injection remains a key factor in the growth of the pandemic in both Russia and Ukraine, as well as in Estonia and Moldova. More than half of those diagnosed in eastern Europe with HIV/Aids had used contaminated syringes, according to UNAIDS. Of those who inject drugs, roughly one in four are believed to

be HIV-infected. However, in Switzerland and some other west European countries efforts to reduce the number of new cases among injecting drug users have made progress;

- prostitution – often combined with drug abuse – is clearly dangerous. In the Russian Federation, studies indicate that more than 30% of females drawn into prostitution had contracted HIV. In Ukraine, the prevalence in this group was estimated to range between 13 and 31%, with even higher figures in the largest cities;

  prisoners also tend to have a higher infection rate than the general population. In Latvia, it has been estimated that prisoners may comprise a third of the total population in the country living with HIV. For Ukraine, UNAIDS reported in 2009 that no less than 10 000 prisoners were infected.

It is believed that a majority of those who live with the HIV today are unaware that they have the virus, and may therefore not be taking adequate steps to avoid infecting others. More has to be done to promote blood testing and to support newly diagnosed carriers of the infection.

Comprehensive prevention strategies can stop the disease from spreading further. There is a need for effective national action plans – programmes which are underpinned by broad-based awareness-raising programmes and strong educational components. It is absolutely essential that governments take effective action against the illicit drug trade and the trafficking of human beings.

This is a heavy agenda. Although Russia, Ukraine, Estonia and Moldova have a serious HIV crisis, other European countries are affected as well and should be reflecting on how best to take preventive action now.

Climate change: an issue of human rights

The daily lives of millions around the world are already being affected by the effects of global warming: desertification, droughts, flooding or cyclones. Basic human rights – such as the right to life, health, food, water, shelter or property – are under threat. In

Europe, as elsewhere, those who will suffer most are those who are already vulnerable – people living in poverty, especially older people, women and children. This is why the protection of human rights as a whole received a set-back with the failure at the United Nations conference in Copenhagen in December 2009.

The Universal Declaration of Human Rights states that "everyone is entitled to a social and international order in which [their] rights and freedoms … can be fully realized". That order is undermined by the absence of effective action against climate change.

Mary Robinson, the former UN High Commissioner for Human Rights, wrote that "we have collectively failed to grasp the scale and urgency of the problem. Climate change shows up countless weaknesses in our current institutional architecture, including its human rights mechanisms. To effectively address it will require a transformation of global policy capacity – from information gathering and collective decision-making to law enforcement and resource distribution".[58]

The challenge is to remedy these failures; to start developing a co-ordinated effort to stop further dangerous global warming; and, at the same time, to take steps to redress the environmental degradation which has already taken place or is now inevitable.

This will require a unique spirit of global solidarity. So far, richer countries have contributed most to global warming, whilst the poorer ones have had to deal with the consequences.

The carbon-emission cuts pledged by developed states have not met the expectations of the developing world. Adaptation funds, designed to help poor nations to protect their societies against climate change impacts, have also been slow to materialise. This, in turn, has made developing countries less willing to restrain the increase of their own emissions. We need to recognise our global interdependence.

---

58. Foreword to *Climate change and human rights. A rough guide*, published by the International Council on Human Rights Policy, 2009 (www.ichrp.org).

Another flaw in the climate-change discussion so far has been the lack of emphasis on human rights. Though the reports of the Intergovernmental Panel on Climate Change (IPCC) describe the social consequences of global warming, they have not applied a human rights analysis to their work.

However, the Office of the UN High Commissioner for Human Rights has published a report on the relationship between climate change and human rights. The document describes the effects of climate change on individuals and communities, and underlines the treaty-based obligations of governments to protect those whose rights are affected by the impact of global warming or by the policies and measures designed to address climate change.[59]

Another report – published by the non-governmental organisation International Council on Human Rights Policy – argues that the disciplinary boundaries between environmental and human rights law should be breached. The study shows that both the policy to reduce emission levels (mitigation) and the efforts to strengthen capacities of societies to cope with the impact of climate change (adaptation) can be more effective if linked to human rights.

A human rights analysis would indeed add an important and different perspective to the climate-change negotiations. At the very least, it would ensure that the discussion was grounded in the concrete consequences of climate change on the daily lives of people: it would remind us that climate change is about human suffering.

If our response to the environmental challenge is to be effective, we must know who is at risk and how they could be protected. Consideration of the human rights impact of certain actions/inactions on individuals and communities will hopefully encourage greater preparedness to prevent chain effects such as mass displacement and conflict. A human rights approach should guide the targeting of assistance to the most vulnerable groups.

---

59. http://www2.ohchr.org/english/issues/climatechange/study.htm.

Human rights standards and principles also provide safeguards which should be integrated into plans and policies to address climate change. Economic and social rights are to be protected to the maximum extent of available resources: in other words, they are to be given priority. This in turn requires that affected populations have the right to be well informed and to participate in relevant decision-making through genuinely democratic processes.

These safeguards are reflected in the 1998 Aarhus Convention: the convention has provisions for pro-active information sharing and for the involvement of affected people in the preparation of plans and programmes to combat environmental risk.[60]

There is also a burning need to discuss accountability. By using human rights standards, states can define minimum requirements for both mitigation and adaptation policies. This starting point would oblige all states to make it clear that damage to the environment that goes beyond a certain threshold, causing harm to certain basic human rights, is unacceptable and illegal.

In the article cited earlier, Mary Robinson also mentioned the need to adapt human rights mechanisms so that they can better handle the new challenges arising as a result of climate change. Care needs to be taken to establish effective procedures aimed at securing accountability and providing reparation to victims. However, it will not be easy to assign legal responsibility: there are often many perpetrators involved, and they often do not reside in the countries where the damage occurs.

The European Court of Human Rights has recognised environmental rights (mostly in connection with Article 8 of the European Convention). In one case, the Court noted that "severe environmental pollution may affect individuals' well-being and prevent them from

---

60. The Aarhus Convention on Access to Information, Public Participation in Decision-making and Access to Justice in Environmental Matters (1998).

enjoying their homes in such a way as to affect their private and family life adversely".[61]

The Court has also confirmed the obligation of states to carry out proper studies before allowing an activity which might cause environmental damage, and to bring those studies to the public's knowledge.[62]

A violation of the right to life has been found by the Court in a case where, even though the authorities were aware of an increasing risk of a large-scale mudslide, no preventive action was taken and the local population had not been informed of the risk.[63]

The European Social Charter provides for the right to health and requires state parties "to remove as far as possible the causes of ill-health" (Article 11). On this basis the European Committee of Social Rights has required that states show measurable progress in lowering levels of pollution.[64] The same ruling would cover nuclear hazards, risks related to asbestos, or food safety.

These are only first steps. With growing awareness of the harm caused by climate change, it will be necessary to clarify further those state obligations that must surely flow from an individual's right to a healthy environment.

Already, the first UN Conference on the Environment in Stockholm 1972 declared as a right for humans to have "adequate conditions of life, in an environment of a quality that permits a life of dignity and well-being".

The statement did not end there: it also unambiguously declared that we all have "a solemn responsibility to protect and improve the environment for present and future generations".

---

61. *Lopez Astra v. Spain,* judgment of 9 December 1994.
62. *Taşkın and Others v. Turkey,* judgment of 10 November 2004.
63. *Berdyaev and Others v. Russia,* judgment of 20 March 2008.
64. European Committee of Social Rights decision in the case *Sarantopoulos Foundation for Human Rights (MFHR) v. Greece,* Complaint No. 30/2005, decision on the merits of 6 December 2006, paragraphs 203 and 205.

Enforcing social rights standards

The protection of social rights is being further tested during the current economic crisis. As with other human rights they are enshrined in treaties agreed by governments, one being the European Social Charter. The challenge is to ensure that these agreements are enforced in practice. This requires informing people about their rights and giving them an opportunity to complain when they find their rights violated. In this regard, active civil society groups can provide a valuable contribution.

Support for the European Social Charter and the later revised European Social Charter has broadened in recent years after ratifications by Hungary, the Slovak Republic, the Russian Federation, Serbia and Montenegro. A clear majority of the Council of Europe member states have now bound themselves to respect the Charter in its original or its revised version.[65]

This is progress. However, the key point about human rights standards is their enforcement in real life. To ensure realisation of the Charter, a monitoring body, the European Committee of Social Rights (ECSR), was set up and the committee assesses and advises on implementation in the course of reviewing state reports. The conclusions of the ESCR are then submitted for further action to the Committee of Ministers via a Governmental Committee.

The procedure of reporting and oversight is now well developed and provides a useful mechanism for collegial support to member states in their efforts to give practical effect to their duties under the Charter. First, member states have to prepare detailed reports indicating their compliance with European standards, and they are encouraged to report any difficulties they face in implementation. Second, the committee provides specialist feedback and guidance to the member state.

---

65. The Charter was adopted in 1961 and the revised Charter in 1996. For details on ratifications see appendix.

My focus here is on a complementary information channel that has been established by the ECSR. Drawing on the experience of the International Labour Organization, which demonstrated the value of accepting submissions from social partners about specific human rights violations, a system of collective complaints has been established through a protocol to the European Social Charter.

This mechanism has existed now for more than a decade but not even a third of the Council of Europe states have so far decided to be party to it. This is a pity because the collective complaints procedure was intended to contribute directly to the enforcement of the social rights guaranteed by the Charter.

Previously, the European Committee of Social Rights was limited to developing its case law under the reporting procedure. The committee examined reports submitted by member states and commented on the extent the state was in conformity with the Charter. With the complaints procedure, the verification process has been given a new dynamic. It allows the committee, in its own words, "to make a legal assessment of the situation of a state in the light of the information supplied by the complaint and the adversarial procedure to which it gives rise".[66]

Collective complaints may be submitted by European organisations of employers and trade unions which participate in the work of the Governmental Committee,[67] international non-governmental organisations enjoying participatory status with the Council of Europe, as well as national organisations of employers and trade unions of the contracting parties concerned. In addition, each state may, in a special declaration, authorise national non-governmental organisations to lodge complaints. Only Finland has so far agreed to this last measure.

---

66. Decision as to the admissibility: *ICJ v. Portugal* (Complaint No. 1/1998), 10 March 1999, paragraph 10.
67. European Trade Union Confederation (ETUC), BusinessEurope (formerly UNICE) and the International Organisation of Employers (IOE).

The complaints are examined by the ECSR and declared admissible if the formal requirements are met. Then a written procedure is set in motion, with an exchange between the parties. Other states parties, as well as employers' organisations and trade unions, may also submit observations.

The ECSR may decide to hold a public hearing. Subsequently, it takes a decision on the merits of the complaint, which it forwards to the parties concerned and to the Committee of Ministers, in a report which is made public within four months. The Committee of Ministers adopts a resolution on the basis of the report and, where appropriate, it may recommend that the state concerned takes specific measures to bring itself into line with the Charter.

Despite the low number of states parties to the procedure, and its quasi-judicial character, the collective complaints mechanism has exceeded expectations. The committee has been able to respond to concrete complaints and to deal with key issues of vulnerability and discrimination:

- insufficient protection for autistic children;
- discrimination both in law and in practice against Roma in the field of housing;
- insufficient medical assistance to the children of illegal immigrants;
- corporal punishment of children;
- inadequate state action to prevent negative environmental impact in the main areas where lignite was mined, and the lack of appropriate strategies aimed at preventing and mitigating health hazards for local people;
- unsatisfactory implementation of domestic law preventing evictions and the lack of measures to provide re-housing solutions for evicted families;
- discrimination in the education of children with intellectual disabilities;

- environmental hazards and lack of adequate health care for Roma.[68]

In its role as authentic interpreter of the European Social Charter, the ECSR has demonstrated that it does not operate in a vacuum. It has built on the Council of Europe's standards with particular reference to the European Convention on Human Rights and, when relevant, to other important international standards such as the UN Convention on the Rights of the Child. Its case law is now also an important reference for my work as Commissioner for Human Rights, and the European Court of Human Rights recently explained how ECSR case law can be useful as a source of interpretation.[69]

The procedure of collective complaints has a preventive dimension. The complaints lodged before the ECSR do not deal with individual cases but with alleged general shortcomings in law and practice. Assessments made by the committee can assist states in taking required measures to remedy a situation, thus also pre-empting individual applications before the Strasbourg Court. The committee can also refer to an issue dealt with in its complaints procedure when submitting its regular reports on state compliance with the Charter: thereby further assisting member states in their efforts to prevent violations.

Indeed, several states have redressed a situation brought to light by way of this procedure. In November 2006, I welcomed the adoption by the Greek Parliament of a law on domestic violence which prohibited corporal punishment of children. The law's adoption had been prompted by a decision of the ECSR on a collective complaint against Greece.

In response to a complaint concerning housing rights, France undertook to take into account the decision of the European Committee of Social Rights when implementing its legislation on the enforceable right to housing.

---

68. For the full listing of the collective complaints lodged to date see: www.coe.int/t/dghl/monitoring/socialcharter/Complaints/Complaints_en.asp.
69. *Demir and Baykara v. Turkey*, judgment of 12 November 2008.

In the case concerning the right to education for children with autism, the French Government declared that it would bring the situation into line with the revised Charter and that measures were being taken to this effect.

The collective complaints procedure has several advantages. It is relatively fast and non-bureaucratic. Its admissibility criteria are more flexible than those applicable to actions taken to the Strasbourg Court. A complaint may be declared admissible even if domestic remedies are not exhausted (a big source of delay in seeking redress at the European Court of Human Rights), and even if a similar case is pending before national or international bodies.

I hope that more governments will open this channel for complaints relating to their own countries. And I hope that trade unions, employers groups, and other civil society organisations will use this mechanism more systematically in order to protect social rights.

Chapter 9: Police, courts and prisons

Corruption in the justice system often goes hand in hand with political interference. Ministers and other leading politicians do not always respect the independence of the judiciary and instead signal prosecutors or judges on what is expected of them. Conditions in prisons are appalling in several European countries. In some cases the treatment of inmates is clearly inhuman and degrading.

Photo © Council of Europe.

Police violence

Police brutality remains a serious problem in several European countries. During my missions I have received numerous allegations against the police of unprovoked violence before, during and after arrest. When I have asked victims why they have not filed complaints, the answer has often been that they feared being beaten up again. Others, however, have taken their case to the European Court of Human Rights in Strasbourg, which has passed a great number of judgments against states for excessive or abusive use of force by the police.

The role of the police in a democratic society is to defend the general population against crime, especially violent crime. Illegal behaviour by police officers is particularly damaging. The entire system of justice risks being derailed when law enforcement officials break the very laws that they are employed to uphold.

This fact is of course recognised throughout Europe and great efforts are made to recruit reliable personnel. Training is aimed at preparing police officers to cope, within the limits of the law, with a range of difficult situations, including when and how force may be used. Steps are being taken to discourage corruption, and to promote professional codes of ethics. Despite this, cases of police brutality occur.

The solution to tackling abuses of police powers is not to focus solely on the individuals involved. The police sometimes have to work in very difficult situations, and acts of police brutality are often not isolated incidents but form part of a wider mentality about dealing with crime. In several transition countries, there is still a strong belief that a good police officer is one who "solves" cases, and the pressure on the police to secure confessions is considerable. Courts also rely excessively on signed statements from the accused. In combination, these factors can act as an incentive to obtain confessions by coercion.

The fight against crime (including terrorism) does not justify any and every means. Human rights require that the security of all is protected, but not at the cost of fundamental human rights. The Strasbourg Court has clarified that there is a limit:

> *The Court, being aware of the danger ... of undermining or even destroying democracy on the ground of defending it, affirms that the Contracting States may not, in the name of the struggle against espionage and terrorism, adopt whatever measures they deem appropriate.*[70]

There are situations when the use of police force can be justified, for instance, to control a riot or to apprehend a suspect. However, the use of force should be strictly regulated. One requirement is legality; it is particularly important that the laws covering such situations be clear.

The Strasbourg Court has stated that "[the] legal and administrative framework [must] define the limited circumstances in which law enforcement officials may use force and firearms. ... Police officers [are not] to be left in a vacuum when performing their duties, whether in the context of a prepared operation or a spontaneous chase against a person perceived to be dangerous".[71]

Another requirement is that of proportionality. The use of force is justified only in a situation of absolute necessity and even then should be practised with maximum restraint. Police operations must be planned and controlled with this in mind.

Yet the allegations of police brutality that come to my office often relate to police violence being used on individuals deprived of their liberty – prisoners or detainees being interviewed.

Prisoners often complain that they are beaten and kicked when being moved between places of detention. Except in extreme cases of self-defence, it is quite unacceptable for state agents to violate the physical integrity of people already in their custody.

---

70. *Klass and Others v. Germany*, judgment of 6 September 1978.
71. *Makaratzis v. Greece*, judgment of 20 December 2004.

Ill-treatment during interrogation remains common in too many countries. During my visits, I have been informed about the frequency of such abuses and have asked the authorities to take firm action to stop such malpractices.

The Strasbourg Court has made clear that there is a legal obligation to undertake effective inquiries into serious allegations of such violations. Any inquiry should be adequate to lead to the identification and the prosecutions of those responsible, and must be independent, transparent, prompt and thorough. All cases of deaths in custody should automatically be subject to an impartial examination.

The European Committee for the Prevention of Torture and Inhuman or Degrading Treatment or Punishment (CPT) has issued policy guidelines for such investigations, and underlined that, among other requirements, justification has to be provided for any inaction to initiate an investigation into serious allegations. Neglect on this point might in itself – according to the CPT – amount to a violation of the European Convention on Human Rights.

In order for the investigations to be credible, it is necessary that those conducting the inquiry have no relationship to the law enforcement staff implicated in the case.

Different models for dealing with complaints against the police exist throughout Europe. One is to involve personnel from other police districts in such investigations. Several countries have specialist investigative departments within the police to monitor police conduct, but these are not always as independent as they need to be.

Countries seeking more independence have transferred the investigation of police complaints to a court prosecutor with a specialised team to review such cases. Alternatively, a general or specialised police ombudsman has been assigned the responsibility. Another option has been to create a complaints commission involving members of civil society.

The goal must be to establish a system that is independent, while having sufficient legal powers to investigate complaints effectively. The Police

Ombudsman for Northern Ireland is a particularly interesting model combining both independence and strong investigative powers.[72]

When in Dublin, I visited a similar agency for Ireland – the Garda Síochána Ombudsman Commission.[73] The Commission receives complaints from the public and seeks to provide an independent and effective oversight of policing. It is a serious agency with more than 80 staff members, about half of whom are trained investigators, many of them recruited from abroad. The Garda Ombudsman can initiate mediation but also recommend disciplinary action or criminal prosecution when police misconduct has been discovered.

Yet an effective complaints system – however good – deals with problems only after the fact. A further challenge for the authorities is to take additional steps to reduce the possibility of wrongdoing – in other words, to encourage a new policing culture. Clear guidelines for police conduct, drafted in line with international human rights principles, are essential. The European Code of Police Ethics is of guidance here. Thorough initial and continuous training of police personnel to increase their awareness of the importance of respect for human rights in their work is also crucial.

The building of a new culture of policing requires frank open debate in order to develop public trust in the police. As the Strasbourg Court reiterated in a recent judgment: "in a democratic state governed by the rule of law the use of improper methods [by the police] is precisely the kind of issue of which the public have the right to be informed".[74]

Police officers are on the front-line of upholding the rule of law and are the most visible part of the criminal justice system, having regular interaction with members of the public. Abuse of power by law enforcement officials undermines public confidence in the system

---

72. See also article on lessons from Northern Ireland; the website for the Police Ombudsman for Northern Ireland sets out the uniquely independent functions of the office – www.policeombudsman.org.
73. www.gardaombudsman.ie.
74. *Voskuil v. the Netherlands*, judgment of 22 November 2007.

of justice overall. To ensure the highest standards of professionalism – the democratic accountability, powers, recruitment, training and disciplinary systems applied to the police must be regularly reviewed.

The "ticking bomb" argument

Torture and other cruel, inhuman or degrading treatment or punishment are prohibited under international law. No exceptions are allowed – ever. Torture was made unthinkable – or at least impossible to defend – after the total ban had been inscribed in United Nations human rights treaties, the Geneva conventions on the laws of war and the European Convention on Human Rights. However, this great achievement to overcome barbarity, and for human rights, has been undermined during counterterrorism actions.

In spite of all these efforts to outlaw torture, it has continued to be used on a distressing scale, even in recent times. This requires strengthening existing protection mechanisms. Instead, misguided responses to the threat from terrorism have challenged the very consensus against torture.

The devious "ticking bomb" argument has returned and even been taken seriously by some leading opinion makers, not least in the United States where it was used during the period of the Bush administration to defend one of the most cruel torture methods, so-called "water boarding" (a form of mock drowning).

The argument is a familiar one, built on a hypothetical scenario in which police or security forces could save lives by torturing someone who knows where a bomb is placed and thereby obtain information to prevent the explosion. The purpose of this argument is to question the absolute prohibition of torture: if there is a case in which you would save lives by torturing – how could the ban be general and total? This line of reasoning may appear reasonable at first glance, but is flawed and dangerous.

The scenario itself is built on a series of assumptions, the combination of which is extremely unlikely in reality. The exercise requires that (a) the captured person has the necessary information; (b) the police know that this is the case; (c) the accused person will talk under torture; (d) he or she will not talk for any other inducement; (e) he or she will tell the truth; (f) he or she will talk in time and with the level of detail to save lives; (g) no other means are available to obtain the information in time and that (h) no other action could be taken to avoid the harm feared.

The obvious intention of setting out the "ticking bomb scenario" is to create legal room for exceptions to the absolute ban on torture, but making exceptions would have alarming consequences. The use of torture would become a relative issue of ends and means, a question of judgment from case to case. This would lead us to a "slippery slope" where torture would inevitably spread.

Even today, in Europe, despite the clear and absolute ban in national and international law, torture is used in a considerable number of cases, not least before and during interrogations. Any confusion about its illegality would almost certainly increase the prevalence of torture. This is also why the attempts of the previous US Government to "redefine" torture – while Europe was largely silent – were so disquieting.

What is needed is further solid underpinning of the legal ban. Every government must make clear that nothing but zero tolerance is acceptable. The judiciary must react decisively to reported cases of ill-treatment, and evidence produced as a result of torture in police investigations must be ruled inadmissible in any judicial or administrative procedures.

No one must be deported to countries where they are at risk of torture. Attempts to overcome this prohibition through "diplomatic assurances" should not be accepted. Governments which have used torture are already in violation of all international human rights law; they cannot be trusted to make an exception in an individual case simply because of a bilateral, less binding agreement. Moreover, respect for such promises is very difficult to monitor. It is wrong to put individuals at risk by relying on such dubious assurances.

Each government should put in place an effective programme of prevention. Police and security staff must be instructed on legal methods of interrogation. Capacity for disciplined, lawful behaviour must be a key factor when recruiting law enforcement personnel; unsuitable officers must be removed.

Safeguards must be put in place to guarantee that anyone arrested has prompt access to a lawyer and an impartial medical examination upon arrival and release. There must be an effective system of continuing, independent monitoring of all places where people are held and deprived of their liberty.

Effective monitoring to prevent torture is the motivation behind the 2002 Optional Protocol to the United Nations Convention Against Torture (OPCAT). One obligation for states which have ratified the protocol is to establish an independent national preventive mechanism to monitor police detention cells, prisons, psychiatric hospitals, detention centres for refugees and migrants, institutions for young offenders and any other place where persons are held involuntarily.[75]

In most European countries, there are already systems for independent visits to such places. The value of the protocol is that it clarifies the mandate of these local, national and regional mechanisms, and promotes their constructive co-operation with the United Nations sub-committee established under the protocol.

In France, a new institution was created – a *Contrôleur Général*. In the UK, several previously existing monitoring bodies now share this responsibility and work more closely together. In several other countries this monitoring task has been given to the Parliamentary Ombudsman.

---

75. As of July 2010, the protocol has been ratified by 27 Council of Europe member states while another 10 have signed but not yet ratified it.

Whatever model is chosen, it is important that the mechanism be fully independent and authorised to undertake visits without forewarning to all places of detention, without exception. It should be staffed and funded in a manner which guarantees its independence.

There is one effect, which the setting-up of a national preventive mechanism should certainly not have, and that is to limit access by non-governmental organisations to places of detention. Even where national preventive mechanisms exist, NGOs continue to be essential to the work against ill-treatment in all places of detention.

Final abolition of the death penalty

Step by step the death penalty is being abolished. Most countries of the world have now stopped using this cruel, inhuman and degrading punishment. Some 95 states have decided on total abolition, nine have abolished the penalty for all ordinary crimes, and 35 others have it on the statute book but have not executed anyone for more than 10 years. Europe is nowadays close to being a death-penalty-free zone. However, the abolitionist cause has not yet been won.

The most populous countries in the world still retain the death penalty: China, India, Indonesia and the United States. This means that the majority of the world's people live in countries which continue to practise execution as punishment.

Public opinion appearing to support the death penalty can make this a taboo issue. The Russian Federation gave an undertaking when joining the Council of Europe to do away with the death penalty. A moratorium was introduced and extended by a decision in the Supreme Court in 2009, but the Duma does not appear to be ready yet for de jure abolition. After the monstrous terrorist attack against a school in Beslan in September 2004, there were strong emotions in favour of executing the sole attacker who survived the disaster. However, the judicial authorities in Russia were loyal to the moratorium decision, even in this extreme situation – the death sentence was transformed into a sentence of life imprisonment.

Surveys of public opinion about the death penalty have usually shown a majority to be in favour of retaining this punishment. This has been the case particularly when a brutal and widely publicised murder has taken place. However, opinion polls on this issue are not easy to interpret. There is a great difference between asking an interviewee for their gut reaction to a brutal crime, and soliciting a considered opinion about the ethics and principles relating to legalising state killing.

It is certainly worthy of note that there have been no widely based demands for the re-introduction of the death penalty in Europe. Where re introduction is canvassed by politicians, this does not normally attract support from the larger political parties.

Despite this abolitionist trend, I still believe it is important to regularly revisit and argue strongly against killing as a judicial sanction. This is a debate which will routinely recur and it is vital that younger generations are educated afresh on the topic.

It can for example be convincingly argued that the death penalty is ineffective. It has not had the intended deterrent effect. The crime rate is not lower in countries which have retained the penalty and nor has criminality increased in countries where it has been abolished. If anything, the trend is the opposite.

What has been demonstrated, however, is the real risk of executing an innocent person. No system of justice is infallible; judges are human beings and mistakes are made in the courtroom. When the convicted person is executed, it is too late to correct the mistake. There have been a number of such cases – some of them revealed afterwards thanks to new DNA techniques – and there are no guarantees that they will not occur in the future.

It has also been demonstrated that the death penalty regime has a clear tendency to discriminate against the poor and against minorities. Privileged people run much less risk of such punishment than others who have committed the same crime. The greatest risk is run by those who are anyway marginalised (by their minority status, colour, religion, economic status, etc.) since they tend to be disadvantaged in the judicial process generally, and at greater risk when the death penalty is a judicial option.

These arguments are strong. However, it is not enough to cite concerns about effective crime prevention, judicial certainty or discrimination. The death penalty goes to the essence of human rights.

The universal declaration states that no one shall be subject to torture or to cruel, inhuman and degrading treatment or punishment. There have been attempts to find means of execution which involve little pain, in order to make the process more "humane". This has failed: there have been recent examples of prolonged suffering in the electric chair, or after a person has been injected with poison. Even if this physical pain could be avoided, how does one avoid the psychological pain created when awaiting execution? The death penalty is cruel, inhuman and degrading – and will always be so.

The most compelling human rights argument against the death penalty, however, is that it violates the right to life. State killing is indeed the ultimate denial of human rights. That is why it is so essential that we continue to act for abolition.

The Council of Europe has been at the forefront of this effort. All member states have ratified Protocol No. 6 to the European Convention concerning abolition in peace time, and the majority has also agreed to be bound by Protocol No. 13 regarding abolition in all circumstances (including in situations of war). The remaining states should join this growing consensus.[76]

It should also be made clear that Belarus can only aspire to membership of the Council of Europe, or obtain observer status, after it has abolished the death penalty. Governments in the United States and Japan should be reminded that their observer status is in question because of their position on this issue.

---

76. Azerbaijan and the Russian Federation have not signed nor ratified Protocol No. 13; Armenia, Latvia and Poland have signed but not ratified; the remaining 42 member states have ratified.

In the meantime, the successful diplomatic initiatives undertaken in the United Nations should continue. A resolution was adopted with a broad majority in the General Assembly in 2007 which recommended a global moratorium on the use of the death penalty. A similar resolution was agreed in 2008, again stressing that the moratorium should be established "with a view to abolishing the death penalty".[77]

Our position on the death penalty indicates the kind of society we want to build and live in. When the state itself kills a human being under its jurisdiction, it sends a message: it legitimises extreme violence. I am convinced that the death penalty has a brutalising effect in society. There is an element of "an eye for an eye" in each execution. A civilised society should expose the fallacy behind the idea that the state can kill someone to make the point that killing people is wrong.

Corruption undermines justice

In several European countries there is a widespread belief that the judiciary is corrupt, and that the courts tend to favour people with money and personal contacts. This perception may sometimes be exaggerated, but it has to be taken seriously. No system of justice is effective if it is not trusted. There are also indications that people's suspicions are well justified in a number of cases.

Complaints are often made in member states about corruption as it affects the judiciary, the police and prison personnel. Such allegations may be groundless, and are in many cases difficult to verify. Still, it has become clear to me that corruption in the justice system is a problem in several European countries. I am convinced that the problem is a real one and not merely one of perception.

In reports from official visits, I have raised this concern and recommended strong action. One of several examples is my report on Albania – where the government has given priority to this problem

---

77. The vote in the General Assembly in 2007 (A/62/PV.76) was 104 for, 54 against and 29 abstentions; in 2008 (A/63/PV.7) the result was 106 for, 46 against and 34 abstentions. The text of the resolutions can be found at www.un.org (click on resolutions).

– but I still had to conclude that "[m]ore effective and efficient measures addressing corruption in the justice system need to be taken in order to restore public confidence and enable fair trials and due process".[78]

A report on Azerbaijan also recognised that a number of legal and other measures had been taken to put an end to corrupt practices. However, some aspects of the administration of justice still seem to be influenced by pecuniary interests. I concluded that problems of corruption and dependence on the executive still marred Azerbaijani justice "as in many countries in fast transition from the former Soviet system".[79]

Corruption in the justice system often goes hand in hand with political interference. Ministers and other leading politicians do not always respect the independence of the judiciary and instead signal to prosecutors or judges what is expected of them. This is sometimes referred to as "telephone justice". The distorted effect of such practices is even worse in countries where there are close links between the political leaders and business interests. This is where greed tends to trump justice.

Corruption threatens human rights and in particular the rights of the poor. Police officers are often badly paid and some try to add to their income by asking for bribes: the result is that people who cannot pay bribes are treated badly. I have met prisoners who have had no family visits because their relatives could not pay the unofficial "fee" for entry into the prison.

There are also cases of court officials whose influence has been bought – either with money under the table, or with other less obvious favours such as a promise of career advancement. This is one revealing

---

78. Report by the Commissioner for Human Rights on his visit to Albania, 27 October-2 November 2007, CommDH(2008)8.
79. Report by the Commissioner for Human Rights on his visit to Azerbaijan, 3-7 September 2007, CommDH(2008)2.

explanation for some trials being excessively drawn out whereas others are speeded up.

What is needed is a comprehensive programme to stamp out corruption at all levels and in all public institutions. There is also a need to react effectively to corrupt practices in private business, since they tend to spill over into the public sphere.

We need legislation which clearly criminalises acts of corruption. However, such laws cannot address all aspects of the different problems in this field. It is extremely difficult to define the criminal dimension of some corrupt practices, such as nepotism and political favouritism. Issues relating to "conflicts of interest" must also be assessed in this context. In other words, more focused standards and effective follow-up mechanisms are necessary.

Clear procedures for the recruitment, promotion and tenure of judges and prosecutors are essential, and should confirm the firewall between party politics and the judiciary. As I stressed in my report on Ukraine,[80] the process of appointing judges should be transparent, fair and based on merit. Requirements concerning judicial integrity should be defined clearly and early in the recruitment process, and should be made part of initial and routine training for all judges.

Judges should be adequately paid in order to minimise the temptation of corrupt practices. However, a higher salary is only one aspect of this picture and not always effective – greed sometimes grows with income.

Codes of conduct can help to enhance the integrity and accountability of the judiciary. The standards should regulate behaviour in office but also outside activities and remuneration. Independent disciplinary mechanisms should be in place to deal with complaints against court officials and they must be capable of receiving and investigating complaints, protecting complainants against retaliation, and provide for effective sanctions.

---

80. Report by the Commissioner for Human Rights on his visit to Ukraine, 10-17 December 2006, CommDH(2007)15.

Experience suggests that judicial complaints mechanisms should not operate in a political setting, but rather through a special and independent body within the judicial system itself. Clearly no undue influence (including from colleagues) should be allowed, and allegations of corruption must be investigated according to procedures which are scrupulously fair.

Useful recommendations have been presented by the Group of States against Corruption (GRECO), a body set up by the Council of Europe to fight bribery, abuse of public office and corrupt business practices. GRECO has developed a system for the regular review of anti-corruption measures among its participating member states and GRECO reports have encouraged important reforms at national level.[81]

Legally binding standards for measures against corruption are set forth in two important international treaties which should inspire national action. The Council of Europe has adopted the Criminal Law Convention on Corruption and the Civil Law Convention on Corruption, which entered into force in 2002 and 2003 respectively.[82] There is also the United Nations Convention against Corruption, which entered into force in 2005.

These treaties stress the need to protect those individuals who report their suspicions in good faith. Such whistle-blowers have too often been hit by retaliation – dismissals or worse. This in turn may well have silenced or intimidated others. People seeking to promote ethical behaviour need to be protected against overt sanctions, but also the more subtle forms of retribution, for example by being denied promotions or by being socially ostracised.

---

81. In May 1998, the Committee of Ministers authorised the establishment of the Group of States against Corruption – GRECO – in the form of an enlarged partial agreement and, on 1 May 1999, GRECO was set up by 17 founding members.
82. The Additional Protocol to the Criminal Law Convention on Corruption, which entered into force in 2005, complements the Convention's provisions aimed at protecting judicial authorities from corruption.

The media has exposed judicial and other corruption scandals, and freedom of expression is indeed key. This is one reason why it is essential to promote the freedom and the diversity of media and to protect the political independence of public service media. The European Court of Human Rights has recognised that the press is one means by which politicians and public opinion can verify that judges are discharging their responsibilities in a manner that conforms to the task entrusted to them[83] (see the media discussed elsewhere in more detail).

Freedom-of-information legislation should also promote governmental transparency. The public should in principle have access to all information which is handled on their behalf by the authorities. Confidentiality is necessary – for instance, in order to protect privacy and personal data – but should be seen as exceptional and it must be justifiable and justified. Progress is being made in Europe, but transparency is far from the general rule.

Governments have an obligation to ensure that the public has effective access to information. The European Court of Human Rights has emphasised that the public must have information on the functioning of the judicial system, given the centrality of this institution for any democratic society: "The Courts, as with all other public institutions, are not immune from criticism and scrutiny".[84]

When reporting on Ukraine, I had to stress the importance of such transparency: "With the exception of the judgments of the highest courts, only a small percentage of judicial decisions are published. Accurate and reliable records are an exception".

Parliamentarians can play a particularly important role in confronting corrupt practices, both in their own profession and across the justice system generally. They must set a good ethical example themselves, and openly declare their income and capital assets, as well as all relevant activities, connections and interests. Furthermore, they should act as watchdogs monitoring for any risk of corruption within the

---
83. *Prager and Oberschlick v. Austria*, judgment of 26 April 1995.
84. *Skalka v. Poland*, judgment of 27 May 2003.

government administration. They are well placed to ask questions which others might have difficulty in pursuing. They should ensure that strong oversight legislation and procedures are in place and functioning well.

Some non-governmental organisations already play an important role in combating corruption. At the international level, Berlin-based Transparency International has made a major contribution, and also succeeded in encouraging the World Bank to treat the problem more seriously than it had done previously. Transparency International has national sections in many countries and there are also other groups which expose bad practice and seek reform to counter corruption.

In some countries, ombudsmen and other independent national human rights structures are actively working against undue political influence and other corrupt practices that undermine the justice system. The public defenders in Georgia and Armenia have described how poor and destitute people are particularly vulnerable when corruption takes hold: the poor need legal aid, not pressure to pay bribes, and they need proof that no one is above the law.

We all need systems of justice that are free from corruption, that are fair and unbiased, and where everyone is equal before the law.

Judges must be independent

Countries in central and eastern Europe face the challenge of moving from a system in which judges served the political interests of the regime, to an order based on the rule of law. While progress has been made, I have observed that the independence of judges is still not fully protected in some countries I have visited. Political and economic pressure still influences the courts.

This problem must be addressed. Persons seeking to influence judges in any manner should be subject to sanctions by law. Corrupt action by one judge may tarnish the system as a whole.

Political interventions and corruption undermine the credibility of the entire justice system and threaten the right to a fair trial as defined in the European Convention on Human Rights: "everyone is entitled to a fair and public hearing within a reasonable time by an independent and impartial tribunal" (Article 6, paragraph 1). These failings should be tackled with priority and in a systematic manner.

The independence and integrity of the judiciary are essential for the rule of law. Legal protection for these principles is necessary; most European countries have inscribed the principle of the separation of powers between the executive, the legislature and the judiciary in their constitutions.

Judicial independence needs to be underpinned by a number of measures, for example:

- there should be a judicial appointment system which is shielded from improper party political or other partisan control; neither the government nor its administration should recruit judges;
- judges should not have to fear dismissal after unpopular decisions. Security of tenure, until a mandatory retirement age or expiry of a fixed term of office, is a prerequisite for independence;
- to avoid abuse, disciplinary action against judges should be regulated by precise rules and procedures, managed inside the court system, and not be amenable to political influence;
- judges should receive appropriate remuneration and adequate pension provision, commensurate with their responsibilities.

The credibility of the judiciary also depends on the conduct of the judges themselves. Accordingly, they must decide the cases before them impartially, on the basis of the facts, and in accordance with the law. Judges need to secure the trust of society as a whole, and this presupposes impartiality when adjudicating between parties.

There must therefore be no bias on the part of the judge or tribunal, and if any party to a dispute has a legitimate doubt as to the impartiality of the judge, this should be addressed. Justice must not only be done, but be seen to be done. The perception and the reality of fairness require that:

- the allocation of cases between judges should not be influenced by any of the parties directly involved;
- cases should not be withdrawn from a judge without good reason; and
- decisions of judges should not be the subject of revision beyond the normal appeals procedure.

To protect the reputation of the judiciary it is also necessary to ensure genuine competence. Judges should be appropriately qualified and be individuals of integrity and ability. All countries must provide ongoing training for judges. Other factors essential to ensure judicial competence include:

- appointments or promotions must be based on objective criteria such as merit, qualifications, integrity and efficiency;
- there must be no discrimination on any grounds when appointing judges. On the contrary, it is important that the diversity of society (in terms of, for instance, gender and ethnicity) will be considered as an aspect of competence;
- training in the jurisprudence of the European Court of Human Rights should be organised to ensure, to the extent possible, that issues are resolved at the domestic level.

The judicial system must also function in an efficient manner: the Strasbourg Court is inundated with applications complaining about excessively lengthy judicial proceedings at the domestic level (see following article). An efficient judiciary demands:

- appropriate working conditions, including the recruitment of a sufficient number of judges; and
- the provision of adequate support staff and equipment.

Judges must also be able to exercise their functions without fear of the consequences. Their safety must be ensured by including security guards on court premises or providing police protection when necessary.

All member states should routinely review the systems in place to safeguard the independence, impartiality, competence and efficiency of their judiciary and the court system.

Lengthy court proceedings

Judicial processes in Europe are not perfect. Excessively lengthy proceedings are an unfortunate reality in many countries. In spite of a broad recognition that "justice delayed is justice denied", too little has been done at the domestic level to complete court actions within a reasonable time. We know this because of the huge number of complaints, from many countries, brought before the European Court of Human Rights.

Unduly delayed court proceedings are a violation of the European Convention which provides that "everyone is entitled to a fair and public hearing within a reasonable time" (Article 6, paragraph 1). This provision applies to both civil and criminal trials, as well as to disciplinary and administrative proceedings.

The European Convention provides that everyone arrested or detained has the right to be brought promptly before a judicial authority and is entitled to a trial within a reasonable time (Article 5, paragraph 3).

The Committee of Ministers has stated in a number of resolutions that excessive delays in the administration of justice constitute a danger for the rule of law, over and above the problems created for the individuals directly concerned.

Inordinately long court proceedings undermine the credibility of the justice system as a whole. Justice becomes an illusory concept if the public loses confidence in the ability of the state to dispense justice in a timely fashion.

Legal certainty requires that matters of dispute be resolved and peaceful coexistence restored, and therefore those having recourse to the courts should be able to foresee when the proceedings are likely to end. Unpredictability creates a sense of frustration and fuels feelings of powerlessness.

Excessive delays may also have negative consequences for parties to the proceedings, whether claimant or defendant:
- as time passes, evidence disappears and new evidence has to be adduced; this may cause practical as well as financial difficulties;
- witnesses may become less reliable as they forget the events at issue, lose credibility or move on;
- court costs increase.

Lengthy proceedings may also result in breaches of other human rights. In custody or parental authority cases, for example, delays in deciding matters between parents can have harmful or irreversible consequences for one or more of the parties.

Some cases of course do necessitate lengthy examination: complex cases (either legally or factually) or those spanning a number of levels of appeal, for example. Nevertheless, long periods of inactivity on the part of the court should be scrutinised closely and challenged.[85]

An effective remedy before a national authority is particularly important in cases involving complaints of unreasonable length of proceedings. This has been emphasised by the Strasbourg Court. National authorities are better placed than the European Court to act quickly to accelerate pending proceedings or to provide compensation.[86]

Following the impetus given by the European Court through this judgment, member states have pursued several solutions to provide effective remedies. Domestic solutions have allowed for violations to

---

85. The Council of Europe's European Commission for the Efficiency of Justice (CEPEJ) published in December 2006 two reports on this problem: "Length of court proceedings in the member states of the Council of Europe based on the case law of the European Court of Human Rights" and "Time management of justice systems: a northern Europe study".
86. *Kudla v. Poland*, judgment of 26 October 2000.

be found and adequate redress to be provided. Measures to accelerate proceedings, as well as financial reparation for damage incurred, have been introduced.

Introducing a legal remedy for lengthy court proceedings is a first step, but more work still needs to be done to tackle the root causes. A combination of better case management, improved judicial training, penalties for late submission of documents/evidence, the setting of strict deadlines and increased professional staffing (judges, court clerks, assistants, etc.) is required. The rule of law requires no less.

Enforcement of court decisions

In several European countries, court decisions are often enforced only partly, after long delays, or sometimes not at all. This is one of the most frequent and serious problems identified by the European Court of Human Rights. Flawed execution of final court decisions must be seen as a failure to uphold the rule of law.

The non-execution of court judgments constitutes a breach of the right to a fair trial as defined in Article 6 of the European Convention on Human Rights. The Strasbourg Court has affirmed that the "right to a court ... would be illusory if a Contracting State's domestic legal system allowed a final, binding judicial decision to remain inoperative to the detriment of one party".[87]

The Court observed also that member states, by ratifying the Convention, have undertaken to respect the principle of the rule of law. To ignore the implementation of judicial decisions would be incompatible with this principle. Where administrative authorities delay, refuse or fail to comply, the guarantees under Article 6 are undermined.

Every judgment must be enforced, including those delivered against the governmental administration. This is an important principle. Therefore, it is particularly worrying to see when even senior political

---

87. *Hornsby v. Greece,* judgment of 19 March 1997.

decision makers hide behind different pretexts to disregard judicial decisions, or make public statements conveying a lack of respect for the judiciary.

These flawed responses to domestic judicial decisions constitute a structural problem requiring priority action from the national authorities in several European countries.

The non-enforcement of court judgments can affect large groups of people and vulnerable groups in particular. When state authorities ignore judicial decisions, for example, that social benefits (such as pensions or child allowances) should be paid, this can have profoundly negative economic or other consequences for whole families. Having recourse to the courts is often seen as a remedy of last resort. People's confidence in the rule of law is damaged if, having secured a positive result, they then witness the court's rulings being casually ignored.

A great number of cases of non-enforcement of domestic judicial decisions are raised among the complaints to the Strasbourg Court, which has found numerous violations in this area. It has stated that the complexity of the domestic enforcement procedure or of the state budgetary system cannot relieve the state of its obligation to guarantee to everyone the right to have a binding judicial decision enforced within a reasonable time. Nor is it open to a state authority to cite lack of funds or other resources as an excuse for not honouring a judgment debt.

Several Council of Europe bodies have focused on the structural problems highlighted by non-enforcement. This has been a focus of attention for the Parliamentary Assembly, for specialised organs such as the European Commission for the Efficiency of Justice (CEPEJ), and for the Committee of Ministers in the framework of the execution of judgments of the European Court of Human Rights.

The Council of Europe has a special department which assists the Committee of Ministers in supervising the execution of the judgments of the European Court. This department has also organised discussions to address the problem of delayed action, or inaction, on domestic court decisions.

The conclusions drawn have stressed the need for a legal and regulatory framework which will ensure the enforcement of domestic court decisions:
- there should be clear procedures, adapted to national budgetary contexts compatible with the need for rapid and proper execution of judgments;
- an effective and independent bailiffs service should be established;
- the accountability of national officials for the execution of domestic judgments should be increased, both by increasing their personal responsibility, and through stricter oversight;
- there should be effective domestic remedies to accelerate execution proceedings and compensation for non-execution should be provided.

This last requirement (penalties for failure) is essential. In a pilot judgment (*Burdov v. Russia (No. 2)*, 15 January 2009), the Strasbourg Court further specified the requirements and criteria for efforts to verify the effectiveness of preventive or compensatory remedies to ensure adequate and sufficient redress at domestic level.

Several countries have initiated a number of measures, for example through action plans or national strategies, reforms of the bailiffs systems, laws introducing remedies or new enforcement systems.

It is clear, however, that for these efforts to be effective greater expertise is needed on the part of all involved. Exchanges of experiences between the countries concerned and Council of Europe specialist bodies are essential in this respect.

These efforts to render the judicial system effective require more awareness-raising, and action, by key national actors. Parliamentarians should push for the rapid introduction of necessary legal reforms. Independent state authorities such as ombudsmen have an important role to play in monitoring progress: they can inform citizens about new laws regulating domestic remedies in cases of non-enforcement; and they can put pressure on the authorities to uphold the law.

The credibility of the justice system is at stake. It is not sufficient to reform legislation, increase the resources of the courts, or encourage the public to settle their disputes in court. Members of the public who have placed their trust in the judicial system should obtain satisfaction, not only in theory, but also in practice. The full and prompt execution of court decisions is one of the hallmarks of a democratic society.

Prison conditions

Conditions in prisons are appalling in several European countries. In some cases the treatment of inmates is inhuman and degrading. This is not acceptable: prisoners have human rights.

The purpose of a prison sentence is to punish the offender and prevent continued criminal activities. A related objective is to ensure the rehabilitation and reintegration of prisoners in society after release. Agreed international and European standards are based on these assumptions.

The European Prison Rules adopted by the Council of Europe recognise that convicted prisoners lose their right to freedom, but not to all other rights. The prison rules also require that detention shall be managed so as to facilitate the reintegration of the prisoners into society at the end of their sentence. In practice, these rules are inadequately respected, which may explain why recidivism rates are high and why so many prisoners return to crime on their release.

In almost every European country prisons and pre-trial detention centres are overcrowded. In some countries there are more than twice as many inmates as foreseen when the institutions were built. The guidelines defined by the European Committee for the Prevention of Torture and Inhuman or Degrading Treatment or Punishment (CPT) – at least 4 square metres per inmate in multi-occupancy cells, or dormitories and 7 square metres in single-occupancy cells – are often not respected. In some cells, prisoners have to sleep in shifts.

Overcrowding means a constant lack of privacy – even when using toilet facilities. Such conditions increase tension and result in violence between prisoners and between prisoners and staff. The CPT has concluded on more than one occasion that overcrowding has resulted in inhuman and degrading conditions of detention. Whilst the ideal would be to explore creative alternatives to imprisonment (especially for less serious crimes), some countries are addressing the problem of overcrowding by building new prisons.

Special security measures are sometimes necessary in order to prevent collusion and continuing criminal activities by certain prisoners. The authorities must also be able to prevent "gang rule" inside the prison. Such restrictions should, however, be proportionate to the legitimate purpose for which they are imposed. Disciplinary procedures to deal with violence and other types of misconduct by inmates should reflect principles of justice and fairness, and provide for the possibility of appeal. Some disciplinary cells I have seen during my missions are quite unacceptable for human use. Solitary confinement can be damaging, especially when extended for long periods.

The European Prison Rules state that lack of resources cannot justify conditions which infringe the human rights of prisoners.

Depriving someone of liberty entails a moral duty of care. The authorities must give particular attention to the conditions of imprisonment – for example:

- prisoners should have adequate access to medical treatment: in many countries, prison inmates suffer from tuberculosis, hepatitis and HIV; they often also have a history of drug abuse. Too few prisons offer appropriate treatment or support in such cases. Many inmates are poorly educated and some are illiterate: education and job training increase the chances of reintegration upon release;
- prison work should be seen as a positive element of the prison regime; recreation and exercise should be incorporated into the daily activities of prisoners;

- prison will be a solely negative experience if prison officers, who are often under great pressure, experience poor working conditions. Jobs in the penal system are often seen as "low status" and are badly paid. Prison staff must be sufficient in number, reasonably paid, and appropriately qualified and trained.

As prisons are by nature closed institutions, they must be inspected through regular visits by a genuinely independent body with the authority to open all doors and interview every detainee in privacy.

The CPT has contributed greatly to the improvement of conditions in places of detention through its missions and advice. The International Red Cross Committee, which organises regular prison visits, is another important international actor.

However, these efforts need to be complemented by effective national monitoring systems, as stipulated in the Optional Protocol to the UN Convention Against Torture and Other Cruel, Inhuman or Degrading Treatment or Punishment, a role that could be given to an ombudsman or a similar institution operating independently.

In a few European countries, special monitoring teams have been set up with strong support from and participation by non-governmental organisations. This has given the inspection system both energy and a greater level of independence.

Life sentences

There is a trend in Europe towards more life sentences. For instance, in the United Kingdom one in six prisoners is now serving a life or indeterminate sentence of imprisonment for public protection. Many of those sentenced are deprived of the possibility of ever being released; they are actual "lifers".

This trend to life sentencing is a reaction to violent and organised crime. However, it seems also to be a response to the perception that politicians have to demonstrate firm purpose in the face of public demands for tougher punishments. Yet, the use of life sentences should be questioned: Are they necessary? Are they humane? Are they compatible with agreed human rights standards?

During visits to member states, I have met "lifers" in several prisons. Many are held in harsh conditions. In too many cases, the authorities keep these prisoners under a special regime, treating them as particularly dangerous and cutting them off from contact with the outside world and often from other inmates as well. Prison guards also face the difficult task of dealing with lifers who have no incentive to demonstrate good behaviour.

A distinction should be made between the length of the sentence imposed and the degree of security restrictions considered necessary. "Lifers" are not necessarily more dangerous than others and should therefore not automatically be kept under a "maximum security" regime. There should be an individual assessment of each prisoner to determine the threat posed to the safety and security of both the prisoner and others.

This issue was addressed in a Recommendation adopted in 2003 by the Council of Europe Committee of Ministers on the management by prison administrations of life sentence and other long-term prisoners. The policy document sets out a number of important guiding principles:

- individualisation: there should be individual plans for the implementation of the sentence that take into account the personal characteristics of the prisoner;
- normalisation: prison life should resemble as much as possible life in the community;
- responsibility: prisoners should be given opportunities to exercise personal responsibility in daily prison life;
- security and safety: a clear distinction should be made between any risks posed by life sentence (or other long-term prisoners) to the external community, to themselves, to other prisoners and to those working in or visiting the prison;

- non-segregation: consideration should be given to not segregating life-sentence and other long-term prisoners on the sole ground of their sentence.

I have seen for myself that these principles are not fully applied in a number of member states. The same conclusion can be drawn from reading reports of the CPT. The committee has also highlighted a range of psychological problems among this category of prisoners, including loss of self-esteem and impairment of social skills.

The UN Convention on the Rights of the Child prohibits life sentences without the possibility of release. Similar universal provisions banning such sentences in relation to adults do not yet exist. It is, however, significant that the Rome Statute of the International Criminal Court – dealing with the most serious crimes of genocide, crimes against humanity and war crimes – stipulates a review of prison sentences after 25 years.

My opinion is that sentencing to indefinite imprisonment is wrong: the prisoner needs some clarity about the future. The law in some countries in Europe does not allow for life sentences, irrespective of the crime. This is, for example, the case in Norway, Portugal, Spain and Slovenia, although very long fixed-term prison sentences can be handed down. Other countries permit reviews after a certain period of time, during which the behaviour of the prisoner is normally one criterion.

However, an increasing number of prisoners can nurture little or no hope of ever being released. There are reports about cases of severe depression and other psychological problems among this category of inmates.

Life imprisonment without the possibility of release raises human rights concerns. Especially, in combination with "maximum security" conditions, such a penalty could amount to inhuman or degrading punishment, and thereby violate Article 3 of the European Convention on Human Rights.

Life sentences also negate the human rights principle that people can change. There are of course recidivist criminals but there are also examples of prisoners who have reformed. Court decisions assuming that someone constitutes a permanent threat to society are therefore misplaced. The principle of rehabilitation should be protected, not undermined.

There is also a need to discuss a new category of "lifers" that has emerged in a growing number of countries: offenders who have never been given a life sentence but might well serve one in practice. By virtue of new laws adopted in the name of public security, serious offenders may be denied not only conditional release, but even release once they have served their full sentence. Such decisions to continue to hold the prisoner would be taken if the offender is defined as dangerous by experts. In such cases, if release is denied persistently until the end of a detainee's life, this would amount to de facto life imprisonment.

Moreover, such legislation raises concerns about its compatibility with the rule of law: the principle of legal certainty, and the right not to be tried or punished twice. These are important principles of our penal law systems and international human rights standards.

Are prisoners who face the prospect of indefinitely prolonged detention not in a situation of "mounting anguish", condemned by the European Court in relation to death rows? The present trend in the use of life sentences must be challenged.

Remedies for victims of human rights violations

Torturers and others who violate human rights should be brought to account but it is also vital not to forget their victims. Victims have often been caused distressing trauma; their lives have been severely disrupted; and their futures have been placed in serious jeopardy. Justice requires that the victims achieve redress.

The right to a remedy and reparation is indeed a basic human right which is enshrined in numerous international human rights instruments and tribunals, including Article 13 of the European Convention on Human Rights. Victims of violations of human rights and humanitarian law have a right to redress for the suffering and harm caused to them.

Reparation is the last step in the achievement of full human rights protection. Violations of human rights should be prevented. If a violation does take place, it must be investigated by the state authorities, promptly, thoroughly and impartially. Victims should have access to justice. And finally, victims have the right to receive adequate reparation.

The fact that reparation is the last step in the achievement of human rights may explain why there has been so little international focus on this issue to date.

In 1993, Professor Theo van Boven, in a United Nations study concerning the right to restitution, compensation and rehabilitation for victims of gross violations of human rights and fundamental freedoms, concluded that the question of reparation had received little attention. He urged that it be addressed more consistently and thoroughly both at the national and international levels.[88]

In recent years, in the cases of the many individuals who have been wrongfully detained and tortured during the "war on terror", there have been few clearly and publicly expressed opinions about the necessity for just compensation. Governments have ducked the issue and left it to the former prisoners themselves to fight for their rights in complicated court procedures.

An exception was made in November 2010 when the British Government decided to pay compensation to 16 former Guantánamo detainees, all of them UK citizens or with a residence permit. Some

---

88. UN Commission on Human Rights, "Study concerning the right to restitution, compensation and rehabilitation for victims of gross violations of human rights and fundamental freedoms", Theo van Boven, special rapporteur, July 1993 (reference E/CN.4/SUB.2./RES/1993/29).

of them had filed law suits accusing the government agencies of complicity in the incarceration and torture they had suffered.

What does reparation entail? Financial compensation is the most widespread form of reparation. Some damage can be easily estimated in monetary terms, for example loss of earnings or legal expenses, while other forms cannot. How does one compensate someone adequately for physical, mental or moral damages?

However, financial compensation is not the only remedy which victims seek. Other forms of reparation include the following:
- restitution: restitution of the situation before the violation took place. This could mean the release of detainees, restitution of property confiscated, restoration of employment;
- rehabilitation: legal and social services, as well as mental and physical care;
- satisfaction: which could include verification, public disclosure of the facts, a public apology or memorialising of the victim(s);
- revelation of the truth: this is a vindication for the victims themselves and often a form of catharsis for the society in question;
- guarantees of non-repetition by, for example, amending laws or reforming institutions to uphold the rule of law.

These various forms of reparation were highlighted in "The United Nations Basic Principles on the Right to a Remedy and Reparation for Victims of Gross Violations of International Human Rights and Serious Violations of International Humanitarian Law", adopted by the General Assembly on 21 March 2006.

By taking a victim-oriented approach, we affirm our solidarity with victims of gross violations of human rights and we seek to compensate these victims for the fact that the state either caused damage and harm, or failed to protect them.

Reparation can never fully undo the damage that has been done. Gross violations of human rights are irreparable. But this must not impede just redress for victims. The UN basic principles are a good starting point for implementing the various aspects of reparation – a key element to full human rights protection.

Applications to the Strasbourg Court

During my country visits, I have met persons who told me that they wanted to submit an application to the European Court of Human Rights, but feared that this would mark them out as troublemakers. Such an atmosphere undermines the spirit of the Convention.

The European Convention on Human Rights states that "the Court may receive applications from any person, non-governmental organisation or group of individuals claiming to be the victim of a violation by one of the High Contracting Parties of the rights set forth in the Convention or the protocols thereto. The High Contracting Parties undertake not to hinder in any way the effective exercise of this right" (Article 34).

This right is a key component of the European human rights system. Everyone living within the jurisdiction of the states parties shall enjoy this right – refugees, stateless persons and irregular migrants are all included.

The Strasbourg Court is a unique institution. Its creation was a historic achievement aimed at the protection of freedom and security of all individuals in Europe; it has established an important precedent as a role model for other parts of the world.

The European Convention is now part of the national legal framework in all 47 member states of the Council of Europe. The judgments of the Court are therefore directly relevant as the authoritative interpretations of important elements of the law of the land throughout Europe.

This incorporation of regional standards into domestic law should result in domestic remedies that will genuinely protect human rights so that individuals will see no need to "go to Strasbourg" in future. This is our vision. We will, however, only move in that direction if governments fully co-operate with the Court, and protect the right to individual petition.

It is of particular importance that governments do not hinder submissions to the Strasbourg Court. The Court has stated that applicants or potential applicants should be able to communicate with it freely, without being subjected to any form of pressure from the authorities to withdraw or modify their complaints.

The Court has described such pressure as including "not only direct coercion and flagrant acts of intimidation against actual or potential applicants, members of their family or their legal representatives, but also other improper indirect acts or contacts designed to dissuade or discourage applicants from pursuing a Convention remedy".[89]

A report prepared by the Parliamentary Assembly of the Council of Europe in 2007 gives examples of alleged intimidation against applicants, potential applicants, their lawyers and members of their families, preventing them from applying to the Court.[90]

It also refers to information that individuals have been warned not to appeal to national courts, thereby preventing them from exhausting domestic remedies, which normally is a condition for an application to be deemed admissible in the Strasbourg Court.

These are very serious allegations. Any such allegation should be thoroughly investigated and any tendency towards such abuse prevented as a matter of urgency.

Politicians and others in position of authority should demonstrate that they do not object to complaints, and that "going to Strasbourg" is not in any way regarded as unpatriotic or an act of political opposition.

The right of individuals to appeal to the European Court of Human Rights in Strasbourg has to be protected. Governments must not hinder anyone from submitting a complaint and they must co-operate

---

89. *Mamatkulov and Askarov v. Turkey*, judgment of 4 February 2005.
90. "Member states' duty to co-operate with the European Court of Human Rights", Doc. 11183, 9 February 2007.

fully when the Court examines a case – relevant documentation should be willingly provided.

The report of the Parliamentary Assembly also contains a wide range of examples where the respondent state has failed to co-operate with the Court, or to provide the necessary existing evidence. Case files, or other relevant documents such as medical files, have not been disclosed, and witnesses have not been made available.

Such lack of co-operation violates a specific provision of the European Convention which makes it an obligation for states parties to provide all necessary information to the Court for the effective conduct of its examination of the case (Article 38).

States also sometimes fail to comply with binding interim measures which the Court issues in order to avoid an irreversible situation – such as an extradition to a country where there is a risk of torture. When this happens, the Court is no longer in a position to examine the application properly, nor to ensure that the applicant obtains effective protection.

The Court itself has addressed this problem and stated that states parties must refrain from "any act or omission which, by destroying or removing the subject matter of an application, would make it pointless or otherwise prevent the Court from considering it under its normal procedure".[91]

Acts to discourage applications, and the failure to fully co-operate with the Court, are serious matters which require more open discussion. The Committee of Ministers in Strasbourg has addressed these issues and will have to do so again.

The time has come for all the Council of Europe member states to sign and ratify the important treaty adopted in 1996, which enables the right of individual petition to be exercised effectively: the European

---

91. *Mamatkulov and Askarov v. Turkey*, judgment of 4 February 2005.

Agreement relating to Persons Participating in Proceedings of the European Court of Human Rights.[92]

The Parliamentary Assembly is right to put this high on its agenda and pressure from parliamentarians is needed to ensure that all member states support and fully co-operate with the Court.

---

92. Council of Europe Treaty Series (ETS) No. 161. Entered into force on 1 January 1999. As of 16 July 2010, the treaty is not signed by: Armenia, Azerbaijan, Bosnia and Herzegovina, Montenegro, the Russian Federation and Serbia; it is not ratified by: Estonia, Malta, Poland, Portugal, San Marino and "the former Yugoslav Republic of Macedonia".

Chapter 10: Fighting terrorism while respecting human rights

The tragic mistake after 11 September 2001 was not the determination to respond, but the choice of methods: terrorism must not be fought with terrorist means. The "war on terror" violated core principles of human rights. Thousands of individuals have been victimised; many were totally innocent. It is urgent that the damage now be repaired.

Photo © US Navy via ABACA.

Counterterrorist methods and European complicity

Effective and co-ordinated action to prevent and punish terrorist acts is needed. The tragic mistake after 11 September 2001 was not the determination to respond, but the choice of methods: terrorism must not be fought with terrorist means. The "war on terror" violated core principles of human rights. Thousands of individuals have been victimised; many were totally innocent. It is urgent that the damage now be repaired.

The use of illegal methods by democratic states might well be what terrorist leaders had hoped for. It has seriously harmed the international system for human rights protection, and damaged a fundamental principle that respect for human rights, basic freedoms and the rule of law be upheld even in times of tension and crisis, by everyone and for everyone.

The first step to restore the primacy of these values is to recognise the facts. In an editorial of January 2008, the *New York Times* summarised the main points:

> *In the years since September 11, we have seen American soldiers abuse, sexually humiliate, torment and murder prisoners in Afghanistan and Iraq. A few have been punished, but their leaders have never been called to account. We have seen mercenaries gun down Iraqi civilians with no fear of prosecution …*
>
> *Hundreds of men, swept up on the battlefields of Afghanistan and Iraq, were thrown into prison in Guantanamo Bay, Cuba, so that the White House could claim they were beyond the reach of U.S. laws. Prisoners are held there with no hope of real justice, only the chance to face a kangaroo court where evidence and the names of their accusers are kept secret, and where they are not permitted to talk about the abuse they have suffered at the hands of American jailers.*
>
> *In other foreign lands, the CIA set up secret jails where "high-value detainees" were subject to even more barbaric acts, including*

simulated drowning. These crimes were videotaped, so that "experts" could watch them, and then the videotapes were destroyed, after consultation with the White House, in the hope that Americans would never know.

The CIA contracted out its inhumanity to nations with no respect for life or law, sending prisoners – some of the innocents kidnapped on street corners and in airports – to be tortured into making false confessions, or until it was clear they had nothing to say and so were let go without any apology or hope of redress.

What this editorial highlights is a flagrant defiance of the core principles of justice on which human rights are built: protection against torture; the presumption of innocence; no deprivation of liberty without due process; the right to a fair trial; the right of appeal; and the right to reparation.

European citizens were also among the victims. Some were brought to Guantánamo for indefinite detention and interrogation in violation of the United Nations Convention Against Torture. Others were "blacklisted" by the UN Security Council at the suggestion of the US Government. Without legal procedures and the possibility to appeal, they had their bank accounts frozen and were prevented from travelling.

European governments did not defend their citizens in these situations with sufficient vigour. They were also slow to condemn the methods employed, and they have yet to fully clarify the facts about European co-operation with US intelligence services in this counterterrorism policy.

Some European national security services handed over suspects to the CIA, or looked the other way when people were being secretly abducted. European agents facilitated flights with prisoners on board, and provided information to the CIA. They must take their share of responsibility for the abductions, renditions, secret detentions and unlawful interrogations.

Independent and effective national investigations should be established whenever there are credible allegations of unlawful renditions or secret detentions. Indeed, states are required by the European Convention on Human Rights to investigate such human rights violations.

The Lithuanian government – after some prompting – commissioned a parliamentary inquiry which established that the national security service had indeed co-operated with the CIA in organising at least one place of secret detention for terrorist suspects. It has not yet been confirmed whether this facility was actually used for detention purposes and if so which detainees were held there.

In Poland – after a period of official denial – a prosecutor has been engaged since 2008 in an investigation into the possible involvement of Polish officials in the operations of a secret CIA prison opened in December 2002 at Stare Kiejkuty. Two of the CIA's so-called "high-value detainees" (HVDs), Abd al-Nashiri and Abu Zubaydah, have been granted "victim status" in the prosecutor's investigation. It is understood that at least three further HVDs, all presently held at Guantánamo Bay, were also detained and interrogated in Poland. The situation regarding the likely trials of these suspects in the US is therefore complicated, from a European perspective, by the prospect that they may face the death sentence.

Romania has also been mentioned in connection with reports about illegal detention of such suspects. However, the authorities in Bucharest continue a policy of denial.

The Macedonian authorities had not at the time of writing provided any relevant information in the case of Khaled el-Masri, a German citizen who was seized by Macedonian security forces and detained incommunicado for 23 days before being turned over to the CIA, flown to Kabul and severely tortured until the US security agency realised that they had got the wrong man. This case has been brought to the European Court of Human Rights.

Another case which has still to be resolved is the Swedish handover to CIA agents of two asylum-seeking Egyptians, Ahmed Agiza and

Mohammed al-Zari, at Bromma airport in Stockholm. They were flown to security cells in Cairo and subjected to "harsh" interrogation. The handling of this case was severely criticised by the United Nations Committee Against Torture. The Swedish Government has admitted mistakes, but it has not yet agreed to a full investigation into all the circumstances of the case.

The avoidance of inquiries into what actually happened in this and other cases may partly be due to the political bullying and scaremongering of the Bush government at the time. There is also a widespread presumption that national security matters cannot or should not be openly discussed. Governments have been anxious that transparency might hamper co-operation between security agencies, and hinder future exchanges of information.

However, human rights violations committed by executive bodies should not be shielded from accountability under the pretext of "state secrets". It is essential to create effective safeguards. The introduction of safeguards, with the right political will, is entirely feasible and does not lead to the exposure of facts that must be kept confidential. The Canadian Government set an excellent example when establishing its commission into the case of Maher Arar – a Canadian citizen who was stopped at a US airport, handed over to the Syrian security police and badly tortured. The commission demonstrated that a thorough and fair investigation is possible without endangering a country's intelligence system.

Democracies should never accept the use of secrecy doctrines to excuse lack of action to prevent or punish serious human rights violations. It must be absolutely clear to all that security agents are also accountable: parliamentary and judicial scrutiny must be ensured. One lesson from the mistakes made during the "war on terror" has been the need to keep national security agencies under more effective democratic control.

It has also become evident that even government leaders were not always kept in the picture, and that parliamentary and judicial control has been minimal. In other words, intelligence services have pursued inter-agency co-operation with little democratic oversight.

The Venice Commission published a report in 2007 on the organisation of democratic control to ensure state accountability. Although the study does not explicitly cover military and foreign intelligence services, the analysis of the commission is useful. It deals with four forms of accountability: parliamentary, judicial, expert and complaints mechanisms and concludes:[93]

- the formal authority of security agencies should be subject to parliamentary supervision. The parliament could itself establish an oversight body whose members would have to respect the necessary confidentiality. Such a mechanism might convince the broader population that continuous review exists, even if the facts about activities are withheld from the public;

- decisions to authorise special investigative measures could rest with the judiciary, which also has a role in reviewing measures after the fact. The commission noted with concern that data-mining and other information-gathering methods tend to escape judicial oversight;

- expert bodies could be established to assist in overseeing security activities. This model may be preferable when there is a need to ensure both independence and expertise. There are also models of oversight bodies which combine both experts and parliamentarians.

Individuals who claim to have been adversely affected by the security services must have a possibility of redress before an independent body. Action aimed at redressing individual cases might also prove effective in strengthening mechanisms for accountability and encouraging improvements in the intelligence and security system as a whole.

---

93. www.venice.coe.int/docs/2007/CDL-AD(2007)016-e.asp.

Intelligence secrecy: no excuse

All the necessary lessons have still to be drawn from the breakdown of human rights which followed the "war on terror" initiated in the wake of 11 September 2001. More and more detailed and shocking information has emerged about systematic torture, secret detentions and other serious human rights violations. Yet, political authorities have been reluctant to face the facts. It is urgent to improve the democratic oversight of intelligence and security agencies and to regulate cross-border co-operation between them.

Terrorism is a grim reality and states must seek ways to combat this threat. However, some of the counterterrorism measures in use today are both illegal and counterproductive. This was the conclusion of an international panel of eminent judges and lawyers, convened by the International Commission of Jurists, in an authoritative report issued in 2009.[94]

The panel found that the failure of states to comply with their legal duties had created a dangerous situation whereby terrorism and the fear of terrorism were undermining basic principles of international human rights law.

One trend the panel documented was the acquisition by intelligence agencies of new powers and resources without legal and political accountability keeping pace. This tendency has become more marked since 2001.

The Council of Europe's Guidelines on Human Rights and the Fight against Terrorism sets out conditions for counterterrorism efforts: they must conform to domestic law provisions; they must be deemed proportionate to the aim of the interference with other rights; and they must be supervised or monitored by an independent authority.

---

94. "Assessing damage, urging action; report of the Eminent Jurists Panel on Terrorism, Counter-terrorism, and Human Rights", February 2009, International Commission of Jurists, www.icj.org.

Standards also exist in relation to the collection and processing of personal data.[95]

Most European countries today have some oversight arrangements to hold intelligence and security services accountable, to ensure that laws are respected, and abuses avoided.

However, it is clear that several European states need to improve the democratic control of their agencies. Good models exist: the Norwegian Parliamentary Oversight Committee, for instance, has the authority to review all records and archives and appears to actively control inter-agency communications. There are other countries, however, where the oversight bodies seem to have little access to sensitive information or even discussions about strategies.

There have, however, been cases where embarrassing lapses have been evident and these seem often to apply in situations where bilateral or multilateral arrangements were involved.

One example is the case mentioned in the previous article of the two Egyptians who were handed over to the CIA at Bromma Airport in Stockholm. The Swedish Parliamentary Committee on Constitutional Affairs reviewed the case but failed to obtain all the relevant facts. It was only through subsequent investigative journalism that it became known that this operation was conducted in close co-operation with the CIA and that the deportees had been handed over to CIA agents on Swedish soil. In this case, the Swedish Government subsequently argued that it had not been possible to report fully to the parliamentary committee as this might have jeopardised intelligence operations with the CIA.

In the United Kingdom, the government tried to prevent the High Court from releasing a key document which would have thrown light on the nature of inter-agency co-operation in the rendition and torture of Binyam Mohamed. The argument again was that the US

---

95. "Guidelines on Human Rights and the Fight against Terrorism", Committee of Ministers, 11 July 2002.

Government might have reacted negatively and, if they had, that this could reduce the UK's effectiveness in responding to terrorism. Other governments in similar situations have made the same point.

This argument requires a response. Although cross-border co-operation between intelligence services is essential, it is not acceptable to use such "understandings" to prevent investigations into possible human rights violations, or to limit democratic oversight of intelligence exchanges.

There is an obvious risk that arguments of maintaining good relations with agencies in other countries will be misused – by one side or by both – to cover up illegal actions, including human rights violations or other misconduct. When this happens, the principle of accountability is seriously undermined.

There is also a danger that information which is secretly shared might be inaccurate, but might still be acted upon – with grave consequences for the individuals involved and with no possibility for the innocent victims to rectify mistakes. There have been cases where this has led to serious injustice against individuals and has also harmed their family and friends.

The trading of information between intelligence services has increased dramatically in recent years. Previously established domestic control systems will be of little value unless they also address these bilateral and multilateral information exchanges.

Thanks to the Council of Europe, the European Parliament, the media and non-governmental organisations, some facts have emerged about human rights violations which took place as a result of secret inter-agency collaboration.

These revelations have not undermined the struggle against terrorism. Although embarrassing to some, several revelations have led to crucial discussions on how to render the struggle against terrorism more effective by halting human rights violations and upholding human rights and democratic principles. One conclusion, for example, has been that exemptions to freedom-of-expression legislation based on national security considerations should be strictly limited.

There are facts which clearly should not be made public and aspects of intelligence work which should legitimately be kept confidential. That is precisely why oversight bodies are needed: they should seek to balance the public interest in transparency against the need for confidentiality with regard, for example, to informants. Only in this way can the agencies be effectively held to account, and can public confidence in their work be maintained.

To perform their functions properly, oversight bodies must also be able to monitor inter-agency co-operation. A first step is to stipulate that such co-operation is permissible only according to principles established in law, and when authorised or supervised by parliamentary or expert control bodies.

Both the supply and receipt of data should be regulated by law through explicit agreements between the parties, as is the case, for example, in the Netherlands. The agreements should include human rights safeguards and be overseen by the relevant oversight body.

The supply of data to others should be made conditional upon clear restrictions on its use, and any further distribution of data should be strictly regulated. The use of information for intelligence purposes should not be allowed in immigration or extradition proceedings.

The rule should be that information can be disclosed to foreign agencies only if they undertake to apply the same controls as exercised by the "donor" agency, including guaranteeing respect for human rights safeguards. Likewise, "recipient" agencies should make imported data subject to full scrutiny by their national oversight mechanism.

It would be easier for individual European countries to conclude bilateral agreements with other states if they had all agreed on common principles to apply in inter-agency co-operation. The European Commission suggested in June 2009 a common "information model" which would define criteria for gathering, sharing and processing information obtained for security purposes. The Council of Europe is well placed to promote such initiatives.

While extensive international co-operation now exists between the intelligence and security services, this is not the case for national oversight bodies. The modest network that has been set up to facilitate contact between oversight bodies needs to be developed further. Models of national mechanisms from which others can learn exist.

National parliaments have a role in promoting such contacts in order to facilitate better control of inter-agency collaboration. Above all, they must make clear that such co-operation must comply with human rights standards.

Terrorist blacklisting

Innocent victims of counterterrorism measures must have their names cleared and receive compensation. Steps must also be taken to prevent similar injustices in future. Those suspected of association with terrorism must not find themselves on so-called "blacklists" without any prospect of having their case heard or reviewed by an independent body.

"Blacklisting" is a striking illustration of how human rights principles have been ignored in the fight against terrorism. "Blacklisting" refers to procedures under which the United Nations or the European Union may order sanctions targeting individuals or entities suspected of having links with terrorism. These sanctions include the freezing of financial assets.

The formal basis for such procedures lies in a Security Council resolution in 2000 which established a list of individuals suspected of having connections with al-Qaeda, Osama bin Laden and the Taliban.

The European Union followed suit with its own regulations, taking the view that European Community action was also essential. Consequently, EU regulations freeze the funds and other economic resources of persons and entities whose names appear on the UN list.

These measures have affected a number of the rights of the targeted individuals, including the right to privacy, the right to property, the right of association, the right to travel or freedom of movement. There has been no possibility of appeal, or even to know all the reasons for the blacklisting, which means that a person's right to an effective remedy and to due process have been ignored.

Imagine the following scenario: you are placed on the terrorist sanctions list at the UN level, which also means that your financial assets will be frozen within the European Union. You would like to challenge the assertion that you are linked to a terrorist group, but you are not allowed to see all the evidence against you. The delisting procedure at the UN level allows you to submit a request to the Sanctions Committee or to your government for removal from the list. The process of delisting, however, is purely a matter for intergovernmental consultation. The guidelines to the committee make it plain that applicants submitting a request for removal from the list may in no way assert their rights during the procedure. The applicant may not even be legally represented before the Sanctions Committee for that purpose. Only the government of his or her residence or citizenship has the right to submit observations.

This sounds Kafkaesque but it is the reality. In Sweden, three citizens of Somali origin found themselves on such a list. When I met them they were in despair, not knowing how to pursue their case. Their bank accounts had been frozen, and neither their employers nor the social authorities were permitted to provide them with the means to live.

The listing and delisting procedures have of course been questioned. In 2007, Council of Europe Parliamentarian Dick Marty issued a report which criticised the delisting procedures and the limited means of appeal available to individuals or entities on the lists.[96]

Following a discussion of the report, the Council of Europe's Parliamentary Assembly found that "the procedural and substantive

---

96. Doc. 11454. The Assembly adopted a recommendation based on the report, 23 January 2008: Recommendation 1824 (2008).

standards currently applied by the United Nations Security Council and the Council of the European Union ... in no way fulfil the minimum standards laid down ... and violate the fundamental principles of human rights and the rule of law".

Many individuals have been targeted by these measures. The UN Special Rapporteur on Human Rights and Terrorism stated in a 2007 report that the listing regime "has resulted in hundreds of individuals or entities having their assets frozen and other fundamental rights restricted".[97]

The European Court of Justice delivered a landmark decision on this issue on 3 September 2008. The case was about Yassin Abdullah Kadi, a resident of Saudi Arabia, and Al Barakaat International Foundation, established in Sweden by the three Somali-Swedes I had met. Both were designated by the UN Sanctions Committee as being associated with Osama bin Laden, al-Qaeda or the Taliban. As a result of being placed on the list of suspects developed by the committee, their bank accounts in the European Union were frozen in 2001 by means of European Council regulations.

The European Court of Justice in Luxembourg found that the European Council regulations, implementing within the EU the decisions of the UN Sanctions Committee to freeze funds and other economic resources, had infringed the fundamental rights of the applicants – notably their right to property and their right to a review of those decisions.

The Court stated that "respect for human rights is a condition of lawfulness of Community acts and that measures incompatible with respect for human rights are not acceptable in the Community". As a result of the judgment in the Kadi and Al Barakaat case, the European Union was requested to remedy the shortcomings in its implementation of the sanctions and the listing procedure.

---

97. A/HRC/4/26, 29 January 2007.

What are the lessons from this judgment, and what future action should be taken at the international level?

The importance of the global fight against terrorism should not be underestimated. All Council of Europe member states are under a duty to fight terrorism and have a positive obligation under human rights law to protect the lives of their citizens. The response to terrorist financing is a global problem and deserves international attention and action.

Yet at the same time, fundamental human rights protections for all form the basis of European Community law. Measures taken for the maintenance of peace and security must respect the rights enshrined in the European Convention on Human Rights and the European Union's Charter of Fundamental Rights.

As the Advocate General Poiares Maduro wisely observed in his opinion on the Kadi and Al Barakaat case, "the claim that a measure is necessary for the maintenance of international peace and security cannot operate so as to silence the general principles of Community Law and deprive individuals of their fundamental rights".

The ruling of the Luxembourg Court should trigger a change in the Security Council procedures. Some changes of the listing and review process were introduced by Security Council Resolution 1822 (in 2008) and, more importantly, Resolution 1904 (in December 2009). An institution of a special independent ombudsman was created with authority to scrutinise decisions to place individuals on such lists, and to assess the justification of such decisions in the light of actual facts and circumstances.

If the supreme authority of the Security Council is to be protected, the council itself must act in harmony with agreed international human rights standards. It is therefore welcome that the council has to some extent recognised the need for an independent review mechanism as a last stage of the Security Council decision-making about listings. Such procedures should ensure the right of the individual to know the full case against him or her, the right to be heard within a reasonable time, the right to an independent review mechanism, the right to counsel in these procedures and the right to an effective remedy.

The UN Special Rapporteur on Human Rights and Terrorism has argued that such a quasi-judicial body, composed of security classified experts, serving in an independent capacity, would possibly be recognised by national courts, the Luxembourg Court and regional human rights courts as a sufficient response to the requirement of the right to due process.

There may indeed be other ways of responding constructively to the Luxembourg Court ruling. What is important is both that human rights deficiencies at the global level are remedied before they are replicated at the European Union level; and that intergovernmental bodies such as the UN and the EU themselves respect the human rights standards on which they are based.

Terrorism – Lessons from Northern Ireland

In recent years Europe has been subjected to the most vicious terrorist acts. We still remember with horror the attacks in Beslan, Istanbul, London, Madrid, Moscow and several other cities. Effective measures must be taken to prevent such evil crimes in future. One crucial lesson we have learnt is that terrorism should not be fought with methods violating human rights. Such means undermine those values which we want to defend against the enemies of democracy; they are also ineffective.

Immediately after 11 September, the "war on terror" was set in motion. It is now more obvious than ever that the approach of the Bush administration was deeply flawed. The "warfare" was not only ineffective – there are clear indications that, on the whole, the methods were counterproductive: the "collateral damage" planted seeds for further extremism.

People were kidnapped and detained for several years without due process – some of them were even brought to secret prisons. Torture was approved at the highest level in the US administration and systematically practised. People were blacklisted with no possibility of defending themselves and they had their bank accounts frozen. Bugging, phone-tapping and other surveillance techniques were surreptitiously introduced.

The human rights of a large number of innocent people were violated during this "war". In particular, Muslims and persons coming from Arab countries or South Asia were targeted. "Profiling" of a racist or an Islamophobic nature was used.

European countries co-operated with this policy or looked the other way when US security agents were active on their soil. This attitude is also what made rendition flights possible.

It is urgent that all counterterrorism measures in Europe be reviewed. Such a review requires a sober approach, without either scaremongering or hysteria. The time has come to resurrect respect for the human rights principles we once all agreed upon, but which have been compromised in recent years.

I would recommend taking a close look at the experiences of Northern Ireland which suffered from terrorism for more than thirty years. The Committee on the Administration of Justice (CAJ) – a cross-community human rights group based in Belfast – has published an interesting and well-documented 120-page report: "War on terror: lessons from Northern Ireland".[98] In this publication, the CAJ worked together with the International Commission of Jurists in Geneva and, in particular, with its Eminent Jurists Panel (whose work was referred to in an earlier article).

Out of a population of only 1.6 million, more than 3 600 persons were killed during the "Troubles". After numerous emergency and counterterrorism measures being introduced, at last the 1998 Good Friday/Belfast Agreement turned the tide, and peace building could start. The CAJ report defines the good and bad lessons from these experiences. Many of them are relevant for other parts of the world.

---

98. See www.caj.org.uk.

A major lesson was that emergency legislation can easily lead to serious human rights abuses and therefore be counterproductive. The experience in Northern Ireland was that such laws corroded the normal criminal justice system and politicised the rule of law.

Such legislation also proved ineffective in deterring terrorism as it tended to demonise and alienate the very communities that could be of most assistance in fighting terrorism. It fuelled the violence it attempted to contain, by making real or perceived grievances worse, by normalising violence and by giving potential propaganda victories to those engaged in violently attacking the state.

When special legislation was introduced in Northern Ireland, supposed human rights safeguards were also adopted, such as regular reviews of the emergency powers, but these safeguards were not enough to keep in check a state with extraordinary powers. The review processes were mostly ineffective. Their terms of reference were too limited. The reviewers themselves were also unwilling to take clear principled positions. Even the judges failed to be immune to the climate of fear that was dominant at the time.

References to "national security" tended to hamper any independent analysis. The executive was left largely unchallenged in determining what constituted national security, and what needed to be done to uphold it.

Counterterrorism legislation was not balanced by stronger protections for human rights. This adversely affected policing in Northern Ireland and there were frequent allegations of ill-treatment, lethal force and discriminatory stop-and-search practices. As part of the political negotiations, it was agreed to establish an independent international commission to address these problems in detail.[99]

---

99. The commission (called the Patten Commission, after its chair, Chris Patten, now Lord Patten of Barnes) issued its report in September 1999: www.cain.ulst.ac.uk/issues/police/patten/patten99.pdf.

The commission proposed a series of measures to ensure that the police became more representative of society as a whole; that they received thorough human rights training; that effective accountability mechanisms were introduced; that a completely independent complaints system was established; and that greater community involvement with the police was actively encouraged.

The fact that the police commission in Northern Ireland developed wide-ranging and extensive practical recommendations for change clearly built trust. Such measures could have had a preventive effect, and avoided serious human rights violations, had they been taken at an earlier stage. The independent complaints system established in Northern Ireland is also an impressive model for others to consider.[100]

A further lesson is that it is crucial to protect the rule of law and the principle of due process. Public confidence in the justice system breaks down if people engaged in criminal acts are not arrested, or if innocent people are imprisoned.

The report listed numerous lessons about an effective criminal justice and policing response to violence. For example:
- long or indeterminate pre-trial detention is unacceptable;
- ill-treatment of detainees and prisoners must be actively prevented and allegations must be immediately and independently investigated;
- false allegations of torture or ill-treatment can be avoided by ensuring independent medical examinations, immediate and confidential access to legal advice and to family, audio and video recording of interrogations, and by unannounced visits to places of detention by independent observers;
- coercive interrogations should also be avoided by good police training, detailed custody records, a court's refusal to accept confession evidence secured through unacceptable interrogation

---

100. The Office of the Police Ombudsman for Northern Ireland is arguably the most independent of all police complaints bodies; details of powers and activities can be found at: www.policeombudsman.org.

methods and serious penalties for wrongful behaviour on the part of interrogators;

- the principle of "innocent until proven guilty" requires that suspects be allowed to retain their right to silence and their right not to self-incriminate;
- trials should be promptly held, thereby avoiding any risk of "internment by remand"; bail should be available for all but the most serious of charges;
- trials should be fair and ensure equality of arms with full disclosure of evidence to defence solicitors, speedy access by the accused to independent legal advice and an adequate legal aid system.

The experience in Northern Ireland underlines once again the importance of addressing the underlying causes of conflict. Effective programmes to tackle poverty, educational inequalities and discrimination are necessary as human rights requirements, and to prevent social exclusion, anger and the violence that can flow from a sense of alienation.

A remaining challenge in Northern Ireland is how to deal with the tragedies of the past, not to provoke new tensions between the different communities but to engage with the rights of the individual victims. Lasting peace and security requires that complaints of gross injustices be heard and handled by way of proper procedures in accordance with national and international human rights standards. This has to be handled with care and it cannot be ignored (see further discussion about dealing with the past in the next chapter).

The CAJ report also comments on the impact of interventions from the Council of Europe and other international human rights bodies. The experience was largely positive and the report argues that external interventions contributed to the protection of human rights. "Sometimes international pressure can be much more influential than local efforts, though of course such pressure is best exerted when it is informed by local knowledge and expertise."

Privacy and data protection

Surveillance technology is developing with breathtaking speed. This trend creates new instruments that are valuable in countering terrorism and organised crime, but it also raises fundamental questions about everyone's right to privacy. Individuals should be protected from intrusions into their private life and from the improper collection, storage, sharing and use of data. We must combat terrorism and organised crime, but not by using means which undermine our basic human rights.

Nowadays, technologies exist which allow for millions of telephone and e-mail communications to be monitored, screened and analysed simultaneously; for the use of virtually undetectable listening and tracing devices; and for the surreptitious installation of "spyware" on someone's computer capable of secretly monitoring the online activities and e-mails of the user, and even turning on the computer's camera and microphone.

It is sometimes said that only those who have something to hide should be fearful about these new measures. However, the notion that if you have nothing to hide you have nothing to fear puts the onus in the wrong place. It should be for states to justify why they seek to interfere with an individual's right to privacy – not for individuals to justify why they are concerned about attacks on their basic human rights.

The use of such new surveillance facilities by the police and security services requires enhanced democratic and judicial control.

Already, the storing of enormous amounts of personal data in social security, medical and police databases is a matter of concern. The UK's National DNA database contains over 5 million profiles. In 2007, the government accidentally lost two disks with confidential benefits data on 25 million people, amply illustrating some of the risks involved. In December 2008 in a judgment against the UK, the Strasbourg Court found a violation of Article 8 of the Convention (right to respect for one's private life) due to the blanket and indiscriminate nature of the powers of retention of fingerprints and DNA profiles of persons suspected but not convicted of offences.[101]

Banks, insurance companies and other business enterprises also develop customised databases on clients and their transactions. Understandably, there is widespread concern that these various databases can be combined – raising the question of whether there is sufficient protection against such interlinking. What are the consequences if interlinking is extended to public-sector databases, and used as the basis for decision making in anything from health and social security benefits to suspicion of involvement in crime or terrorism?

People who travel face invasive new security measures, such as fingerprinting and other biometric identity control methods, and even "strip-search" body scanners. One example is the demand that airlines going to the US should provide personal data on all their passengers, including names, phone numbers, e-mail addresses, credit card numbers and billing addresses. This information is to be available to the US security services and will be stored for several years. Preparations are under way to introduce a similar system for travellers to and from European Union countries.

Police and secret services already have a massive amount of data available to them. The intention when they process information is not only to find previously identified criminals but, increasingly, they seek persons who match predetermined "profiles" of persons who are supposedly more likely be a terrorist. These search methods are increasingly extended to non-terrorist crimes. However, the profiles can (even unwittingly) have built-in biases which may in reality result in unchallengeable discrimination against whole "suspect communities", or out-groups.

Obviously, it is essential that data protection rules cover the police, the judiciary and the security services. One of the shortcomings in the EU Council Framework Decision on the Protection of Personal Data is that it applies neither to domestic data processing relating to

---

101. *S. and Marper v. the United Kingdom*, judgment of 4 December 2008.

European police and judicial co-operation, nor to any processing of personal data by the security services, or indeed by the police when they act in relation to national security.

As terrorists and other organised criminals increasingly act across borders, co-operation between law enforcement forces in various countries has become more urgent. A principle of "availability" is being established within the European Union, to promote unhindered sharing of information. The idea is that the national law enforcement agencies in any one EU country should in principle have full and prompt access, with few "bureaucratic obstacles", to all the data held by other such agencies in any other member state.

This means that every piece of information in any national law enforcement database will be available across large parts of Europe – and possibly to other countries as well, notably the United States of America. If it functions as envisaged, this may well facilitate police work. On the other hand, any mistake or misreporting will have a potentially very serious and negative impact on the individual involved. This calls for a developed data-protection regime within the Union, based on agreed common high standards.

If the "availability" process is opened for authorities in different countries (including the United States), it is necessary to ensure that all involved genuinely respect common standards of data protection. Europe should not compromise on these important rules in order to satisfy their US counterparts.

The European data-protection authorities have stressed the need for a stronger data-protection regime. In a declaration in May 2007 they stated:

> *In view of the increasing use of availability of information as a concept for improving the fight against serious crime and the use of this concept on both national level and between Member States, the lack of harmonised and high level of data protection regime in the Union*

creates a situation in which the fundamental right of protection of personal data is not sufficiently guaranteed any more.[102]

This was a serious warning from official expert watchdogs working at the national level across Europe. It is important to listen to them, as these problems are complex and it is not easy for ordinary people, or even politicians, to fully grasp the implications of the many changes proposed or already decided.

Confidence in one's right to privacy and proper data protection has been badly undermined during the "war on terror". Previously accepted safeguards have been undermined by governments. In the United States, library records and a range of other data have been accessed using "National Security Letters" without court oversight. Extensive telephone surveillance of US citizens was approved by President Bush, but kept secret even from Congress, damaging public confidence. The situation of non-US citizens (for example, Europeans) is in fact worse, because spying on them by US security is not subject to any control or constitutional guarantees at all.

In Europe, there is a need for a deeper discussion on how to combine methods of preventing terrorism and other crimes, and the protection of the right to a private life. In recent years, human rights requirements have not been given sufficient emphasis in the debate about surveillance. Moreover, when intrusive methods have turned out to be ineffective, public debate has been circumscribed by the supposed need for secrecy.

In some discussions, the argument has even been made that good data protection is an obstacle to effective law enforcement. This is a mistake. It has to be realised that there are competing rights here that need to be considered.

There is, on the one hand, an imperative duty on states to uphold the rights of their populations by protecting them against possible terrorist

---

102. Declaration adopted by the European Data Protection Authorities in Cyprus on 11 May 2007; for the full text see: www.edps.europa.eu/EDPSWEB/Jahia/EDPSWEB/edps/lang/en/pid/50.

acts. On the other hand, governments also have an obligation to protect the privacy of individuals and ensure that private information on them does not get into the wrong hands or is not otherwise misused.

It is urgent that the rule of law be reasserted in this area. The European Convention on Human Rights with its case law, and the Convention for the Protection of Individuals with regard to Automatic Processing of Personal Data and its additional protocol specify the appropriate standards. Important guidance is also given by the Council of Europe recommendation on data protection in the police sector.[103]

The following are some of the key principles I find particularly relevant for a future discussion on privacy and data protection in the fight against terrorism:

- all processing of personal data for law enforcement and anti-terrorism purposes must be based on clear, specific, binding and published legal rules;
- within the sweeping categories of "fighting (organised) crime" and "the fight against terrorism", the purpose of particular police and secret service actions should be more specifically defined. There should be recognition of the fact that methods that are proportionate for some purposes (such as countering an immediate threat from a terrorist bomb) will not meet that same test if being applied to lesser threats (such as trying to prevent young people from being "radicalised" or "supporting extremism"). Fundamental European democratic values are undermined when the concept of "terrorism" is excessively widened, or when draconian measures – adopted to deal with a very specific and serious threat – are applied to a range of lesser law enforcement challenges;
- the collection of data on individuals solely on the basis of, for example, ethnic origin, religious belief, sexual behaviour or political opinions should be prohibited;

---

103. Recommendation No. R (87) 15 of the Committee of Ministers on regulating the use of personal data in the police sector.

- the collection of data on persons not suspected of involvement in a specific crime, and not posing a threat, must be subject to particularly strict "necessity" and "proportionality" tests;
- access to police and secret service files should only be allowed on a case-by-case basis, for specified purposes, and under judicial control;
- there must be limits to the length of time for which collected information can be retained. Except in exceptional circumstances, DNA data on arrested persons should be deleted, and samples destroyed, where the individual was not subsequently prosecuted and convicted; in all instances, there should be clear rules and a right of appeal;
- strong safeguards should be established by law to ensure appropriate and effective supervision over the activities of the police and the secret services. This supervision should be carried out both by the judiciary and through parliamentary scrutiny;
- all personal data processing operations should be subject to close and effective supervision by independent and impartial data-protection authorities.

National authorities have an obligation to ensure that these standards will be fully respected by the recipients before any personal data is shared with another country. The principle of making data available to other authorities should not be used to circumvent European and national constitutional data-protection standards.

Chapter 11: Gross violations in the past

Coming to terms with history is always important, but it is particularly necessary when massive atrocities and gross violations of human rights have occurred. Such crimes cannot be ignored without risking severe consequences. Prolonged impunity or a lack of acknowledgement, especially over several generations, creates bitterness among the victims and those who identify with them. This in turn poisons relations between people who were not even born when the events in question took place.

Photo: June 1944, the arrival of Hungarian Jews at Auschwitz-Birkenau concentration camp where some 1 million Jews were exterminated by the Nazis during the Second World War (© dpa/ABACA).

Lessons from history

Gross violations of human rights committed in the past continue to haunt today's Europe. In some cases, an acknowledgement of the violations that occurred has generated understanding, tolerance and trust between individuals and peoples. In other cases, the crimes committed have been denied or trivialised or exploited, thereby feeding division and hatred. False interpretations of history have been used to justify discrimination, racism, anti-Semitism and xenophobia.

Acknowledging and coming to terms with gross violations of human rights committed in the past is essential. Ignoring such crimes has severe consequences: it sows bitterness among those who identify with the victims and poisons relations between people who were not even born at the time.

European powers have been reluctant – even long afterwards – to recognise the full extent of the suffering caused, and the legacy created, by their colonial policies. European representatives vehemently opposed a proposal at the World Conference against Racism in Durban in 2001 to refer to such historic facts in the outcome document. This opposition resulted in a bland compromise formulation which was justifiably criticised.

The crimes of Nazi Germany, and in particular the Holocaust, were denied, trivialised or ignored by many when the killings were taking place. Afterwards, the world community adopted the concept of genocide and an international convention to prevent and punish such crimes in the future. Post-war Germany has made enormous efforts to expose Nazi crimes, to compensate victims, to punish perpetrators when possible and to educate younger generations about the crimes that were committed. All this has been absolutely necessary; nothing less would have been acceptable.

Authorities in other countries have been less open about co-operation and collusion in the executions of Jews committed on their soil. The mass killings of Roma have not been given sufficient attention. The murder of homosexuals and the medical experiments on, and killings of, persons with disabilities have also tended to be set aside.

The crimes of Stalin in the Soviet Union have been documented and exposed, especially by the non-governmental organisation Memorial, but the full scale of Stalinist repression has still to be fully established and acknowledged.

The discussion in some European countries in 2009-10 about the role of the Soviet army during the Second World War was not understood in the Russian Federation, where many felt that the sacrifices of their nation during "the Great Patriotic War" were not recognised. Even worse, some saw the debate as equating their efforts to combat Nazism with the brutalities of Hitler's army. These exchanges illustrated the need, when history is discussed, to make important distinctions. In this particular instance, there was a need to make a clear distinction between Stalin's dictatorial policies on the one hand and the efforts by Soviet soldiers and civilians on the other to defend their nation and combat Nazism.

This distinction was made by President Boris Yeltsin when he went to Warsaw in 1992, bringing with him key documents – including Stalin's personal order authorising the murder of 22 000 Poles in Katyn in 1940. This was a breakthrough contradicting the Soviet claim that these killings had been committed by Nazi troops. Yeltsin's move opened up a process of acknowledgement and conciliation. The 70th anniversary of this crime was marked in a joint Polish-Russian ceremony.

I hope that a genuine process of understanding and acknowledgement will also start between Armenia and Turkey. The very description of the enforced mass displacement and the ensuing deaths, as well as the outright killings of ethnic Armenians in 1915 under the Ottoman Empire, continue to be extremely controversial. Even though these events occurred before the creation of the new Turkish Republic, there has been an unwillingness to discuss these crimes in Turkey. Writers and journalists who have tried to raise the issue have been brought to trial. Some steps towards recognising the facts are now being taken – largely through academic discussion – but much more needs to be done.

One group of people whose tragic history has been grossly neglected in Europe is the Roma. Not only have the Nazi crimes against them been largely ignored, but accounts of their brutal repression and systematic discrimination in several European countries, both before and after the Nazi period, have not been recognised. Official apologies have been slow to come, if at all (see chapter on Roma rights).

In the Balkans, different versions of historic events – some going back several centuries – were replayed in the conflicts of the 1990s and severely undermined international peace efforts. New atrocities were also committed, the scope and even the existence of which became disputed. Human rights organisations throughout former Yugoslavia have been asking for a regional truth commission – an important initiative which could help to avoid distortions of history becoming the cause of future tensions.

In most zones of conflict, there is more than one historical narrative, based on different perspectives and emphasising different aspects. It is important for groups in society to become aware of the diversity of these competing historical accounts – and to accept that differences of viewpoint may persist, even after the basic facts have been established.

An example of a non-governmental project to create understanding of this kind was initiated in Northern Ireland, where a dialogue was organised to encourage the opposing sides to discuss and acknowledge their different experiences. Official efforts have also been launched to address historic cases, including the events which occurred on "Bloody Sunday" in 1972. Judgments of the European Court of Human Rights on the unsatisfactory investigations into political and sectarian killings in Northern Ireland also play their part in this historical reconstruction.

After the fall of the junta in Greece in 1974, trials were held to establish accountability. Similar efforts in post-dictatorship Portugal focused on the activities of the secret services.

Establishing the facts and an honest accounting of previous human rights violations are essential to underpin subsequent efforts to build the rule of law, bring those responsible to justice, compensate victims and take remedial action aimed at preventing the recurrence of such crimes.

Establishing the truth is also important in a longer-term perspective. Those who suffered were human beings, not numbers. Survivors, as well as the children and grandchildren of victims, have the right to know what happened and to grieve in dignity. The opportunity to remember and commemorate must be protected.

Society as a whole must learn from what happened, document the events, establish memorial sites and help the next generation to understand through proper education.

The Council of Europe now has extensive experience in fostering multiperspective history teaching through interactive teaching materials and bilateral co-operation. It has developed teaching kits for key events of the 20th century and the European dimension of history. Giving more visibility to the history of women in the 20th century has been part of these endeavours. New materials aimed at ensuring a diversity of perspectives are being prepared to assist in the portrayal of "the Other" in the teaching of history.

In Bosnia and Herzegovina, the Council of Europe co-ordinated the preparation of common guidelines which led to the drafting of new history and geography textbooks and teaching manuals, with teachers taking an active part, and demonstrating enthusiasm for a multiperspective history approach with new interactive teaching styles.

The Parliamentary Assembly of the Council of Europe has highlighted the role of history teaching for reconciliation. It has stressed the need to deal with controversial questions without resorting to the politically expedient approach of only presenting one single interpretation of events. An acceptance that there may be several well-documented but competing views is now emerging.

Controversies about history should not hold human rights hostage. One-sided interpretations or distortions of events should not result in discrimination against minorities, xenophobia and a renewal of repression and conflict. Future generations must not be blamed or made to suffer for the crimes of their forefathers.

What is important is an honest search for the truth, sober discussion based on fact, and an understanding that the contest involving competing versions of history is part of the process of coming to terms with a violent past. Only then can the right lessons be learned.

Accountability in post-totalitarian states

Countries in transition have to settle past accounts. Persons who have committed gross human rights violations must be prosecuted and barred from holding public office. The judiciary, law enforcement agencies and government administration must be reformed and screened. Countries in transition need to find a sensible approach towards those who collaborated with the former repressive system.

Lustration was an administrative measure used in some European post-communist countries to exclude from public institutions persons who worked for or collaborated with communist security services. Vetting is a more general term used for measures to purge from public institutions those who lack integrity – in other words, those who cannot be trusted to exercise governmental power in accordance with democratic principles.

In 1996, the Council of Europe's Parliamentary Assembly proposed guidelines to ensure that lustration laws complied with the requirements of a state based on the rule of law.

The Assembly stated that due process must be fully respected. This should include the following rights to:

- benefit from counsel;
- confront and challenge the evidence used;

- have access to all evidence;
- be able to present one's own evidence;
- have an open hearing if one so requests; and
- appeal to an independent judicial tribunal.

Furthermore, the Strasbourg Court has concluded that if a state is to adopt lustration measures, it must ensure that those affected enjoy all procedural guarantees under the European Convention on Human Rights.[104]

Experience has shown that even the most urgent vetting exercise can be compromised if strict procedures are not followed. In December 2006, I visited Sarajevo to discuss complaints from 260 police officers who had been barred from police service, or "de-certified" through a vetting procedure organised by the UN International Police Task Force. The police officers had limited possibility to challenge the merits of the decision to de-certify them.

The decision not to grant a certificate was for life and therefore had a severe economic and social impact on the individuals concerned. The UN decision had also given them a certain stigma in society which had further worsened their situation. This goes to show that vetting is a very complex process which must be handled with great caution.

Under the previous version of the lustration law in Poland, which came into effect on 1 March 2006, public figures, including senior officials, judges, teachers, journalists, diplomats, municipal officials and heads of state-owned companies, would all have had to make a declaration as to whether they had co-operated with state security organs of the Polish People's Republic from 1944 to 1990. This declaration was then to be verified by the Polish Institute of National Remembrance. If information in the state archive files showed that a person had in fact collaborated, he or she could be dismissed from office.

I was informed that this law could affect more than 300 000 people. The scope was extremely broad and questions were raised regarding

---

104. *Turek v. Slovakia*, judgment of 14 February 2006.

whether people in all these professions posed a significant danger to human rights and democracy – especially given the time that had elapsed since the system changed. The procedures left little room for recognising different forms of "collaboration", or for the possibility that individuals might have changed their attitudes and habits during the years which had passed since the end of the communist regime.

This law was changed as a consequence of the public debate. One lesson was that relying on illegally collected information, stored in incomplete secret services files, is highly problematic. Fair vetting procedures can hardly be based on such archives.

All persons affected should be able to examine the files kept on them by the former secret services. However, the privacy of individuals, victims and witnesses must also be protected according to human rights standards. Files can be leaked and unsubstantiated information can damage the reputation of individuals in violation of the principle that everyone should be treated as innocent until guilt is proven.

Lustration is only one aspect of dealing with the past. Prosecuting those responsible for serious crimes, providing compensation to victims, uncovering the truth and educating society about the past are all measures which should complement any vetting procedures.

Council of Europe parliamentarians stated in their 1996 resolution that "the key to peaceful coexistence and a successful transition process lies in striking the delicate balance of providing justice without seeking revenge".

Any risk of vetting being misused for political or personal reasons has to be avoided and this requires strict and fair procedures.

The International Criminal Court

The atrocities in the Balkans in the early 1990s were a reminder of the need for an effective and independent international justice mechanism to end impunity for the gravest of crimes: genocide, crimes against humanity and war crimes. The Rome Statute was agreed in 1998 after lengthy intergovernmental negotiations and the International Criminal Court (ICC) was established in 2002 after 60 states had ratified the treaty. Now with 114 states parties, the court still faces major challenges.

Previous US administrations looked upon the court with suspicion and hostility. Within the Clinton administration, there was fear that the court might be misused for politically motivated prosecutions against US nationals. Yet, President Clinton signed the statute on 31 December 2000, the very last day it was open for signature. He said that ratification (the next step) was not imminent and that such a proposal to the Senate would depend on whether the International Criminal Court demonstrated political impartiality.

His successor was unwilling to go even that far. Just before the entry into force of the statute, President George W. Bush declared, in a letter to the UN Secretary-General, that his administration would not ratify the treaty and that it did not accept the obligations following from its signature. This "unsigning" meant that the US Government no longer felt obliged to refrain from acts which would defeat the object and purpose of the Rome Statute.[105]

Thereafter the US engaged in a full-scale campaign against the ICC. In 2002, it pushed the UN Security Council to adopt a resolution which requested the ICC not to begin investigation or prosecution "involving present or former officials or personnel" from a state which had not ratified the statute. This exception was renewed in June 2003 for a 12-month period, but later attempts to renew it did not win sufficient support. The US finally withdrew the resolution.

The next step was to request other governments to conclude bilateral immunity agreements with Washington which would shield current or former US Government officials, military and other personnel, including non-US citizens working for the US and other US nationals,

---

105. Article 18(a) of the 1969 Vienna Convention on the Law of Treaties stipulates that a state which has signed a treaty is obliged to refrain from acts which would defeat the object and purpose of the treaty in question.

from the jurisdiction of the court.[106] No guarantee was provided that suspects would be prosecuted in a national criminal justice process.[107]

The political and diplomatic pressure exerted to obtain these agreements was exceptional. Programmes of military training and even development assistance were terminated for those states which refused to co-operate. In 2002, the American Service-Members Protection Act (ASPA) prohibited the US from engaging in bilateral and multilateral activities aimed at co-operating with or supporting the ICC, and authorised the use of force to liberate any US citizen detained in The Hague by order of the Court.

In addition, an amendment to a law on economic assistance named after its initiator, Congressman George Nethercutt, badly affected several poorly-off countries when they took a principled position not to undermine the Rome Statute.

European institutions were clearly sceptical towards both the substance and the methods of this campaign, and governments seeking good relations with both the European Union and the US were placed in an unenviable position. Romania and Azerbaijan, for instance, signed the Bilateral Immunity Agreement with the US, though they never subsequently ratified it.

---

106. These agreements were also called "Article 98" agreements. Article 98(2) of the Statute states that the Court "may not proceed with a request for surrender which would require the requested State to act inconsistently with its obligations under international agreements pursuant to which the consent of a sending State is required to surrender a person of that State to the Court, unless the Court can first obtain the cooperation of the sending State for the giving of consent for the surrender". Many experts agreed that such agreements were contrary to international law and the Rome Statute.
107. The Rome Statute offers comprehensive safeguards against abuse for political purposes. The preamble of the Rome Statute says that the International Criminal Court shall be complementary to national criminal jurisdictions, and its Article 17 provides that the Court may exercise its jurisdiction only when the state which has jurisdiction over the case is unwilling, or genuinely unable, to carry out the investigation or prosecution.

The Parliamentary Assembly of the Council of Europe discussed this issue in various sessions. In 2003, it regretted the ongoing US campaign, stated that the agreements sought were in breach of the Rome Statute, and continued:

> The Assembly condemns the pressure exercised on a number of members states of the Council of Europe to enter into such agreements, and regrets that the contradictory demands made on them by the United States on the one side, and the European Union and the Council of Europe on the other, confronts them with a false choice between European and trans-Atlantic solidarity. The Assembly considers that all countries should be left free to decide on their stance vis-à-vis the ICC on the basis of considerations of principle alone.[108]

In the end only four European governments ratified the immunity agreement: Albania, Bosnia and Herzegovina, Georgia and "the former Yugoslav Republic of Macedonia". In my subsequent discussions with government representatives from these countries, I did not detect any enthusiasm for the agreement.

Significantly, not even half of the agreements became legally binding, as many governments never followed up on their first promises to the US administration. Of the 101 signed agreements, only 21 were ratified by parliament, and only 18 others were described as executive decisions, which would not require ratification.[109]

Even within the Bush administration, enthusiasm appeared to fade with time: the number of exceptions to APSA increased, and, in the end, punitive actions were no longer sought.

The Obama administration is certainly showing a more positive attitude towards the court. The sanctions foreseen by the bilateral agreements have been waived and Secretary of State Hillary Clinton stated to a Senate committee that the "hostility" to the ICC would end. The

---

108. Council of Europe Parliamentary Assembly (PACE) Resolution 1336 (2003).
109. Statistics from the Coalition for the Criminal Court: www.iccnow.org.

US endorsement of the ICC action on Sudan may anticipate a new era for international justice.

The US Government should restate its support for the ICC by reactivating its signature, repealing APSA and fully engaging in the Review Conference. The Obama administration should ask the Senate to ratify the Rome Statute and contribute to making the court an effective instrument of last resort against impunity for crimes that have too often gone unpunished despite their appalling character.

European representatives should engage in a renewed dialogue with the US Government on this issue. Remaining US worries, if any, should be clarified and remedied. Such dialogues should also encourage those European states which have still to accept the Rome Statute to come on board.

We should aim for universal support and participation. Crimes committed since the treaty was adopted in 1998 have unfortunately proved just how much the International Criminal Court is needed.

Chapter 12: Media freedom and freedom of expression

The purpose of journalism is not to please those who hold power or be the mouthpiece of governments. Instead, I argue that the media have an important role as a "public watchdog". The media's role is to inform the public about relevant developments in society, even when that information may embarrass.

Photo: Anna Politkovskaya seen on CCTV camera footage as she enters the building where her assassin was waiting (Courtesy of Novaya Gazeta*).*

Blasphemy and hate speech

The famous little mermaid in the port of Copenhagen was one day found dressed in a headscarf. No one took responsibility for this action – maybe it was a joke, maybe it was intended to be provocative, or maybe it sent a message about the lack of respect for Muslims. Anyhow, it was a reminder that the public debate about how to combine freedom of expression and respect for religious belief is far from concluded.

I was one of those who felt that the publishing of the Danish cartoons was stupid, irresponsible and a reflection of Islamophobia.[110] The damage was considerable and the hurt among Muslims very deep. However, I was not in favour of any legal action against the Danish newspaper *Jyllands-Posten*. I also did not feel that the cartoons illustrated a need for stronger blasphemy laws. My opinion is that we should try to tackle such differences through a free and open discussion.

Freedom of expression, as articulated in Article 10 of the European Convention on Human Rights, is not an absolute right; it has limits. The freedom carries with it duties and responsibilities, and may be subject to restrictions to protect public order and the rights of others if this is "necessary in a democratic society" and also regulated by law.

Article 10 specifies that the freedom may be limited "in the interests of national security, territorial integrity or public safety, for the prevention of disorder or crime, for the protection of health or morals, for the protection of the reputation of others, for preventing the disclosure of information received in confidence, or for maintaining the authority and impartiality of the judiciary".

These provisions may not be easy to interpret in individual cases. One thing, however, is clear: hate speech is not allowed. The European Court of Human Rights has ruled that freedom of expression gives

---

110. In 2005 a controversy broke out around cartoons printed in the Danish media considered by some to be disrespectful to the Muslim faith.

no entitlement to hate speech, since this "is incompatible with the values of the Convention, notably tolerance, social peace and non discrimination".[111] The same line is followed in a 1997 recommendation of the Committee of Ministers of the Council of Europe.

Indeed, the International Covenant on Civil and Political Rights makes it an obligation for states to prohibit incitement to racial and religious hatred (Article 20). The key aspect here is deliberate incitement which can lead to discrimination or other human rights violations. The term hate speech is carefully defined as "advocacy of national, racial or religious hatred that constitutes incitement to discrimination, hostility or violence".

In practice, it may not always be easy to draw the line between hate speech and other types of scathing criticism. However, the limitation on hate speech is definitely not intended to restrict or prohibit speech that is merely uncomfortable or irritating for others. The Court made this clear in a frequently quoted ruling that freedom of expression was not only applicable to information and ideas which were inoffensive "but also to those that offend, shock or disturb the State or any sector of the population".[112] This was an important interpretation.

Banning information or the expression of opinion should be seen as exceptional – a measure which must be decided upon by democratic means and justified as a matter of absolute necessity. There may, otherwise, be a risk that certain statements are prohibited merely because some influential person or group does not like them.

Freedom of expression is essential for the very functioning of democracy itself. We experience the centrality of this right when exposing social problems, monitoring people in power and promoting tolerance. These values must be protected – even at the cost of accepting some dubious media reporting.

---

111. Decision as to the admissibility of Application No. 23131/03, *Norwood v. the United Kingdom*, 16 July 2003.
112. *Handyside v. the United Kingdom*, judgment of 7 December 1976.

The Venice Commission of the Council of Europe was asked to prepare an overview of national law and practice relating to blasphemy, incitement to hatred, and freedom of expression. The commission wrote that "religious groups must tolerate, as other groups must, critical public statements and debate about their activities, teachings and beliefs, provided that such criticism does not amount to intentional and gratuitous insult and does not constitute incitement to disturb the public peace or to discriminate against adherents of a particular religion".[113]

The legal situation in Europe today appears to be as follows:

- practically all Council of Europe member states have legislation outlawing incitement to hatred, including religious hatred;
- most states also provide for specific, often more stringent or severe, provisions relating to incitement to hatred through the mass media;
- religious insults are a criminal offence in just over half of the member states;
- denial of certain historic facts, such as the Holocaust or genocide, is an offence in certain countries;
- blasphemy is an offence in only a minority of member states and where this is the case, it is, nowadays, rarely prosecuted.[114]

The Venice Commission concludes that there is no need for new specific legislation on blasphemy, religious insults and inciting religious hatred. The focus should rather be on the full, proper and non-discriminatory implementation of existing general legislation.

This is a wise conclusion. New legislation would give the impression of favouring further restrictions to freedom of expression rather than

---

113. Venice Commission, "Report on the relationship between freedom of expression and freedom of religion", CDL-AD(2008)026, paragraph 72.
114. Article 19, a London-based international non-governmental organisation defending freedom of speech, has compiled more information about blasphemy laws, denial laws and hate speech laws; www.Article19.org.

accepting that an open discussion of controversial issues is vital for democracy. In fact, what is needed is a review of existing laws and to repeal those that are overly restrictive.

As rightly stressed by the Venice Commission, it rests with the national courts to apply the relevant legislation in a non-discriminatory manner. National judges should build on the principles offered by the European Court and, in their test of proportionality, take into account the opinions issued, and the context in which they are expressed.

Media diversity

Governments often complain about the mass media in their country, claiming that their messages are distorted and unfairly criticised. True, there are unprofessional media outlets. However, this problem should not be exaggerated and is not an excuse for draconian interventions or state control. Instead governments should promote a media policy which encourages self-discipline and allows for a wide variety of media voices. This is what democracy requires. Indeed, media diversity enhances further democratisation.

Editors and other media representatives should take careful note of criticism of the quality of some their reporting. Improved professional training for journalists and effective systems of self-regulation (including codes of ethics and press councils) are of paramount importance.

However, the main problems facing the media are that too little meaningful information is circulated, and too few voices are heard.

Although the Internet has created new possibilities for more democratic dialogue on political matters, the mass media will surely continue to function as the main form of conveying news that is of interest to society as a whole and as the key arena for public debate.

All over the world, governments and business interests dominate mass media production, in television especially. This is to some extent inevitable given the heavy investment costs involved. However, this makes it even more essential to actively encourage competition, and to democratise media structures. A minimum requirement is that there is transparency about who owns, controls and influences the various media outlets.

It is sometimes said that consumers act as a natural and sufficient corrective. Media outlets which are too propagandistic do tend not to be read, viewed or listened to. However, when there are no or few alternatives, there is a problem. Increased possibilities for tuning into foreign radio transmissions or satellite television helps, but language and other barriers make this an unrealistic option for many.

Some principles are essential for diversity in the media: governments and parliaments must encourage genuine competition; the official public service media must act impartially and in the interests of all people in society; and governments must be transparent and allow access to the information they hold.

Competition

Some European governments and parliaments have actively subsidised smaller media – often those run by minorities – in order to secure a broader output. Other governments, however, have sabotaged competition by actively undermining the media they do not like.

The way frequencies for television and radio are allocated is a test which several governments have failed. State agencies deciding on this should work according to agreed, objective criteria and not discriminate against more independent applicants.

Another problem in some countries is that the government buys advertisement space only in the "loyal" media, signalling to business to follow their lead. As a consequence, independent media are effectively boycotted.

A number of other discriminatory measures have been taken against independent media – some clearly intended to force them into bankruptcy. Tactics such as repeated defamation charges in court, or obstacles to buying paper, or barriers to printing and distributing papers are deployed. Such actions must be seen as violations of freedom of expression.

It is important that there are real alternatives. I once asked the ombudsman in one of the former republics of the Soviet Union what reform he would consider the most important for human rights protection in the country. His answer was: "A truly independent TV channel!" This, in his opinion, would be the most efficient way of promoting an open, free debate and an honest monitoring of problems in society.

Role of the "official" media

These media must operate in an impartial manner in the interest of the population at large. They could indeed be an essential counterbalance to the business-driven entertainment media. The "public service" media – often financed from tax money or other public resources – should never be used as propaganda instruments by particular politicians or partisan political interests. The independence and impartiality of this sector are of paramount importance and ought to be protected through agreed guidelines and an appropriate procedure of appointing senior staff.

Transparency of public authorities

Media culture is considerably influenced by the attitude of the authorities towards journalists asking for information, especially on sensitive matters. The media have a legitimate interest in requesting information about government decisions and actions. They can serve as representatives of citizens who have the right to know how their elected leaders act on their behalf. Open access to government information is therefore a democratic principle of high priority.

It is not enough that ministers are generous in giving interviews. There should be a formal legal affirmation of the right of citizens, including journalists, to obtain written documents and other information from the authorities. Exceptions to this basic principle of transparency should be strictly regulated and allowed solely on the grounds of legitimate state secrets.

These problems are sometimes most acute in transition countries where news and political information were previously firmly controlled by those in power. However, these questions need discussion throughout Europe: do we have genuine competition in the media market? Does the public service media play the role it should? Are governments genuinely transparent?

Journalists at risk

In Europe today journalists are threatened or even put in prison for merely doing their job. Individuals who provide information to the media about abuses of power or corruption run the risk of dismissal or worse. Such practices undermine democracy and must be countered through a clear rights-based media policy grounded on the principle of freedom of expression.

The purpose of journalism is not to please power holders or be the mouthpiece of governments. Indeed, the media have an important role as a "public watchdog" and to inform the public about relevant developments in society, including those which may embarrass those with power and influence.

When the Court of Human Rights in Strasbourg stated that freedom of expression might include information that "offends, shocks or disturbs", it confirmed that the media must be free to be controversial. This does not mean that there are no limits to the freedom. Hate speech, incitement to violence and the dissemination of child pornography are not allowed. The European Convention clarifies that the state is allowed to introduce restrictions, for instance, to protect national security and public safety.[115]

The room for such exceptions should, however, be regulated by law and be interpreted narrowly. It must be clear that critical reporting is allowed, including about the activities of authorities or private companies as well as individual politicians or business leaders.

---

115. European Convention on Human Rights, Article 10, paragraph 2.

It is a major problem that defamation is still criminalised in several parts of Europe. Laws are in place making it a criminal offence to say or publish true or false facts or opinions that offend a person or undermine his or her reputation. The OSCE Representative on Freedom of the Media has recommended that offences against "honour and dignity" should be decriminalised and dealt with in civil law courts. The mere existence of criminal defamation laws could intimidate journalists and cause unfortunate self-censorship. I agree with this assessment.

Also, civil libel lawsuits should not be misused to achieve similar repressive impact on media freedom. The Supreme Court of the Russian Federation ruled in an interesting decision in September 2010 that the amounts awarded should be "reasonable and justified" and "should not be conducive to media-freedom violations".

In a resolution on decriminalisation, the Parliamentary Assembly of the Council of Europe "takes the view that prison sentences for defamation should be abolished without further delay".[116] A related report within the Parliamentary Assembly suggested that public figures should not have more protection from defamation laws than ordinary citizens.[117]

The fact that the margin for criticism of politicians is broader has already been established by the Strasbourg Court which has stated that politicians have to accept that their words and actions are open to a higher degree of scrutiny by both journalists and the public at large.[118]

This discussion is of paramount importance and should include the role of regulatory mechanisms within the media. There have been encouraging results in countries where media representatives have developed codes of ethics and designed their own special procedures

---

116. Parliamentary Assembly of the Council of Europe (PACE), Resolution 1577 (2007), paragraph 13.
117. "Towards decriminalisation of defamation", Committee on Legal Affairs and Human Rights, rapporteur: Mr Jaume Bartumeu Cassany, Doc. 11305, 14 May 2007.
118. *Lingens v. Austria*, judgment of 8 July 1986.

to enforce professional standards, for instance, through press councils or press ombudsmen. Media outlets have matured, the public have obtained better protection against abuse and the right to reply has been strengthened.

Decriminalising defamation and increasing the relevance of self-regulatory mechanisms would not protect the media from civil law charges. The media should of course not be above the law but the Parliamentary Assembly report mentioned above raises the problem of very high damages being accorded. If these damages are not in proportion to the actual injury, and if they are awarded against individual journalists, this might have a chilling effect.

Some countries have introduced a system of responsible publishers in which legal accountability is placed on one clearly defined authority within the media enterprise – normally the publisher or the editor. Such a system puts the responsibility where it belongs, and protects the individual journalist from the risk of having to pay damages.

Another pillar in a rights-based media policy is to ensure sources of information are protected. Journalists should be free to receive information, including anonymously, from any source – including government employees. This right should be confirmed in national law and no one should be allowed to investigate the sources used by journalists. Not even courts should be able to order the media, still less individual journalists, to reveal confidential sources.

The Strasbourg Court has stated that the protection of journalist sources is one of the basic prerequisites for press freedom. Accordingly, an order to disclose a source is unjustified unless there is an overriding requirement involving the public interest.[119] Indeed, every democratic society should welcome and protect "whistle-blowers" – they are a safety valve against the abuse of power in both the public and private sector.

---

119. *Goodwin v. the United Kingdom,* judgment of 27 March 1996; see also Committee of Ministers Recommendation No. R (2000) 7 on the right of journalists not to disclose their sources of information.

In recent years, some of the best-known leading investigative journalists have not only found their sources scared into silence, they have themselves fallen victim to the most brutal contract killings: Hrant Dink in Turkey, Georgiy Gongadze in Ukraine, Elmar Huseynov in Azerbaijan and Anna Politkovskaya in Russia. No effort must be spared in apprehending and bringing to justice not only the actual killers, but also those who ordered these murders.

Many other journalists have been assaulted and severely ill-treated, not least in Russia, in recent years. Some of the attacks have obviously been organised and conducted by extremist criminal gangs.

Such dreadful crimes may make other journalists more cautious and thereby encourage self-censorship. Governments must demonstrate forcefully that they are prepared to protect freedom of media not only in words, but also by way of concrete action.

An immediate step would be to release all journalists who have been imprisoned because of their work and to declare a moratorium on the use of criminal defamation laws.

Freedom of assembly

Peaceful meetings and demonstrations are one of the most important forms of dialogue between the authorities and civil society. Freedom of assembly must be protected as crucial to pluralism and democracy. In principle, the right is well protected – it is codified in the European Convention on Human Rights (Article 11), and in the domestic law or the constitutions of member states. In Russia, for example, the right to peaceful assembly is enshrined in Article 31 of the constitution.

In fact, in most European countries legislation merely requires the organisers of a meeting to notify the local authorities of their intention to assemble. In other words, there is no need to seek authorisation.

However, in a number of countries where the law only requires a notification procedure, the authorities incorrectly regard such notifications as requests for permission and, by extension, as a possibility for them to deny permission and to consider a demonstration or rally as "unauthorised".

Even when there is no explicit "rejection", local authorities have, in several countries, often resorted to other ways of preventing a demonstration or curbing its impact. One approach is to allow a demonstration to go ahead, but at another time and/or at a less central location, thereby rendering it and its message more or less invisible to the general public.

Another method is to allow or even encourage others – sometimes hostile groups – to organise alternative events at the same time and venue. Such methods have been used in various countries to insult the freedom of assembly of disfavoured or stigmatised groups, such as the LGBT community.

Sometimes authorities prohibit a planned demonstration because of concerns for the safety of the participants, in which case they should normally provide protection instead. A general ban of a peaceful demonstration can only be justified if there is a real danger of disorder that cannot be prevented by reasonable and appropriate measures.

The very purpose of a procedure of notification to the authorities is to give them a possibility to organise protection and take steps to avoid clashes with the rights of others, for instance in the traffic. If there are acute conflicts of interest, the authorities have a possibility to seek an agreement with the rally organisers on some adjustments to the original plans.

This spirit was tested in Russia where since 2009 a non-governmental coalition, calling themselves "Strategy 31" (in reference to Article 31 of the constitution), organised rallies in Moscow, St Petersburg and other cities on the last day of months with 31 days. The purpose was to stress the importance of the constitutional right to demonstrate. Several of these meetings ended with crackdowns by riot police; some participants were beaten and a number also arrested.

The overarching principle in international law is for authorities to respect the peaceful and collective expression of opinion. The

European Court of Human Rights has made it clear that the state has a duty to protect participants in peaceful demonstrations, specifying that "this obligation is of particular importance for persons holding unpopular views or belonging to minorities, because they are more vulnerable to victimisation".[120]

The OSCE Office for Democratic Institutions and Human Rights, ODIHR, together with the Council of Europe's Venice Commission, has published a set of Guidelines on Freedom of Peaceful Assembly, which provide useful guidance for legislators and practitioners.

They specify the obligations of the state, such as the duty to protect a peaceful assembly, to inform the public clearly which body is responsible for taking decisions on the regulation of freedom of assembly (regulatory authority), and to act without discrimination.

If we are to protect the free exchange of ideas and the free association of individuals – especially minorities – we should be wary of any tendency to restrict the right to peaceful assembly in ways that run counter to the principles laid down in these guidelines.

---

120. *Alekseyev v. Russia*, judgment of 21 October 2010.

Chapter 13: Actors for human rights

Even when Andrei Sakharov was locked up and isolated in an apartment in the closed city of Gorky, he continued to write his appeals for prisoners of conscience in the Soviet Union and other countries. He gave Russians and others a strong moral message, the consequences of which continue to be felt today.

Photo: At the railway station on the day of Andrei Sakharov's return to Moscow from Gorky, 23 December 1986 (© Yuri Rost).

Human rights defenders

Human rights defenders must be free to speak out and work without interference. Their work in monitoring human rights and reporting is of the greatest importance for peace and the protection and realisation of human rights. They must be able to work in safe conditions and, in line with international standards, be provided with protection if and when needed.

Even self-confident governments can react negatively when their human rights record is questioned. Such over-reactions may reflect an understanding that good conduct is particularly important in the field of human rights, and that criticism on these grounds is particularly sensitive.

In some cases, however, governments have targeted the messenger instead of answering the questions raised. I have been surprised that leading politicians so often speak badly – in private and even publicly – about those who defend human rights in their own country.

Non-governmental human rights groups, journalists and even ombudsmen have been accused of being unpatriotic when they have reported on human rights violations. This charge is levelled particularly against those who have communicated with international organisations or media abroad.

Factual errors, even minor ones, have sometimes been used to prove that defenders of human rights are irresponsible or are acting in bad faith.

This is not a healthy approach promoting serious dialogue. To require that the reporting of non-governmental human rights organisations must be flawless is unreasonable, especially considering their limited resources and the fact that governments are often secretive and less than forthcoming with information. Most of these groups do very high quality work.

Attempts by some governments to silence defenders of human rights prompted a discussion in the United Nations some 30 years ago. In

1998, after long deliberations, the General Assembly adopted the UN Declaration on the Right and Responsibility of Individuals, Groups and Organs of Society to Promote and Protect Universally Recognized Human Rights and Fundamental Freedom.

The genesis of this declaration lay in repeated reports from around the world of outright repression of people trying to monitor and to report on human rights violations; to mediate between authorities and aggrieved groups; or simply to educate ordinary people about their rights. These individuals were referred to as "human rights defenders" in the declaration.

In some cases, individuals defending human rights have been executed or killed. Others have been arrested and tortured. Some have been deprived of basic freedoms such as freedom of movement, expression, assembly or association, or targeted with criminal prosecutions and made victims of unfair trials. The declaration aims at putting an end to such unjustifiable assaults on human rights work.

One dilemma for the drafters of the text was to avoid the temptation to define human rights defenders as a special group, entitled to receive protection because of belonging to that category. Indeed, it was deliberate that there should be no system of authorisation or "licensing", as this might well create additional dangers for those excluded from any formal definition.

All the rights which defenders should be able to enjoy were already agreed as part of international human rights standards. The declaration, therefore, focuses more on the implementation of those rights that are particularly important for those committed to defending and promoting human rights. The declaration emphasises that everyone has the right to promote, to protect and to defend human rights, at the national and international levels. It reaffirms the right to form, join and participate in non-governmental organisations.

It further states that everyone has the right to hold and to publish information about human rights, and to complain about governmental policies and actions. The declaration also spells out that there is a right to unhindered access to international bodies, and a right to receive and to obtain funding for human rights activities.

The idea is not to give anyone special privileges but to make clear that when individuals – alone or together with others – work or speak out for human rights, they should be free to do so without being accused of extremism or targeted in defamation campaigns, or worse.

The UN wanted to emphasise that these people are badly needed.

When the declaration was adopted the UN Secretary-General, Kofi Annan, stated the obvious, but important, lesson: "When the rights of human rights defenders are violated, all our rights are put in jeopardy and all of us are made less safe."

The example of Andrei Sakharov

Andrei Dmitrievich Sakharov became a voice of moral conscience who could not be silenced. His principled messages inspired others and contributed to the non-violent, revolutionary changes of 1989 and thereafter. He died in the midst of those upheavals but had set an example which continues to influence the work for justice and human rights in Russia and Europe today.

Andrei Sakharov was not meant to become a one-man opposition against Soviet misrule. He was at an early age a brilliant physicist, richly rewarded by the government for his work on the hydrogen bomb. The turning point came with his concern about the risks posed by nuclear weapons, and his appeals for a ban on nuclear tests. He demanded an honest debate about the danger of thermonuclear war, but no one in power listened. Gradually, he became more and more critical: his three-decade long campaign had started.

While Sakharov wanted to influence political decisions, he had no political ambitions for himself – although after his release from seven years of enforced exile in Gorky in December 1986, he became an active reformer. He strove to contribute meaningful content to the move towards "perestroika".

He was seen by many as an unofficial leader of the democratic movement and was elected to the First Congress of People's Deputies in April 1989. There he argued tirelessly for democratic reform. He was appointed to a commission tasked with drafting a new constitution. Typically, he produced his own draft – which contained strong provisions for the protection of human rights – which he presented to General Secretary Mikhail Gorbachev.

Though still seen as a troublemaker by many in government and party circles, Sakharov's ideas could not be ignored. Gorbachev included a number of them when he presented his own goals: honest and transparent government; popular participation; truth-telling about the past; the rule of law; freedom of association; and freedom of media.

Sakharov was constructive as a matter of principle. During his years in exile and through earlier periods of severe KGB harassment, he constantly emphasised that he was seeking a rational dialogue. He wrote numerous letters to the Soviet leaders seeking to convince them of the demands of reason, often referring to provisions in the law.

There were no replies, but the letters became known through informal channels and even reached abroad, and thus built up a case. This is how Sakharov himself evaluated these efforts in his memoirs:

> [They] have produced little in the way of immediate results. But I believe that statements on public issues are a useful means of promoting discussion, proposing alternatives to official policy, and focusing attention on problems. Appeals on behalf of specific individuals also attract attention to their cases, occasionally benefit a particular person, and inhibit future human rights violations through the threat of public disclosure.

Sakharov was a tireless activist. When his appeals went unheard he became involved in non-violent, direct action, sometimes putting his own health at risk. He travelled long distances to monitor trials and, when turned away from the courtroom, he demonstrated outside. He went on hunger strike several times for the release of political prisoners – the first time in 1974.

He and his wife, Elena Bonner, received a growing number of appeals from people who had been victimised by repression. Sakharov became an unofficial ombudsman for minorities such as the Crimean Tatars, for Baptists and others who suffered religious discrimination, as well as for Jews and others who wanted to leave the country.

He was alarmed by the inhumane conditions in Soviet prisons. Another abiding concern was the misuse of psychiatry: the involuntary detention in mental institutions of critics of the regime. These tactics bypassed all pretence of legality and frequently resulted in enforced medication for "health reasons" and other forms of abuse. The reports on these violations created a strong reaction abroad and the number of cases decreased.

Sakharov presented a universal vision for a peaceful and progressive society based on human rights standards. In his writings, not least in his 1975 Nobel Peace Prize lecture, he articulated the deeper significance of human rights and their relationship to a peaceful and better world. He argued that respect for human rights ensures that a country's foreign and security policies are democratically monitored and that this in turn prevents militarisation and limits the risk of war. He also stressed that human rights promote exchanges of information and ideas between people, and that this in turn lowers the level of distrust and thereby the risk of conflict:

> *I am convinced that international confidence, mutual understanding, disarmament and international security are inconceivable without an open society with freedom of information, freedom of conscience, the right to publish, and the right to travel and choose the country in which one wishes to live. I am likewise convinced that freedom of conscience, together with the other civil rights, provides the basis for scientific progress and constitutes a guarantee that scientific advances will not be used to despoil mankind, providing the basis for economic and social progress, which in turn is a political guarantee for the possibility of an effective defence of social rights. At the same time I should like to defend the thesis of*

the original and decisive significance of civil and political rights in moulding the destiny of mankind.

Sakharov identified hatred as a major danger for society. He argued persistently for measures against national and racial prejudice and religious intolerance. He considered that state incitement of hatred for "others" was particularly unforgivable.

He took a clear position against capital punishment, and argued in 1977 for total abolition:

I regard the death penalty as a savage, immoral institution which undermines the ethical and legal foundations of society. The state, in the person of its functionaries (who, like all people, are prone to superficial judgments and may be swayed by prejudice or selfish motives), assumes the right to the most terrible and irreversible act – the taking of human life. Such a state cannot expect an improvement in its moral atmosphere. I reject the notion that the death penalty has any real deterrent effect whatsoever on potential criminals. I am convinced that the contrary is true – the savagery begets only savagery.

Though firmly rooted in Russia, he was a true internationalist. He believed that the fates of all human beings are indivisible. "Mankind can develop painlessly only if it looks upon itself in a demographic sense as a unit, a single family without divisions into nations other than in matters of history and traditions," he wrote in his *Reflections on progress, peaceful coexistence and intellectual freedom*, published in 1968.

This understanding of global interdependence made him express concern about poverty in developing countries, the war in Afghanistan and the fate of refugees. He appealed for a general amnesty for those imprisoned for their views everywhere and inspired Amnesty International to launch a global campaign for the release of all prisoners of conscience in 1982.

As a gifted scientist he realised early on the global dangers if we ignore the environment and the need for ecological balance (he used the term "geo-hygiene"). He became involved in efforts to save Lake Baikal from being poisoned by toxic waste and concluded later that "[t]he salvation of our environment requires that we overcome our divisions and the pressure of temporary, local interests".

The example and thoughts of Andrei Sakharov remain acutely relevant today.

Religious leaders

There is a core of ethical values within all major religions, and certainly within Buddhism, Christianity, Hinduism, Islam and Judaism. The moral guidance given expression to by these religious traditions is comparable to many human rights principles. This is hardly surprising since the universal declaration drew inspiration from these traditions when it was drafted in the aftermath of the Second World War.

Religious leaders and teachers have played a significant role in explaining and defending human rights. In several European countries religious leaders have argued effectively for the rights of the poor, for migrants and for minorities like the Roma. An essential element of this message has been concern for injustice and intolerance towards people who are different – especially those who belong to another community.

There are, however, also examples of religious leaders showing limited tolerance for difference, most particularly in relation to people of differing sexual orientation. Religions have also attracted extremists who have distorted core religious values. Militants have agitated against "the Other" as a threat against their own community and have even portrayed them as enemies. Hostility against others has become the essence of their own sense of identity and community cohesion. This is a tragic perversion; it is also a tremendous challenge for enlightened teachers.

More than ever, there is a need to build bridges. My predecessor as commissioner organised several seminars with religious leaders and thinkers in Europe. I took part in the last one in February 2006 in Kazan in the Russian Republic of Tatarstan and could see the great value of this dialogue as people learnt from one another in a spirit of mutual respect.

The Kazan seminar recommended that a European centre be established to service systematic education about religions (in the plural). The reasoning was logical: ignorance can lead to prejudice that can lead to intolerance that in turn can lead to discrimination and human rights violations.

Ideally, inter-religious dialogue meetings like the one in Kazan ought to be organised also at national level. The purpose would be to facilitate mutual understanding and to define concrete measures to improve education about religions.

Respecting one another is not only a question of avoiding tensions and conflicts, it is also about protecting freedom of belief and religion – a cornerstone of all human rights standards. The European Convention on Human Rights formulates this right as follows:

> *Everyone has the right to freedom of thought, conscience and religion; this right includes freedom to change his religion or belief and freedom, either alone or in community with others and in public or private, to manifest his religion or belief, in worship, teaching, practice and observance.*

"Everyone" means everyone. This right should be implemented without discrimination against any religion or belief, or indeed against anyone without religious belief. Countries with a state religion are, in this respect, faced with a challenge – how do they secure the right of individuals belonging to "other" religions or beliefs to have the same potential for "worship, teaching, practice and observance"? The same dilemma faces those secular states where one religion is dominant in society. In both such societies teaching about other religions is important and relevant. In reality, the struggle for freedom of religion or belief (including atheism) is often about minority rights.

It is also clear that this freedom cannot be absolute. The European Convention recognises that there may need to be limitations of the right to manifest one's religion. However, this can be determined only by law and when necessary to protect the rights of others.

One category of "others" is children. The UN Convention on the Rights of the Child seeks to strike a balance between the right of parents and guardians to guide the child in matters relating to religion, and the right of the child to form his or her own opinions and have them respected. The key phrase here is "the evolving capacities of the child" – the older and more mature the child is, the more obvious that he or she has an individual right of thought, conscience and religion (see chapter on children's rights).

For this to be genuine, it is important that the child can learn about religion in school, including about the faiths of others. The Convention on the Rights of the Child gives support to the spirit of Kazan: that children have the right to know about their own cultural identity but also about cultures and civilisations different from their own.

The two go hand in hand. With a clearer self-image, people tend to be more open to messages which demystify what might otherwise appear strange. The aim should be to promote not only tolerance, but respect for others.

Ombudsmen

It is not enough to approve European and international standards: these standards must be turned into reality at both local and national level. In order for this to happen, local and national government should establish a system for independent human rights monitoring. Ombudsmen and similar institutions have made a great difference, provided their integrity is respected by those in power.

An important development has taken place in Europe in recent years: the idea of ombudsmen has spread, and most countries now have such an office or a similar national human rights institution, appointed by governments or parliaments.

There is a great variety of such bodies, and they tend to differ in name and mandate from country to country. Some focus solely on human rights while others guard against the abuse of power such as corruption. Some are mandated to receive complaints from individuals, have the authority to bring cases to court and to mediate with the authorities. Others are limited to a focus on systemic or structural shortcomings and may act by giving advice to the authorities or publishing reports.

In addition to the national offices, there are also regional ombudsmen in some larger countries, such as Russia and Spain. Specialist ombudsmen or human rights commissioners also exist in some states. For instance, more than 30 countries in Europe now have an ombudsman for children.

Offices have also been established in a number of countries to monitor and prevent the occurrence of racial discrimination and xenophobia. Other areas covered by such mechanisms are gender equality, the treatment of people with disabilities and conditions in penal institutions.

These different models reflect specific national contexts and it would be unwise to try to streamline the approach and press countries to copy one another. However, certain lessons can be drawn from experiences so far.

One is the utmost importance of independence. The ombudsman should stand above party politics and not take instructions from the government. He or she should be able to listen impartially to people who complain.

This is a major point in the Paris principles on national institutions for the promotion and protection of human rights which were first adopted at a UN expert meeting in Paris in 1991 and then endorsed by the UN General Assembly in 1993.[121] These principles also guide the Council of Europe commissioner in his co-operation with national ombudsmen.

The principle of independence should be secured by law and be made manifest through the process of appointment.

The office of the ombudsman must be adequately funded to allow it – according to the Paris principles – "to be independent of the government and not be subject to financial control which might affect its independence".

Governments must respect the integrity of these offices – if not, the ombudsmen will have difficulties functioning. They must be able, without approval from the authorities, to look into any issue falling within their competence. Likewise, they must be able to hear from any person or collect any evidence relevant for their work.

It is important for ombudsmen and similar institutions to reach out to everyone. Their existence, and powers, should be widely known and understood, and they should be easily accessible to the general public. This requires funds so that offices can be opened – or a presence maintained – outside the main metropolitan areas. Resources are also needed to ensure that complaints are handled speedily and effectively, without which the institution will be unable to build sufficient public credibility.

Local authorities

The observance of human rights is also a local matter. Authorities at local or regional level take important decisions on education, housing, health care, social services and policing; these are all areas that are relevant to people's rights. Decision makers should apply European and international human rights standards when they formulate their policies and ensure that their approach respects and upholds these rights.

---

121. General Assembly Resolution 48/134.

While governments and national parliaments ratify international treaties on behalf of the state, the day-to-day work of implementing human rights standards often rests on the shoulders of local and regional authorities. They too are bound by these agreements.

Local and regional authorities are often directly responsible for services related to health care, education, housing, water supply, environment, policing and also, in many cases, taxation. These matters affect people's human rights, not least their social rights.

The geographical and personal proximity between inhabitants and local decision makers has obvious advantages. Local decision makers are usually more accessible, and aware of the needs and challenges in their area. Dialogue with inhabitants and non-governmental groups can be more direct and inclusive at the local level.

Municipalities and provinces with an activist approach to human rights have learnt that much is to be gained from treating persons as "holders of rights" instead of merely trying to meet their needs.

But this requires active awareness-raising by local leaders. It is essential to ensure that individuals understand their rights and those of others.

During my visits to member states, I always try to meet with people who work at the local and regional level, and have been impressed by the commitment and creativity of many.

In Austria, provincial governments have human rights co-ordinators who function as the authorities' network for human rights which is used, for example, when submissions to international human rights monitoring mechanisms are prepared. The City of Graz has established a human rights council at the local level, which scrutinises city regulations and activities from a human rights perspective.

I learnt of initiatives undertaken at the local level in Italy also. In Bologna, social inclusion projects have been developed and access to decision-making facilitated; in Naples, housing projects have been started, although a lack of funds hampered progress. Other local networks facilitated the integration of asylum seekers, refugees and foreign students.

Mayors in some cities across Europe have volunteered, in co-operation with UNICEF, to act as special protectors for children's rights. The Human Rights Cities programme, a non-governmental initiative, supported by UN-HABITAT, has inspired local councils in some cities to address human rights issues in a comprehensive and participatory manner.

In 2007, 20 mayors from different European countries joined together to appeal to their peers to ensure freedom of assembly and association for lesbian, gay, bisexual and transgender (LGBT) groups, particularly in those countries where such rights had been denied or restricted.

Unfortunately, I have also seen examples of xenophobia and lack of understanding at the local level, particularly when it comes to the needs of disadvantaged groups.

In October 2008, the Congress of Local and Regional Authorities of the Council of Europe organised a seminar in Stockholm on local initiatives for the implementation of human rights. The Congress highlighted the importance of awareness-raising campaigns, local action plans, the establishment of local or regional ombudsmen, the local monitoring of human rights implementation, and training local politicians and local authority staff about their human rights responsibilities. This provides an excellent agenda for further work.

- municipalities and regional authorities are encouraged to develop their own action plans. These plans can be tailored to their specific needs, resources and priorities. A number of local agencies in various European countries have developed sector-based action plans, for example, to protect children's rights, promote gender equality or address the rights of people with disabilities. Through coherent planning, the local human rights situation can be regularly monitored and analysed. Problems as well as solutions can be directly discussed with civil society, the public and others.

Experience gained at the local level can also contribute to human rights planning at the national level;

- the existence and work of ombudsmen and similar human rights institutions need to be known to the public, and must be easily accessible, not just to those living in the capital or major cities. Particularly in larger countries, accessibility may require the establishment of satellite offices of the national ombudsman outside metropolitan areas. Another solution is to set up local or regional ombudsmen;

- for public officials to identify and address human rights issues in the course of their work, they must benefit from human rights training;

- the human rights consequences of the widespread privatisation of education, health or social services call for discussion. Though various service functions can be outsourced, the responsibility for the enforcement of international human rights standards cannot be delegated to the private sector. Consequently, there is a need to establish a system of accountability and service monitoring within the respective agencies;

- the local budget is usually a good indicator of the level of political commitment to human rights. Local politicians are often faced with the task of prioritising competing needs. Budget review from a human rights perspective is a way to ensure that elected representatives and officials are fully informed of the consequences – in human rights terms – of their decisions.

To promote human rights the Congress set up a monitoring committee in 2010. Guidelines have been drawn up for local and regional authorities and the Congress plans to scrutinise the implementation of the rights on these levels.

The human rights approach at the local level empowers hospital patients, pupils, older people, the homeless and others to claim their rights and, thereby, to improve their situation. Local politicians and public officials should seize the opportunity to enhance the quality of life of their communities by giving practical effect to human rights in their day-to-day work.

Parliaments

The ideal parliamentarian is also a defender of human rights. Elected representatives of national parliamentary bodies should give priority to the promotion of freedoms and the protection of justice. More discussion is, however, needed about how this responsibility can be best exercised to tackle current human rights failings. Parliamentary work can also help to develop a sustainable human rights culture for the future.

The role played by parliaments in adopting legislation is crucial for building a system of justice based on respect for human rights. Through the ratification process, parliaments also take positions on international (and European) human rights treaties.

Law making and ratifications must inter-relate so that national laws reflect international agreements on human rights. The incorporation of the European Convention on Human Rights into domestic law in all member states of the Council of Europe has been of great importance in ensuring this link.

Parliaments should analyse all new legislative proposals to ensure that they comply with the European Convention on Human Rights. They should follow the case law of the European Court of Human Rights in order to make sure that existing domestic law and practice is in line with the Court's jurisprudence.

The Parliamentary Assembly of the Council of Europe has underlined the importance of the role of national parliaments in monitoring the execution of judgments coming from the Strasbourg Court on many occasions. Unfortunately, some countries are extremely slow in responding to Court rulings, not least when it comes to taking action on the measures required to prevent further violations of a similar nature in the future.

Law making is not the only aspect of parliamentary work relevant to human rights. The adoption of a state's budget also has far-reaching implications for human rights.

The UN Convention on the Rights of the Child stipulates that states should undertake measures "to the maximum extent of their available resources" for the realisation of the rights defined in that treaty. The UN Covenant on Economic, Social and Cultural Rights has a similar provision. The purpose is to signal that the rights specified in these conventions should be given priority when decisions are made about the allocation of resources. Ideally, parliament should analyse the rights dimension of all budgetary proposals before final decisions are taken.

The promotion and protection of almost all human rights requires financial resources. An effective criminal justice system is resource intensive, and ensuring the right to education and adequate health care are similarly major undertakings which weigh heavily on the central budget.

A human rights approach to budget analysis should include particular scrutiny of the effect on vulnerable groups in society, such as children in difficult circumstances, older people and persons with disabilities. Human rights principles require that conditions for these and other disadvantaged groups should be a collective responsibility, and a question of justice rather than one of charity.

Several national parliaments in Europe adopt specific action plans in the field of human rights. Some plans are requested or instigated by international treaties or conferences, for instance those on children's rights, gender equality, action against human trafficking or the rights of persons with disabilities.

Within the Council of Europe, the development of comprehensive national plans for systematic implementation of human rights has been recommended. A conference on this approach was held in Stockholm in November 2008.[122]

When parliaments adopt action plans on human rights they must also request progress reports from the executive in order to check implementation.

Parliaments should also ensure that there is a human rights mechanism which allows for individual complaints and secures remedies. One possibility is to appoint an independent ombudsman, public defender or commission (the titles differ between countries) to receive complaints and seek solutions to the problems raised.

All member states of the Council of Europe now have some structure of this kind, although their mandates differ. In some countries the office holders are appointed by the government; in others, they are elected by the parliament. My own view is that it is preferable for parliaments to take an active interest in these structures, that they are involved in the recruitment of the key office-holders, and also receive and discuss their reports.

A somewhat different approach is taken by the elected assemblies in Germany, both at the federal and *Land* level, where special parliamentary committees have been set up to receive individual complaints from the public. Complaints are then followed up by putting the complainant in contact with the relevant authority, with a parliamentary motion or with a parliamentary initiative.

One positive effect of this process is that the politicians involved become deeply acquainted with human rights concerns among the public. The reports from the committees can give an indication of deeper structural problems needing to be resolved.

Several parliaments have established a human rights committee. One of the most powerful is probably the UK's Joint Committee on Human

---

122. "Rights work! Make them real!", conclusions from the International Conference on Systematic Work for Human Rights Implementation held in Stockholm on 6 and 7 November 2008: www.sweden.gov.se/rightswork.

Rights, which consists of 12 members from the House of Commons and the House of Lords. The committee undertakes thematic inquiries on human rights issues and it reports its findings and recommendations to the parliament. It scrutinises all government bills and selects those with significant human rights implications for further examination. It also analyses what government action has been taken in response to judgments of the Strasbourg Court.

In some European parliaments, the human rights committee is of an informal and consultative nature. Discussions leading to decisions on human rights issues tend to take place in standing committees such as those dealing with legal or social affairs. In Italy, the Senate established a committee on human rights, while the other chamber discusses human rights in a sub-committee of the Foreign Affairs Committee.

By having active discussions about human rights at the parliamentary level we underline that these issues engage important political questions. However, party politicisation of human rights matters can be harmful. It can happen that parliamentarians from the majority party argue more in defence of the government, rather than in support of human rights principles.

A great number of European parliaments include individuals who act as human rights defenders. Typically, many are also members of the Council of Europe's Parliamentary Assembly. Indeed, their dual role as domestic and European parliamentarians is an important factor in helping to promote human rights, the rule of law and democracy at the local level. Others have their roots in minority communities and represent their diverse interests.

The importance of such voices in the parliamentary debate should not be underestimated. For this reason, rules which protect the immunity of those elected must not easily be waived. By way of example, I felt that the decision last year of the Armenian Parliament to lift the immunity of four of its members was not justified. After all, parliamentarians have a popular mandate.

In a parliamentary democracy, governments must ensure that they have the support of parliament. However, this dependency does not work the other way round: parliaments do not need the blessing of the executive. As an elected body, parliaments have their own distinct role and can establish their own approach. In fact, governments benefit from a parliament committed to reminding it of its human rights obligations.

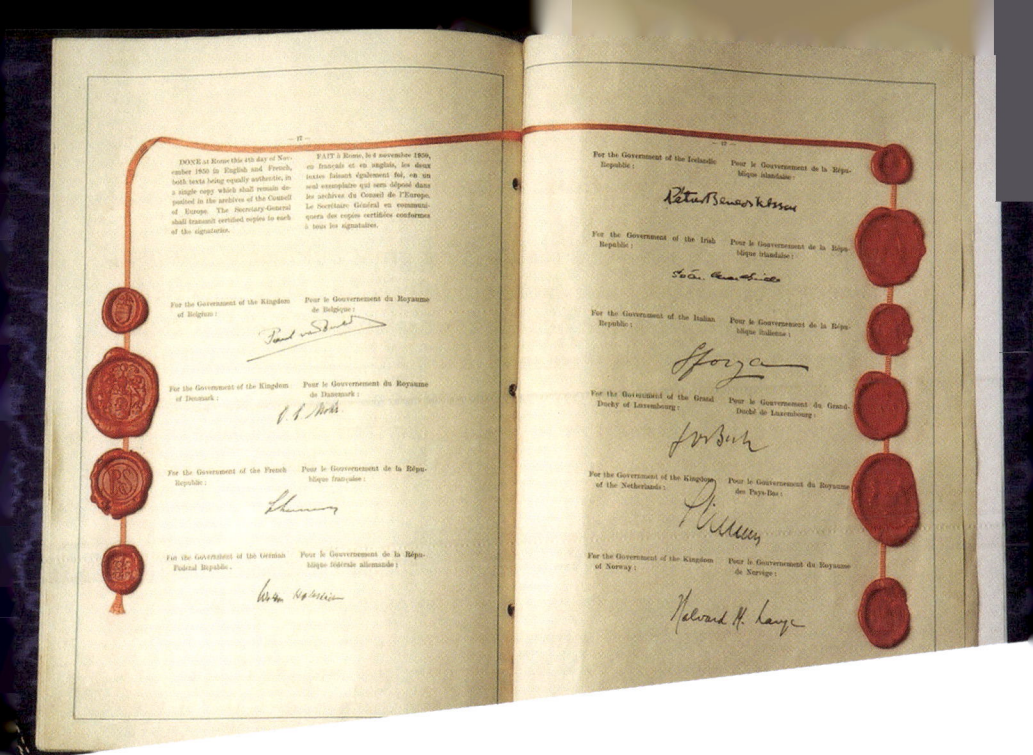

Chapter 14: Systematic measures for human rights implementation

Governments should draw up national action plans for the protection and promotion of human rights. The idea is to bring together all major stakeholders in a process which would lead to a comprehensive plan covering all substantial human rights issues. Objectives and a coherent framework of benchmarks would be defined. Where this has been tried, the action plan has been found to be useful: for instance, to improve the protection of the most vulnerable groups who otherwise often tend to be forgotten or marginalised.

Photo: The European Convention on Human Rights was adopted in Rome in November 1950 and went into force in September 1953 (© Council of Europe).

National implementation

Human rights are not yet a reality for a great number of people all over Europe. The standards are not fully enforced or respected; there is an implementation deficit. The massive inflow of cases to the Strasbourg Court demonstrates that many individuals feel that their rights have not been protected. However, the European system cannot act as a substitute for national systems. The conclusion must be that much more must be done to protect human rights at home, at domestic level.

In order to bridge the implementation gap, all European governments need to work out a systematic and comprehensive strategy that would ensure the full realisation of the international human rights treaties, starting with the European Convention and the case law of the Strasbourg Court. The development of a national plan for the implementation of the human rights obligations would be an ideal framework for such an approach.

The 1993 World Conference on Human Rights – concerned about the gap between agreed standards and reality in a number of countries – recommended that all governments should produce such a plan. However, only a few countries in Europe have done so, among them Azerbaijan, Lithuania, Moldova, Norway, Spain and Sweden. Several others, though, are reported to be in the process of developing theirs.

Baseline study

The process could be initiated with a national baseline study to establish a broad picture of the current human rights situation in the country. A thorough evaluation of existing policies and practices and recognition of problematic areas would be the starting point. Reviews of the record on ratification of international human rights treaties, gaps in legislation and shortcomings in judicial proceedings would be part of the process, as well as an analysis of the problems highlighted by international treaty bodies and other human rights mechanisms.

An obvious area for review is the functioning of existing national monitoring systems, such as ombudsmen or national human rights institutions. Human rights education is an area which also deserves special attention – both the situation in schools and universities as well as specialist training for professionals (see separate article for more discussion).

It is essential that views from minorities or marginalised groups are obtained for this baseline study. The relationship between the authorities and civil society should be looked at critically. A media policy which respects freedom of expression and encourages multiple voices to be heard is an issue for examination in a number of countries.

Normally, there is no lack of information about human rights shortcomings. Local non-governmental groups, ombudsmen and international bodies usually provide such information, as do the media and relevant authorities. Such data should be collated and analysed in a structured manner for planning purposes.

The appointment of an interministerial committee for this task – as Poland and Sweden have done – can be very helpful.

Action plan

The baseline study should lay the ground for discussion about priorities and what actions ought to be taken. A comprehensive human rights action plan or a series of more specific action plans can be drawn up. Observations and recommendations from international human rights bodies – including those from the Council of Europe – should be of substantial help at this stage.

As financial constraints and lack of human resources make it difficult to address all the problems at once, there is a need to discuss priorities thoroughly, and to plan for the medium and long term. All interested parties should be involved in this discussion, including politicians, representatives of the governmental authorities at different levels and non-governmental groups. This would ensure a comprehensive agenda for action and also create a sense of shared ownership of the eventual product.

To encourage the various authorities to get involved, it is necessary that they perceive this process as directly relevant to their own work. In the long term, a human rights perspective should be mainstreamed in the day-to-day activities of different authorities, including budgetary decisions. Active participation by representatives from the political opposition during the drafting process can contribute to the continuity of the work.

Human rights work involves many, if not all, authorities. Co-ordination and co-operation within government and across different authorities at national, regional and local levels is thus essential. One tested method is to establish a co-ordinating body consisting of representatives from all the relevant ministries and agencies.

Such a mechanism provides a forum for exchanges of experiences and information, discussion and co-operation. It is also useful for reporting to international human rights monitoring mechanisms and may in fact save resources, minimising overlap in reporting obligations.

Actors other than the authorities themselves should also be involved in the continuous work for human rights. Focus groups representing civil society, indigenous and national minorities, national human rights structures and commercial enterprises can be established for this purpose.

It takes time to build effective mechanisms to protect human rights, especially when laws need to be changed and institutions reformed. At the same time, the plan should not project too far into the future, otherwise it risks being too vague. Experience to date indicates that the time frame for such national plans should be four to five years.

Implementation

States should ensure high-level and long-term support for the action plans through the active involvement of politicians and the leadership of the authorities and agencies responsible for the plan's implementation. Action plans stretching over national and local elections should be discussed and adopted by parliaments to ensure continuity.

Human rights planning should be co-ordinated with the budgetary process to secure proper funding for human rights work. It is also necessary to review budget proposals from a human rights perspective to inform politicians of the consequences of their decisions and to hold them accountable.

A significant part of this policy should be to integrate human rights into the everyday work of public administrations and to ensure effective co-ordination and co-operation between authorities at all levels by setting up networks or other fora for discussion and exchange of experiences.

Local authorities should be encouraged to develop comprehensive local baseline studies, action plans or similar documents ensuring regular reviews of the local situation and co-ordinated efforts to address human rights challenges. Adequate systems using a rights-based approach should be established for monitoring the provision of health care, education or social services, whether provided by private or public actors.

It is essential to set up adequate systems for data collection and analysis, including data on disadvantaged groups of people. Collection of sensitive data should be accompanied by proper safeguards to prevent the identification of individuals belonging to a particular group. Official data should be complemented with relevant information from national human rights structures and from NGOs.

Evaluation

Action plans should be monitored and evaluated. It is as important to assess the process – in terms of participation, inclusiveness and transparency – as it is to evaluate the end result. The conclusions of this review should be publicly presented and a debate about the effectiveness of the process encouraged. Those who participated in the planning process should be able to contribute to the evaluation.

The evaluation will provide the foundation for a new cycle of the process. A new baseline study should be developed with an equally inclusive, transparent and participatory approach. If well designed, benchmarks and indicators can be valuable tools for follow-up and evaluation, taking both quantitative and qualitative human rights aspects into consideration.

Systematic work for human rights is a continuous process. Baseline studies, action plans and evaluation exercises are the means to clarify and assess the steps to be taken to reach our objectives. They inform us what has worked and what has not.

Consolidation

States should involve all who have a stake in these processes, including ombudsmen and other national human rights structures, civil society and representatives of disadvantaged groups of people. Such an inclusive approach contributes to the legitimacy of the plan, creates shared ownership and should make implementation more effective.

The independence of the ombudsmen and other national human rights structures must be respected. They should have sufficient resources to fulfil their roles. Consideration should be given to establishing such institutions at the regional or local level to facilitate easy access for the general public. These bodies, if adequately resourced, may also facilitate the establishment of national systems of information on the Convention and the Court's procedures and make this information easily accessible to all interested individuals.

Fostering a human rights culture through the full integration of human rights in education and training, as well as through awareness-raising, is another major building block. It is essential that plain and accessible language be used in all human rights education. The training needs of public officials and other professionals whose actions have an impact on human rights should be assessed to ensure that they have a thorough and up-to-date knowledge of the international standards relevant to their field of competence.

A well-considered package of reforms along these lines would improve the protection of human rights in any country. It would respond to the fundamental principle of subsidiarity which is enshrined in the European Convention. The objective is that each individual is able to seek and receive justice at home.

State budgets

The economic crisis has been a reminder that the state budgets must be screened for their compliance with human rights. The allocation of resources will affect human rights protection – including gender equality, children's rights and the situation of older people or people with disabilities, migrants and other groups that risk being disadvantaged. The way state revenues are obtained will also have an influence on justice and fairness in society: in this regard, no tax system is neutral.

Budget analysis should therefore be seen as a potent instrument in the struggle for human rights. Looking at budget proposals from a rights perspective can assist politicians and planners assign priorities in a way that promotes greater equality, and allocate resources where they are needed most.

Such a human rights-based budget analysis can also be a valuable means of assessing whether governments and parliaments have indeed taken steps to fulfil their obligations once international human rights standards have been ratified. The implementation of these treaties is certainly not cost-free and has to be reflected in the budget. This type of analysis could be used to hold the government accountable.

This is to a large extent a question of democratising the public discussion of budget proposals, which requires a publicly accessible presentation of the proposals and options available. Ministers of finance should clarify how their proposed budgets affect different groups in society, including those who are marginalised and disadvantaged.

Many European governments and European Union institutions have required detailed budgetary accountability from countries receiving development aid, including information about the human rights impact of different choices. However, European states have themselves been slow to apply a similar approach to their own budgets. Obviously, Europeans would also benefit from a transparent analysis of the impact on their human rights of state budgets.

International and European treaties require an end to discrimination on the basis of gender, ethnicity, nationality, social origin, sexual orientation and several other characteristics. Some – for instance, the International Covenant on Economic, Social and Cultural Rights – also specify that the state should use the maximum extent of its available resources to ensure economic and social rights.

Rights-oriented budget analysis is a fairly new approach. In the European context, the most concrete work so far has been done in the area of gender equality. Gender budgeting is a means of translating into the state budget a government's commitments to ensure that women and men enjoy their human rights on an equal basis. Budget analysis can also be used to assess public revenue, especially taxation, against the possible discriminatory effects of fiscal policy. Gender budgeting often applies performance targets and requires inclusive participation to improve efficiency, accountability and transparency.

Austria, Belgium, Finland, France, Germany, Norway, Spain and Sweden are among the countries which have already applied a conscious gender perspective to their national budgetary cycle. The inclusion of gender budgeting in the ministry of finance guidelines has often been a key factor for encouraging a gender-sensitive approach by other ministries.

Gender budgeting has also been used at regional and local levels. In the Federal State of Berlin, the regional parliament has taken a leading role in introducing gender budgeting as an integral part of the financial process. In Switzerland, the City of Basel carries out regular budgetary impact analyses based on gender. The Council of Europe has published a handbook on the practical implementation of gender budgeting.

Human rights budgeting in other areas is still in its infancy in Europe. However, interesting projects, involving both academics and non-governmental organisations, have been initiated to examine the impact of public expenditure on economic and social rights in Northern Ireland through a rights-based analysis. The aim is to identify international best practice as well as to analyse examples of government resource allocation in areas such as housing. The results of the project should also strengthen the advocacy and monitoring capacity of civil society organisations.

Outside Europe, there are several examples of how budget analysis helps to evaluate the compliance of governments' decisions with human rights. Such efforts have moved beyond a singular focus on the gender dimension, though this crucial aspect is incorporated as well.

A good example is work being done by IDASA (the Institute for Democracy in South Africa), an independent public interest organisation.[123] IDASA has analysed the impact of the South African state budget on social development, affordable housing, education, health and reduction of poverty. In its analysis of the 2009 budget, IDASA notes the effect of the economic crisis on South Africa, holds the government accountable for its budgetary decisions and stresses the need to improve the efficiency, effectiveness and equitability of the state budget.

One lesson from the work to date on rights-based budgeting and budget analysis more generally is that there must be reliable disaggregated data in relation to the situation of different groups (children, women, Roma, etc.) in society.

Another lesson is the importance of adopting a participatory approach to budget formulation. Involving different authorities, national human rights structures and civil society organisations makes the approach more meaningful and also contributes to better economic governance. Rights-based budgeting puts an emphasis on results, transparency and accountability.

---

123. See www.idasa.org.za.

The key problem in all human rights work is still the gap between promises and reality. This implementation gap can only be bridged when budget processes and the budgets themselves reflect our vision of human rights for all.

Human rights education

Human rights can only be realised if people are informed about their rights and know how to use them. Education about human rights is therefore central to the effective implementation of the agreed standards. While this was emphasised when the Universal Declaration of Human Rights was adopted in 1948, we are still far from ensuring that people know their rights and understand how to claim them.

The good news is that human rights education now is receiving attention at the European or international level. Resolutions have been adopted, conferences held and action plans issued by the United Nations agencies, not least UNESCO. The Council of Europe is particularly active in this field. Non-governmental organisations have also initiated valuable programmes.

The challenge remains one of translating these recommendations into concrete action at the national level. Human rights education needs to be more than a simple repetition of the various legal conventions with little explanation as to their relevance to ordinary people in their daily lives.

My experience is that a number of governments have not given sufficient priority to human rights education, especially in schools. The allocated time is limited and the pedagogic methods unsuitable. The emphasis has been on preparing the pupils for the labour market rather than on developing life skills which would incorporate human rights values.

More worryingly, it seems that some governments fear that a human rights approach in schools could breed unwanted criticism and even undermine government policies. This is an undemocratic and short-sighted attitude. Educating citizens in their human rights creates an informed society which in turn strengthens democracy.

International actors should focus efforts on assisting countries to develop their own programmes, with education materials tailored to the particular needs of individual countries. The UN World Programme for Human Rights Education, which started in 2005, aims to give guidance on how such national efforts can be planned and enforced. Education for Democratic Citizenship and Human Rights, one of the projects currently being run by the Council of Europe, builds on the experience of a network of national co-ordinators.

A resource centre on education for intercultural understanding, human rights and democratic citizenship has been established in Oslo – the European Wergeland Centre.[124] The centre will carry out and support research, provide in-service training for teachers, disseminate information, and serve as a platform and meeting place for relevant actors. Countries can learn much from one another.

The school system is pivotal when making young generations aware of their rights and how to use them. Not only should the school provide the key facts about human rights standards, and the mechanisms for their protection, but it must also foster values such as respect for others, non-discrimination, gender equality and democratic participation.

Intercultural understanding and respect have to be stressed in such learning. When the Convention on the Rights of the Child lists the values to be promoted internationally, it makes special mention of the respect for "the national values of the country in which the child is living, the country from which he or she may originate, and for civilizations different from his or her own". Human rights education should therefore have an inclusive approach to societal diversity.

School curricula, education materials, pedagogic methods and the training of teachers, all have to be in line with such ambitions. At the same time, it is crucial that a human rights atmosphere pervades all

---

124. www.theewc.org.

aspects of a school's life. There is a need for both human rights through education and human rights in education.

The school itself must demonstrate that it takes human rights seriously. Pupils should be welcome to express their views and to participate in the running of the school as much as possible. The atmosphere in school should be characterised by mutual understanding, respect and responsibility, between all actors. I have seen such schools and noticed that they tend to function much better than those run on an authoritarian model. Pupils learn social and other life skills, not only facts.

Teachers and principals have a key role in developing such schools. In addition, they need the support of local and central authorities, not least the ministry of education. Educational policies should promote a rights-based approach. Teacher training for all teachers, regardless of their specialisation, should be conceived along this model. Pedagogic methods should be promoted which are democratic and participatory, and textbooks and other education material should be consistent with human rights values.

The fact that many children now spend more time looking at computer screens than with teachers (or with their parents) also affects human rights learning. While the technology is value-neutral, the messages picked up or sent may not be. Efforts by schools in the field of human rights may be undermined by impressions received via the screen, and these latter are often dictated by purely commercial interests.

Apart from teachers, other professional groups and opinion builders should be reached for specialised awareness-raising and human rights training. Law enforcement officials, medical personnel, politicians, journalists, religious leaders and civil society organisers all have their role to play in securing a human-rights-respecting society.

Extra efforts are also required in order to ensure human rights education and awareness programmes reach minorities and disadvantaged groups. This requires producing materials in relevant languages, recruiting teachers and trainers from within these communities, and adapting pedagogic methods to different cultures and ages.

Governments have agreed not only to respect human rights, but also to disseminate information on human rights standards and to make people aware of their rights and the rights of others. These words should be put into deeds.

Chapter 15: International action

There is a compelling, principled argument for caring about human rights in other countries. People who are oppressed and silenced are defenceless and they should be able to count on the sympathy and solidarity of others. Individuals I have met in such situations have testified to the enormous importance of knowing that people or authorities in other countries care and are informed.

Photo: European Court of Human Rights, Strasbourg, France (© Council of Europe).

Foreign policy and human rights

Some governments have integrated the promotion of human rights into their foreign policies, while others are more cautious or even oppose what they perceive as meddling in the internal affairs of others. My view is that, in their external relations, just as in the domestic arena, European governments should adhere to their obligations under international treaties, including the European Convention on Human Rights and the European Social Charter.

In 1945, against a background of two world wars, the world's nations reaffirmed faith in human rights, in the dignity and worth of each human being and in the equal rights of men and women. They made the promotion of human rights and fundamental freedoms one of the three central purposes of the United Nations, and pledged to act for their universal respect and observance.

As the Charter of the United Nations makes clear, the protection of human rights is not only a national but also an international concern and responsibility. This principle was further confirmed in subsequent international and regional human rights treaties, and elaborated on by independent expert bodies. The Human Rights Committee, which monitors compliance with the International Covenant on Civil and Political Rights, is explicit that violations of covenant rights by any state party deserves the attention of others. "To draw attention to possible breaches of Covenant obligations by other States parties and to call on them to comply with their Covenant obligations should, far from being regarded as an unfriendly act, be considered as a reflection of legitimate community interest."[125]

In other words, there is a concrete link between respect for human rights and international peace and security which no government can ignore.

---

125. Human Rights Committee, General Comment No. 31 on the nature of the general legal obligation imposed on states parties to the covenant.

To address the bilateral responsibilities of states first – states have an obvious self-interest in stability and peace, not least as it relates to neighbouring countries. As experience has shown – not least in Europe – repression and human rights violations in one country often lead to unrest and even armed conflict which in turn can affect the broader region.

There is also a compelling, principled argument for caring about human rights in other countries. People who are oppressed and silenced are defenceless and they should be able to count on the sympathy and solidarity of others. Individuals I have met in such situations have testified to the enormous importance of knowing that people or authorities in other countries are concerned about their fate and are willing to take action on their behalf.

Nonetheless, for governments to raise human rights issues in their bilateral communications is often seen as controversial and even provocative. This is partly because human rights have a moral dimension: those who violate the standards are seen not only as making mistakes, but responsible for unacceptable, unethical acts.

This is why it is so important that governments are sincere when they criticise others. In-depth knowledge is crucial if dialogue is to be meaningful. Too often, approaches are made without sufficient information and can be easily dismissed as politically motivated. Today, there is no lack of information; in most cases it is possible to ascertain the facts from reports issued by non-governmental organisations and international agencies.

It is also essential to be consistent. Much of the unfortunate politicisation of human rights occurs when governments have been selective in their criticism: when they insist on commending the performance of allies, even when this means ignoring reports by independent human rights bodies that show quite a different picture.

The methods to be used in an active foreign policy require thorough reflection and clear explanation. The choice of quiet diplomacy, for example, is not always understood, even when there may sometimes be good reason for keeping discussions confidential. However, quiet diplomacy has also too often been used as a cover for passivity and silence.

Boycotts and other sanctions have sometimes helped to put human rights problems more firmly on domestic and international agendas, but they can also worsen the situation for the victims. The general trend is to try to solve problems through other methods, although sanctions should not be excluded in very serious cases.

One approach has been to seek the assistance of non-governmental organisations in integrating the promotion of human rights in overseas development assistance programmes. This has had positive results when assistance is free from partisan political ambition and does not compromise the impartiality of recipients. Advisory services and technical assistance are almost always welcome but, to be effective, they must address real problems and be combined with frank discussion and monitoring.

Several governments in Europe are now guided by a strategy directive for human rights in their foreign affairs policy, in some cases approved by parliament. Such directives, together with reports on their implementation, have helped to clarify basic principles and priorities, and provided a sound basis for informed discussions on human rights in foreign relations.

At the multilateral level, governments have agreed to set up mechanisms to monitor and assist in the realisation of international human rights standards. This reflects the recognition that these standards are indeed an international concern and that co-operation for their implementation is desirable.

However, governments have also criticised the very bodies they have helped to establish. Some of this criticism reflects unease about hearing uncomfortable truths, and is not well founded. The capacity and overall efficiency of international human rights mechanisms also needs to improve.

A large number of diverse mechanisms have been established since the adoption of the Universal Declaration of Human Rights in 1948 – within the United Nations and also at European level. However, many lack the necessary resources and funding and this has hampered their work. Members of human rights treaty bodies and rapporteurs serving as independent experts, for example, are usually not paid at all. My own office still has a small staff and modest budget which is totally inadequate for the 47 countries it serves.

Much has to change to enable these mechanisms to discharge their responsibilities effectively.

Governments must be open to well-founded criticism and respond constructively. They should also accept that international representatives talk and listen to non-governmental representatives and groups.

International and regional human rights mechanisms are effective when their independence is recognised and respected. This should guide the definition of mandates and the appointment of office holders, and also means that funding should not create dependency.

Human rights bodies should avoid stereotyping, always stand above party political disputes, and should co-operate and co-ordinate their activities better. Some governments have genuine difficulties in coping with complex reporting requirements and in integrating recommendations into concrete policies. It is not necessarily an advance to create more oversight bodies, and any proposals for new global or European human rights mechanisms require careful examination. In fact, most newly defined issues can be tackled within the existing structures.

Effective co-ordination requires information sharing and a rational division of labour. It is important to avoid confusing overlaps or the sending of conflicting messages, and a principle of subsidiarity should be established. I view co-ordination as worthwhile and devote considerable time to it and to building upon the finding of others in a meaningful manner. Working in concert in this way maximises the potential impact of all our work.

Co-ordination between monitoring mechanisms and assistance bodies has improved. For instance, UNICEF now takes into consideration the concluding observations of the Committee on the Rights of the Child when designing its programmes and the European Union has helped to fund some of the follow-up programmes of my office.

The key aspect in assessing international human rights bodies must obviously be whether they have a real impact and genuinely improve people's lives. As well as a clear mandate and adequate resources, this requires an approach that is strategic – recognising the enormous difficulty of the task and its political sensitivity.

A major challenge is how international human rights actors relate to actors at the national and local levels – the authorities, but also the media and civil society, including representatives of the victims. This is not an easy task. It requires experience to grasp the real problems and to give advice that is useful.

From an international perspective, it is not merely a matter of making sound appointments and sending the right delegates on mission – important though these measures are. International actors must exert great care and not "take over" the role and responsibilities of national actors and institutions, or see themselves at the top of a hierarchy. International monitoring should primarily focus on whether national capacities to address problems are adequate and effective, and focus assistance on strategic issues such as the work of domestic ombudsmen, the functioning of independent specialised agencies and, of course, the judiciary.

International actors should also avoid taking over functions that can be undertaken more effectively by domestic actors. For example, in areas such as education and training, domestic actors often have a better understanding than outsiders of local possibilities and problems, and how best to address them. Where international actors can contribute meaningfully is by sharing knowledge about successful and relevant approaches in other countries.

A wide-ranging evaluation of ways to improve and strengthen the international human rights system is overdue. This could be undertaken by a task force established by leading agencies, with the participation of independent experts, among them persons with first-hand experience of working for human rights in their own societies – persons we have in mind when we talk about human rights defenders.

Questions for any such task force to address would include:

- What can be done to ensure adequate financing of international human rights work, and the recruitment of competent staff?
- What further steps can be taken to facilitate better co-ordination and division of labour across international agencies, and between international and any national "counterparts"?
- How can the independence and integrity of monitoring mechanisms be better protected and upheld?
- How can international advice and assistance be more effectively directed to address the actual and most pressing problems at national level?
- In this regard, what is the experience of "mainstreaming" human rights into development assistance and security programmes, and how should these efforts be pursued?

Such an evaluation would highlight problems but also draw on the successes – and there have been several of the latter. I have seen prisons rebuilt to a better standard after criticism from the European Committee for the Prevention of Torture (CPT), and new laws against racism adopted after recommendations from the European Commission against Racism and Intolerance (ECRI). My predecessor's and my own recommendations have led to the release of prisoners, closure of outdated prison facilities, improvements in asylum procedures, the creation of effective ombudsman institutions, changes in laws concerning the compulsory placement in psychiatric institutions and the adoption of laws against discrimination.

A review of the practical impact of Council of Europe mechanisms in improving respect for human rights in member states was published in 2010.[126] It describes several policy reforms and legislative changes linked to judgments of the European Court of Human Rights, the ECRI, the CPT, the supervisory mechanisms of the European Social Charter and the European Convention for the Protection of National Minorities. While changes are usually the result of multiple forces, the reforms and changes described are indeed encouraging.

However, there is no room for complacency. People throughout the world have placed their hope and trust in our efforts and it is our responsibility to respond.

The accountability of International actors

When an international organisation exercises executive and legislative control as a surrogate state it should be bound by the same checks and balances that bind a democratic government. However, in reality, where international organisations govern, power is sometimes vested in one person or organisation with too little accountability for the decisions taken.

Accountability implies that decision-making processes are transparent, that there is good access to information, and that there is participation from civil society and the wider population.

Accountability also entails that there is a means to review and penalise the misconduct of officials vested with public powers, such as civil servants and state officials. We require our public officials to bear the consequences of their actions.

It has been accepted that principles of accountability must apply to United Nations peacekeeping operations, and the UN has taken steps to prevent and punish abuse and sexual exploitation in its operations.[127]

---

126. "Practical impact of the Council of Europe monitoring mechanisms in improving respect for human rights and the rule of law in member states", H/Inf(2010)7.
127. The UN Secretary General initiated in 2004 wide-ranging reforms covering standards of conduct, investigations, organisational, managerial and command responsibility, and individual disciplinary, financial and criminal accountability. See also UN Security Council Resolution 1820 in the field of women, peace and security.

Accountability must also apply when an international organisation acts as a quasi-government. The UN has now been involved in several territorial administration missions where it acted or acts as a surrogate government, for example in Namibia, Cambodia, East Timor, Bosnia and Kosovo. In these circumstances, the international administrations act both as de facto local public authorities and as an international organisation.

Accountability is important because lack of it may undermine public confidence in the international organisation and thereby in its moral authority to govern. It may also promote a climate of impunity for acts committed by its personnel which would create a poor role model for national governments.

Mechanisms to ensure accountability are therefore clearly needed when an international organisation is in control – it is not enough just to rely on good faith. Such mechanisms would enhance the credibility of the organisation's work and dissuade future abuses of power and misconduct.

This was the reasoning when the European Union decided that its own institutions needed a mechanism for complaints. The European Ombudsman, elected by the European Parliament for the first time in 1995, was established to deal with complaints from citizens concerning maladministration by European Union institutions and bodies. The Court of Justice in Luxembourg is also empowered to review claims from the Council of the European Union, the European Commission, the European Parliament and member states regarding the illegality of European Union acts. Individuals may also challenge decisions which are addressed to them.

I have raised issues related to the accountability of international actors during my visits to Bosnia and Herzegovina and Kosovo.

International organisations are still present in large numbers in Bosnia and Herzegovina. The Office of the High Representative (OHR) in Bosnia and Herzegovina was set to up facilitate the parties' own efforts to implement the 1995 Dayton Peace Agreements. The high representative's powers were later extended to include the power to remove from office public officials who violate legal commitments and the Dayton Peace Agreements, and to impose laws if Bosnia and Herzegovina's legislative bodies fail to do so.

I visited Sarajevo in 2006 to discuss complaints made by some 260 police officers from the national police force; they had been barred from police service ("decertified") and stripped of their social and pension rights through a vetting procedure organised by the UN International Police Task Force. They had been accused of having committed crimes during the war. My concern related to their limited opportunities to challenge the merits of the task force decision and the absence of an appropriate legal remedy.

The Council of Europe's Venice Commission had proposed that the UN Security Council set up a special body to review these cases. After my visit, I called on all parties to find a solution which would give justice to the police officers and thereby enhance the credibility of the international community. However, no legal mechanism was established for review of the cases, though the UN did not object when local authorities rehired some of these police officers who applied for junior positions.

In Kosovo, UNMIK[128] and Kfor[129] and their personnel are immune from any legal process. The intention of this legal immunity has been to ensure that international organisations can perform their tasks without improper interference.

It has also been established that the Strasbourg Court has no jurisdiction over complaints against such personnel. According to the admissibility decisions in 2007 of the European Court of Human Rights

---

128. UNMIK is the acronym for the United Nations Interim Administration Mission in Kosovo.
129. Kfor is the acronym for the Kosovo Force led by the North Atlantic Treaty Organization (NATO).

in two cases, the actions of Kfor and UNMIK are attributable to the United Nations, and not to contributing member states.[130]

There is an obvious risk that this system might lead to a situation of impunity. This was not fully remedied by the establishment in 2005 of the Human Rights Advisory Panel in Kosovo to act as a quasi-judicial body to investigate complaints against UNMIK.

The panel faced several difficulties, including delays in the appointment of its members, lack of sufficient secretariat support and uncertainty over how UNMIK would respond to the panel's recommendations.

I exchanged correspondence with UNMIK's leadership on these matters, emphasising the importance of the United Nations holding the organisation to account, through credible procedures, and that it must also stand ready to provide compensation and redress for violations of human rights. The response was not enthusiastic but some compromises were made.

What types of mechanisms are needed to ensure the accountability of international actors?

- when staff members are accused of being responsible for human rights violations in the course of implementing decisions by an international organisation, the organisation concerned should ensure an independent investigation. Victims should be awarded redress or reparation including compensation. The creation of an independent human rights court or panel in the country in question is a good option;

- other intra-organisational methods, such as complaints or claims commissions, can work, although the temptation may be too great to prevent information which could damage the organisation from becoming public;

---

130. *Behrami and Behrami v. France* and *Saramati v. France, Germany and Norway*, decision of 2 May 2007.

- the creation of an ombudsman's office with a strong mandate is another way to hold international administrations accountable for breaches of authority;
- states which contribute personnel to international peacekeeping missions should ensure independent investigations, and full accountability, of all those responsible for human rights violations, including where appropriate through criminal, administrative and disciplinary procedures;
- the International Criminal Court (ICC) has jurisdiction over crimes against humanity, war crimes and genocide, even when committed by UN peacekeepers. The ICC is a court of last resort, which may exercise its jurisdiction when the state party on whose territory, or by whose nationals, the alleged crimes are committed, is unwilling or unable to conduct an investigation or prosecution;
- reporting obligations at the international level also provide a form of accountability;
- international organisations sometimes engage outside actors to perform independent assessments of their activities, for example when the UN Secretary-General created an independent body to conduct an inquiry into UN conduct during the 1994 Rwandan genocide;
- international and local media and non-governmental organisations have a key role to play as watchdogs.

An international accountability deficit is not good for anyone, least of all the local population. No one, especially not an international organisation with the objective of upholding the rule of law, is above the law.

List of acronyms and abbreviations

ASPA – American Service-Members Protection Act
CAJ – Committee on the Administration of Justice
CAT – United Nations Committee Against Torture
CEPEJ – Council of Europe's European Commission for the Efficiency of Justice
CETS – Council of Europe Treaty Series
CPT – European Committee for the Prevention of Torture and Inhuman or Degrading Treatment or Punishment
CRC – UN Convention on the Rights of the Child
EC – European Commission
ECHR – European Convention on Human Rights
ECJ – European Court of Justice (Court of Justice of the European Communities)
ECRI – European Commission against Racism and Intolerance
ECSR – European Committee of Social Rights
ENOC – European Network of Ombudsmen for Children
ERRC – European Roma Rights Centre
ETS – European Treaty Series
ETUC – European Trades Union Confederation
EU – European Union
FAIR – Forum Against Islamophobia and Racism
FCNM – Council of Europe Framework Convention for the Protection of National Minorities
FRA – European Union Agency for Fundamental Rights
GRECO – Council of Europe's Group of States against Corruption
GRETA – Council of Europe's Group of Experts on Action against Trafficking in Human Beings
HCNM – OSCE High Commissioner on National Minorities
ICC – International Criminal Court

ICCPR – International Covenant on Civil and Political Rights
ICHRP – International Council on Human Rights Policy
ICJ – International Court of Justice
ICRC – International Committee of the Red Cross
IDASA – Institute for Democracy in South Africa
IDP – Internally displaced person
IESCR – International Covenant on Economic, Social and Cultural Rights
IOE – International Organisation of Employers
IPCC – Intergovernmental Panel on Climate Change
Kfor – Kosovo Force led by the North Atlantic Treaty Organization (NATO)
LGBT – Lesbians, gays, bisexuals and transgender persons
Luxembourg Court – European Court of Justice
NGO – Non-governmental organisation
ODIHR – OSCE Office for Democratic Institutions and Human Rights
OHR – Office of the High Representative in Bosnia and Herzegovina
OPCAT – Optional Protocol to the Convention Against Torture
OSCE – Organization for Security and Co-operation in Europe
OSI – Open Society Justice Initiative
PACE – Council of Europe Parliamentary Assembly
Strasbourg Court – European Court of Human Rights
UNAIDS – Joint United Nations Programme on HIV/AIDS
UNESCO – United Nations Educational, Scientific and Cultural Organization
UNHABITAT – United Nations Human Settlements Programme
UNHCR – Office of the United Nations High Commissioner for Refugees
UNICEF – United Nations Children's Fund
UNMIK – United Nations Interim Administration Mission in Kosovo
WHO – World Health Organization

Appendix

Council of Europe human rights treaties: record of ratifications and signatures

Convention for the Protection of Human Rights and Fundamental Freedoms
ETS No. 5

Treaty open for signature by the member states of the Council of Europe and for accession by the European Union

Opening for signature
Place: Rome
Date: 4/11/1950

Entry into force
Conditions: 10 Ratifications
Date : 3/9/1953

Status as of 25/3/2011

Member states of the Council of Europe

States	Signature	Ratification	Entry into force	Notes	R.	D.	A.	T.	C.	O.
Albania	13/7/1995	2/10/1996	2/10/1996			X				
Andorra	10/11/1994	22/1/1996	22/1/1996		X	X				
Armenia	25/1/2001	26/4/2002	26/4/2002		X	X				
Austria	13/12/1957	3/9/1958	3/9/1958		X	X				
Azerbaijan	25/1/2001	15/4/2002	15/4/2002		X	X				
Belgium	4/11/1950	14/6/1955	14/6/1955			X			X	
Bosnia and Herzegovina	24/4/2002	12/7/2002	12/7/2002							
Bulgaria	7/5/1992	7/9/1992	7/9/1992			X				
Croatia	6/11/1996	5/11/1997	5/11/1997		X	X				
Cyprus	16/12/1961	6/10/1962	6/10/1962			X				
Czech Republic	21/2/1991	18/3/1992	1/1/1993	17	X	X				
Denmark	4/11/1950	13/4/1953	3/9/1953			X				
Estonia	14/5/1993	16/4/1996	16/4/1996		X	X				

States	Signature	Ratification	Entry into force	Notes	R.	D.	A.	T.	C.	O.
Finland	5/5/1989	10/5/1990	10/5/1990		X	X				
France	4/11/1950	3/5/1974	3/5/1974		X	X		X		
Georgia	27/4/1999	20/5/1999	20/5/1999			X				
Germany	4/11/1950	5/12/1952	3/9/1953	30	X	X		X		
Greece	28/11/1950	28/11/1974	28/11/1974	29		X				
Hungary	6/11/1990	5/11/1992	5/11/1992			X				
Iceland	4/11/1950	29/6/1953	3/9/1953			X				
Ireland	4/11/1950	25/2/1953	3/9/1953		X	X				
Italy	4/11/1950	26/10/1955	26/10/1955			X				
Latvia	10/2/1995	27/6/1997	27/6/1997			X				
Liechtenstein	23/11/1978	8/9/1982	8/9/1982		X	X				
Lithuania	14/5/1993	20/6/1995	20/6/1995		X	X				
Luxembourg	4/11/1950	3/9/1953	3/9/1953			X				
Malta	12/12/1966	23/1/1967	23/1/1967		X	X				
Moldova	13/7/1995	12/9/1997	12/9/1997		X	X				
Monaco	5/10/2004	30/11/2005	30/11/2005		X	X				
Montenegro	3/4/2003	3/3/2004	6/6/2006	56	X	X				
Netherlands	4/11/1950	31/8/1954	31/8/1954			X		X		
Norway	4/11/1950	15/1/1952	3/9/1953		X	X				
Poland	26/11/1991	19/1/1993	19/1/1993			X				
Portugal	22/9/1976	9/11/1978	9/11/1978		X	X				
Romania	7/10/1993	20/6/1994	20/6/1994		X	X				
Russia	28/2/1996	5/5/1998	5/5/1998		X	X				
San Marino	16/11/1988	22/3/1989	22/3/1989		X	X				
Serbia	3/4/2003	3/3/2004	3/3/2004	56	X	X				
Slovakia	21/2/1991	18/3/1992	1/1/1993	17	X	X				
Slovenia	14/5/1993	28/6/1994	28/6/1994			X				
Spain	24/11/1977	4/10/1979	4/10/1979		X	X				
Sweden	28/11/1950	4/2/1952	3/9/1953			X				
Switzerland	21/12/1972	28/11/1974	28/11/1974			X				

States	Signature	Ratification	Entry into force	Notes	R.	D.	A.	T.	C.	O.
"The former Yugoslav Republic of Macedonia"	9/11/1995	10/4/1997	10/4/1997			X				
Turkey	4/11/1950	18/5/1954	18/5/1954			X			X	
Ukraine	9/11/1995	11/9/1997	11/9/1997		X	X				
United Kingdom	4/11/1950	8/3/1951	3/9/1953			X		X	X	

International organisations

Organisations	Signature	Ratification	Entry into force	Notes	R.	D.	A.	T.	C.	O.
European Union										

Total number of signatures not followed by ratifications:	
Total number of ratifications/accessions:	47

Notes:
(17) Dates of signature and ratification by the former Czech and Slovak Federal Republic.
(29) Ratification 28/03/1953 – Denunciation with effect on 13/06/1970.
(30) Ratification by Saarland 14/01/1953 – Saarland became an integral part of Germany on 01/01/1957.
(56) Dates of signature and ratification by the state union of Serbia and Montenegro.
a: Accession – s: Signature without reservation as to ratification –
su: Succession – r: Signature "ad referendum".
R.: Reservations – D.: Declarations – A.: Authorities – T.: Territorial Application – C.: Communication – O.: Objection.

Source : Treaty Office on http://conventions.coe.int

European Social Charter
ETS No. 35

Treaty open for signature by the member states
of the Council of Europe

Opening for signature
Place: Turin
Date : 18/10/1961

Entry into force
Conditions: 5 Ratifications
Date : 26/2/1965

Status as of: 25/3/2011

Member states of the Council of Europe

States	Signature	Ratification	Entry into force	Notes	R.	D.	A.	T.	C.	O.
Albania				52						
Andorra				52						
Armenia				52						
Austria	22/7/1963	29/10/1969	28/11/1969	51	X					
Azerbaijan				52						
Belgium	18/10/1961	16/10/1990	15/11/1990	52	X					
Bosnia and Herzegovina				52						
Bulgaria				52						
Croatia	8/3/1999	26/2/2003	28/3/2003	51	X					
Cyprus	22/5/1967	7/3/1968	6/4/1968	52	X					
Czech Republic	27/5/1992	3/11/1999	3/12/1999	51	X					
Denmark	18/10/1961	3/3/1965	2/4/1965	51	X		X			
Estonia				52						
Finland	9/2/1990	29/4/1991	29/5/1991	52	X					
France	18/10/1961	9/3/1973	8/4/1973	52	X	X				
Georgia				52						
Germany	18/10/1961	27/1/1965	26/2/1965	51	X		X			
Greece	18/10/1961	6/6/1984	6/7/1984	51	X					

States	Signature	Ratification	Entry into force	Notes	R.	D.	A.	T.	C.	O.
Hungary	13/12/1991	8/7/1999	7/8/1999	52	X					
Iceland	15/1/1976	15/1/1976	14/2/1976	51	X					
Ireland	18/10/1961	7/10/1964	26/2/1965	52	X					
Italy	18/10/1961	22/10/1965	21/11/1965	52	X					
Latvia	29/5/1997	31/1/2002	2/3/2002	51	X					
Liechtenstein	9/10/1991									
Lithuania				52						
Luxembourg	18/10/1961	10/10/1991	9/11/1991	51	X					
Malta	26/5/1988	4/10/1988	3/11/1988	52	X					
Moldova				52	X	X				
Monaco				52						
Montenegro				52						
Netherlands	18/10/1961	22/4/1980	22/5/1980	52	X		X			
Norway	18/10/1961	26/10/1962	26/2/1965	52	X	X		X		
Poland	26/11/1991	25/6/1997	25/7/1997	51	X					
Portugal	1/6/1982	30/9/1991	30/10/1991	52	X	X				
Romania	4/10/1994			52						
Russia				52						
San Marino				51						
Serbia				52						
Slovakia	27/5/1992	22/6/1998	21/7/1998	52	X					
Slovenia	11/10/1997			52						
Spain	27/4/1978	6/5/1980	5/6/1980	51	X					
Sweden	18/10/1961	17/12/1962	26/2/1965	52	X					
Switzerland	6/5/1976									
"The former Yugoslav Republic of Macedonia"	5/5/1998	31/3/2005	30/4/2005	51	X					
Turkey	18/10/1961	24/11/1989	24/12/1989	52	X					
Ukraine	2/5/1996			52						

States	Signature	Ratification	Entry into force	Notes	R.	D.	A.	T.	C.	O.
United Kingdom	18/10/1961	11/7/1962	26/2/1965	51		X		X		

Total number of signatures not followed by ratifications:	5
Total number of ratifications/accessions:	27

Notes:
(51) State signatory to the European Social Charter (revised) (ETS 163).
(52) State Party to the European Social Charter (revised) (ETS 163).
a: Accession – s: Signature without reservation as to ratification –
su: Succession – r: Signature "ad referendum".
R.: Reservations – D.: Declarations – A.: Authorities – T.: Territorial Application – C.: Communication – O.: Objection.

Source : Treaty Office on http://conventions.coe.int

European Convention for the Prevention of Torture and Inhuman or Degrading Treatment or Punishment
ETS No. 126

Treaty open for signature by the member states and for accession by non-member states

Opening for signature
Place: Strasbourg
Date : 26/11/1987

Entry into force
Conditions: 7 Ratifications
Date : 1/2/1989

Status as of: 25/3/2011

Member states of the Council of Europe

States	Signature	Ratification	Entry into force	Notes	R.	D.	A.	T.	C.	O.
Albania	2/10/1996	2/10/1996	1/2/1997							
Andorra	10/9/1996	6/1/1997	1/5/1997							
Armenia	11/5/2001	18/6/2002	1/10/2002							
Austria	26/11/1987	6/1/1989	1/5/1989							
Azerbaijan	21/12/2001	15/4/2002	1/8/2002				X			
Belgium	26/11/1987	23/7/1991	1/11/1991							
Bosnia and Herzegovina	12/7/2002	12/7/2002	1/11/2002							
Bulgaria	30/9/1993	3/5/1994	1/9/1994							
Croatia	6/11/1996	11/10/1997	1/2/1998							
Cyprus	26/11/1987	3/4/1989	1/8/1989							
Czech Republic	23/12/1992	7/9/1995	1/1/1996	3						
Denmark	26/11/1987	2/5/1989	1/9/1989							
Estonia	28/6/1996	6/11/1996	1/3/1997							
Finland	16/11/1989	20/12/1990	1/4/1991							
France	26/11/1987	9/1/1989	1/5/1989							
Georgia	16/2/2000	20/6/2000	1/10/2000			X				
Germany	26/11/1987	21/2/1990	1/6/1990						X	
Greece	26/11/1987	2/8/1991	1/12/1991							

States	Signature	Ratification	Entry into force	Notes	R.	D.	A.	T.	C.	O.
Hungary	9/2/1993	4/11/1993	1/3/1994							
Iceland	26/11/1987	19/6/1990	1/10/1990							
Ireland	14/3/1988	14/3/1988	1/2/1989							
Italy	26/11/1987	29/12/1988	1/4/1989				X			
Latvia	11/9/1997	10/2/1998	1/6/1998							
Liechtenstein	26/11/1987	12/9/1991	1/1/1992							
Lithuania	14/9/1995	26/11/1998	1/3/1999							
Luxembourg	26/11/1987	6/9/1988	1/2/1989							
Malta	26/11/1987	7/3/1988	1/2/1989							
Moldova	2/5/1996	2/10/1997	1/2/1998							
Monaco	30/11/2005	30/11/2005	1/3/2006							
Montenegro	3/3/2004	3/3/2004	6/6/2006	56						
Netherlands	26/11/1987	12/10/1988	1/2/1989						X	
Norway	26/11/1987	21/4/1989	1/8/1989							
Poland	11/7/1994	10/10/1994	1/2/1995							
Portugal	26/11/1987	29/3/1990	1/7/1990							
Romania	4/11/1993	4/10/1994	1/2/1995							
Russia	28/2/1996	5/5/1998	1/9/1998							
San Marino	16/11/1989	31/1/1990	1/5/1990							
Serbia	3/3/2004	3/3/2004	1/7/2004	56						
Slovakia	23/12/1992	11/5/1994	1/9/1994	3						
Slovenia	4/11/1993	2/2/1994	1/6/1994							
Spain	26/11/1987	2/5/1989	1/9/1989							
Sweden	26/11/1987	21/6/1988	1/2/1989							
Switzerland	26/11/1987	7/10/1988	1/2/1989							
"The former Yugoslav Republic of Macedonia"	14/6/1996	6/6/1997	1/10/1997							
Turkey	11/1/1988	26/2/1988	1/2/1989							
Ukraine	2/5/1996	5/5/1997	1/9/1997							

States	Signature	Ratification	Entry into force	Notes	R.	D.	A.	T.	C.	O.
United Kingdom	26/11/1987	24/6/1988	1/2/1989					X		

Non-member states of the Council of Europe

States	Signature	Ratification	Entry into force	Notes	R.	D.	A.	T.	C.	O.

Total number of signatures not followed by ratifications:	
Total number of ratifications/accessions:	47

Notes:

(3) Date of signature by the Czech and Slovak Federal Republic.
(56) Dates of signature and ratification by the state union of Serbia and Montenegro.
a: Accession – s: Signature without reservation as to ratification – su: Succession – r: Signature "ad referendum".
R.: Reservations – D.: Declarations – A.: Authorities – T.: Territorial Application – C.: Communication – O.: Objection.

Source : Treaty Office on http://conventions.coe.int

European Charter for Regional or Minority Languages
ETS No. 148

Treaty open for signature by the member states and for accession by non-member states

Opening for signature
Place: Strasbourg
Date : 5/11/1992

Entry into force
Conditions: 5 Ratifications
Date : 1/3/1998

Status as of: 25/3/2011

Member states of the Council of Europe

States	Signature	Ratification	Entry into force	Notes	R.	D.	A.	T.	C.	O.
Albania										
Andorra										
Armenia	11/5/2001	25/1/2002	1/5/2002			X				
Austria	5/11/1992	28/6/2001	1/10/2001			X				
Azerbaijan	21/12/2001					X				
Belgium										
Bosnia and Herzegovina	7/9/2005	21/9/2010	1/1/2011			X				
Bulgaria										
Croatia	5/11/1997	5/11/1997	1/3/1998		X	X				
Cyprus	12/11/1992	26/8/2002	1/12/2002			X				
Czech Republic	9/11/2000	15/11/2006	1/3/2007			X				
Denmark	5/11/1992	8/9/2000	1/1/2001			X		X		
Estonia										
Finland	5/11/1992	9/11/1994	1/3/1998			X				
France	7/5/1999					X				
Georgia										
Germany	5/11/1992	16/9/1998	1/1/1999			X				

States	Signature	Ratification	Entry into force	Notes	R.	D.	A.	T.	C.	O.
Greece										
Hungary	5/11/1992	26/4/1995	1/3/1998			X				
Iceland	7/5/1999									
Ireland										
Italy	27/6/2000									
Latvia										
Liechtenstein	5/11/1992	18/11/1997	1/3/1998			X				
Lithuania										
Luxembourg	5/11/1992	22/6/2005	1/10/2005							
Malta	5/11/1992									
Moldova	11/7/2002									
Monaco										
Montenegro	22/3/2005	15/2/2006	6/6/2006	56						
Netherlands	5/11/1992	2/5/1996	1/3/1998			X		X		
Norway	5/11/1992	10/11/1993	1/3/1998			X				
Poland	12/5/2003	12/2/2009	1/6/2009			X				
Portugal										
Romania	17/7/1995	29/1/2008	1/5/2008			X				
Russia	10/5/2001									
San Marino										
Serbia	22/3/2005	15/2/2006	1/6/2006	56		X				
Slovakia	20/2/2001	5/9/2001	1/1/2002			X				
Slovenia	3/7/1997	4/10/2000	1/1/2001			X				
Spain	5/11/1992	9/4/2001	1/8/2001			X				
Sweden	9/2/2000	9/2/2000	1/6/2000			X				
Switzerland	8/10/1993	23/12/1997	1/4/1998			X				

States	Signature	Ratification	Entry into force	Notes	R.	D.	A.	T.	C.	O.
"The former Yugoslav Republic of Macedonia"	25/7/1996									
Turkey										
Ukraine	2/5/1996	19/9/2005	1/1/2006		X					
United Kingdom	2/3/2000	27/3/2001	1/7/2001		X		X			

Non-member states of the Council of Europe

States	Signature	Ratification	Entry into force	Notes	R.	D.	A.	T.	C.	O.

Total number of signatures not followed by ratifications:	8
Total number of ratifications/accessions:	25

Notes:
(56) Dates of signature and ratification by the state union of Serbia and Montenegro.
a: Accession – s: Signature without reservation as to ratification – su: Succession – r: Signature "ad referendum".
R.: Reservations – D.: Declarations – A.: Authorities – T.: Territorial Application – C.: Communication – O.: Objection.

Source : Treaty Office on http://conventions.coe.int

Framework Convention for the Protection of National Minorities
ETS No. 157

Treaty open for signature by the member states and up until the date of entry into force by any other state so invited by the Committee of Ministers

Opening for signature
Place: Strasbourg
Date : 1/2/1995

Entry into force
Conditions: 12 Ratifications
Date : 1/2/1998

Status as of: 25/3/2011

Member states of the Council of Europe

States	Signature	Ratification	Entry into force	Notes	R.	D.	A.	T.	C.	O.
Albania	29/6/1995	28/9/1999	1/1/2000							
Andorra										
Armenia	25/7/1997	20/7/1998	1/11/1998							
Austria	1/2/1995	31/3/1998	1/7/1998			X				
Azerbaijan		26/6/2000 a	1/10/2000			X				
Belgium	31/7/2001				X					
Bosnia and Herzegovina		24/2/2000 a	1/6/2000							
Bulgaria	9/10/1997	7/5/1999	1/9/1999			X				
Croatia	6/11/1996	11/10/1997	1/2/1998							
Cyprus	1/2/1995	4/6/1996	1/2/1998							
Czech Republic	28/4/1995	18/12/1997	1/4/1998							
Denmark	1/2/1995	22/9/1997	1/2/1998			X				
Estonia	2/2/1995	6/1/1997	1/2/1998			X				
Finland	1/2/1995	3/10/1997	1/2/1998							
France										
Georgia	21/1/2000	22/12/2005	1/4/2006							
Germany	11/5/1995	10/9/1997	1/2/1998			X				
Greece	22/9/1997									

States	Signature	Ratification	Entry into force	Notes	R.	D.	A.	T.	C.	O.
Hungary	1/2/1995	25/9/1995	1/2/1998							
Iceland	1/2/1995									
Ireland	1/2/1995	7/5/1999	1/9/1999							
Italy	1/2/1995	3/11/1997	1/3/1998							
Latvia	11/5/1995	6/6/2005	1/10/2005		X					
Liechtenstein	1/2/1995	18/11/1997	1/3/1998		X					
Lithuania	1/2/1995	23/3/2000	1/7/2000							
Luxembourg	20/7/1995				X					
Malta	11/5/1995	10/2/1998	1/6/1998		X		A			
Moldova	13/7/1995	20/11/1996	1/2/1998							
Monaco										
Montenegro		11/5/2001 a	6/6/2006	54						
Netherlands	1/2/1995	16/2/2005	1/6/2005		X		X			
Norway	1/2/1995	17/3/1999	1/7/1999							
Poland	1/2/1995	20/12/2000	1/4/2001		X					
Portugal	1/2/1995	7/5/2002	1/9/2002							
Romania	1/2/1995	11/5/1995	1/2/1998							
Russia	28/2/1996	21/8/1998	1/12/1998		X					
San Marino	11/5/1995	5/12/1996	1/2/1998							
Serbia		11/5/2001 a	1/9/2001	54						
Slovakia	1/2/1995	14/9/1995	1/2/1998							
Slovenia	1/2/1995	25/3/1998	1/7/1998		X					
Spain	1/2/1995	1/9/1995	1/2/1998							
Sweden	1/2/1995	9/2/2000	1/6/2000		X					
Switzerland	1/2/1995	21/10/1998	1/2/1999		X					
"The former Yugoslav Republic of Macedonia"	25/7/1996	10/4/1997	1/2/1998		X					
Turkey										
Ukraine	15/9/1995	26/1/1998	1/5/1998							

States	Signature	Ratification	Entry into force	Notes	R.	D.	A.	T.	C.	O.
United Kingdom	1/2/1995	15/1/1998	1/5/1998							

Non-member states of the Council of Europe

States	Signature	Ratification	Entry into force	Notes	R.	D.	A.	T.	C.	O.

Total number of signatures not followed by ratifications:	4
Total number of ratifications/accessions:	39

Notes:
(54) Date of accession by the state union of Serbia and Montenegro.
a: Accession – s: Signature without reservation as to ratification –
su: Succession – r: Signature "ad referendum".
R.: Reservations – D.: Declarations – A.: Authorities – T.: Territorial Application – C.: Communication – O.: Objection.

Source : Treaty Office on http://conventions.coe.int

European Social Charter (revised)
ETS No. 163

Treaty open for signature by the member states of the Council of Europe

Opening for signature
Place: Strasbourg
Date : 3/5/1996

Entry into force
Conditions: 3 Ratifications
Date : 1/7/1999

Status as of: 25/3/2011

Member states of the Council of Europe

States	Signature	Ratification	Entry into force	Notes	R.	D.	A.	T.	C.	O.
Albania	21/9/1998	14/11/2002	1/1/2003			X				
Andorra	4/11/2000	12/11/2004	1/1/2005			X				
Armenia	18/10/2001	21/1/2004	1/3/2004			X				
Austria	7/5/1999									
Azerbaijan	18/10/2001	2/9/2004	1/11/2004			X				
Belgium	3/5/1996	2/3/2004	1/5/2004			X				
Bosnia and Herzegovina	11/5/2004	7/10/2008	1/12/2008			X				
Bulgaria	21/9/1998	7/6/2000	1/8/2000			X				
Croatia	6/11/2009									
Cyprus	3/5/1996	27/9/2000	1/11/2000			X				
Czech Republic	4/11/2000									
Denmark	3/5/1996					X				
Estonia	4/5/1998	11/9/2000	1/11/2000			X				
Finland	3/5/1996	21/6/2002	1/8/2002			X				
France	3/5/1996	7/5/1999	1/7/1999							
Georgia	30/6/2000	22/8/2005	1/10/2005			X				
Germany	29/6/2007									
Greece	3/5/1996									
Hungary	7/10/2004	20/4/2009	1/6/2009			X				

States	Signature	Ratification	Entry into force	Notes	R.	D.	A.	T.	C.	O.
Iceland	4/11/1998									
Ireland	4/11/2000	4/11/2000	1/1/2001		X					
Italy	3/5/1996	5/7/1999	1/9/1999		X					
Latvia	29/5/2007									
Liechtenstein										
Lithuania	8/9/1997	29/6/2001	1/8/2001		X					
Luxembourg	11/2/1998									
Malta	27/7/2005	27/7/2005	1/9/2005		X					
Moldova	3/11/1998	8/11/2001	1/1/2002		X					
Monaco	5/10/2004									
Montenegro	22/3/2005	3/3/2010	1/5/2010	55	X					
Netherlands	23/1/2004	3/5/2006	1/7/2006			X			X	
Norway	7/5/2001	7/5/2001	1/7/2001			X			X	
Poland	25/10/2005									
Portugal	3/5/1996	30/5/2002	1/7/2002		X					
Romania	14/5/1997	7/5/1999	1/7/1999		X					
Russia	14/9/2000	16/10/2009	1/12/2009		X					
San Marino	18/10/2001									
Serbia	22/3/2005	14/9/2009	1/11/2009	55	X					
Slovakia	18/11/1999	23/4/2009	1/6/2009		X					
Slovenia	11/10/1997	7/5/1999	1/7/1999		X					
Spain	23/10/2000									
Sweden	3/5/1996	29/5/1998	1/7/1999		X					
Switzerland										
"The former Yugoslav Republic of Macedonia"	27/5/2009									
Turkey	6/10/2004	27/6/2007	1/8/2007		X					
Ukraine	7/5/1999	21/12/2006	1/2/2007		X					

States	Signature	Ratification	Entry into force	Notes	R.	D.	A.	T.	C.	O.
United Kingdom	7/11/1997									

Total number of signatures not followed by ratifications:	15
Total number of ratifications/accessions:	30

Notes:

(55) Date of signature by the state union of Serbia and Montenegro.
a: Accession – s: Signature without reservation as to ratification –
su: Succession – r: Signature "ad referendum".
R.: Reservations – D.: Declarations – A.: Authorities – T.: Territorial Application – C.: Communication – O.: Objection.

Source : Treaty Office on http://conventions.coe.int

**Office of the Commissioner for Human Rights
Council of Europe**

F-67075 Strasbourg Cedex
Tel.: +33 (0)3 88 41 34 21 – Fax: +33 (90)3 90 21 50 53

E-mail address: commissioner@coe.int
Website: www.commissioner.coe.int

Sales agents for publications of the Council of Europe
Agents de vente des publications du Conseil de l'Europe

BELGIUM/BELGIQUE
La Librairie Européenne -
The European Bookshop
Rue de l'Orme, 1
BE-1040 BRUXELLES
Tel.: +32 (0)2 231 04 35
Fax: +32 (0)2 735 08 60
E-mail: order@libeurop.be
http://www.libeurop.be

Jean De Lannoy/DL Services
Avenue du Roi 202 Koningslaan
BE-1190 BRUXELLES
Tel.: +32 (0)2 538 43 08
Fax: +32 (0)2 538 08 41
E-mail: jean.de.lannoy@dl-servi.com
http://www.jean-de-lannoy.be

**BOSNIA AND HERZEGOVINA/
BOSNIE-HERZÉGOVINE**
Robert's Plus d.o.o.
Marka Maruliça 2/V
BA-71000 SARAJEVO
Tel.: + 307 33 640 818
Fax: + 387 33 640 818
E-mail: robertsplus@bih.net.ba

CANADA
Renouf Publishing Co. Ltd.
1-5369 Canotek Road
CA-OTTAWA, Ontario K1J 9J3
Tel.: +1 613 745 2665
Fax: +1 613 745 7660
Toll-Free Tel.: (866) 767-6766
E-mail: order.dept@renoufbooks.com
http://www.renoufbooks.com

CROATIA/CROATIE
Robert's Plus d.o.o.
Marasoviçeva 67
HR-21000, SPLIT
Tel.: + 385 21 315 800, 801, 802, 803
Fax: + 385 21 315 804
E-mail: robertsplus@robertsplus.hr

**CZECH REPUBLIC/
RÉPUBLIQUE TCHÈQUE**
Suweco CZ, s.r.o.
Klecakova 347
CZ-180 21 PRAHA 9
Tel.: +420 2 424 59 204
Fax: +420 2 848 21 646
E-mail: import@suweco.cz
http://www.suweco.cz

DENMARK/DANEMARK
GAD
Vimmelskaftet 32
DK-1161 KØBENHAVN K
Tel.: +45 77 66 60 00
Fax: +45 77 66 60 01
E-mail: gad@gad.dk
http://www.gad.dk

FINLAND/FINLANDE
Akateeminen Kirjakauppa
PO Box 128
Keskuskatu 1
FI-00100 HELSINKI
Tel.: +358 (0)9 121 4430
Fax: +358 (0)9 121 4242
E-mail: akatilaus@akateeminen.com
http://www.akateeminen.com

FRANCE
La Documentation française
(diffusion/distribution France entière)
124, rue Henri Barbusse
FR-93308 AUBERVILLIERS CEDEX
Tél.: +33 (0)1 40 15 70 00
Fax: +33 (0)1 40 15 68 00
E-mail: commande@ladocumentationfrancaise.fr
http://www.ladocumentationfrancaise.fr

Librairie Kléber
1 rue des Francs Bourgeois
FR-67000 STRASBOURG
Tel.: +33 (0)3 88 15 78 88
Fax: +33 (0)3 88 15 78 80
E-mail: librairie-kleber@coe.int
http://www.librairie-kleber.com

**GERMANY/ALLEMAGNE
AUSTRIA/AUTRICHE**
UNO Verlag GmbH
August-Bebel-Allee 6
DE-53175 BONN
Tel.: +49 (0)228 94 90 20
Fax: +49 (0)228 94 90 222
E-mail: bestellung@uno-verlag.de
http://www.uno-verlag.de

GREECE/GRÈCE
Librairie Kauffmann s.a.
Stadiou 28
GR-105 64 ATHINAI
Tel.: +30 210 32 55 321
Fax.: +30 210 32 30 320
E-mail: ord@otenet.gr
http://www.kauffmann.gr

HUNGARY/HONGRIE
Euro Info Service
Pannónia u. 58.
PF. 1039
HU-1136 BUDAPEST
Tel.: +36 1 329 2170
Fax: +36 1 349 2053
E-mail: euroinfo@euroinfo.hu
http://www.euroinfo.hu

ITALY/ITALIE
Licosa SpA
Via Duca di Calabria, 1/1
IT-50125 FIRENZE
Tel.: +39 0556 483215
Fax: +39 0556 41257
E-mail: licosa@licosa.com
http://www.licosa.com

MEXICO/MEXIQUE
Mundi-Prensa México, S.A. De C.V.
Río Pánuco, 141 Delegacíon Cuauhtémoc
MX-06500 MÉXICO, D.F.
Tel.: +52 (01)55 55 33 56 58
Fax: +52 (01)55 55 14 67 99
E-mail: mundiprensa@mundiprensa.com.mx
http://www.mundiprensa.com.mx

NETHERLANDS/PAYS-BAS
Roodveldt Import BV
Nieuwe Hemweg 50
NL-1013 CX AMSTERDAM
Tel.: + 31 20 622 8035
Fax.: + 31 20 625 5493
Website: www.publidis.org
Email: orders@publidis.org

NORWAY/NORVÈGE
Akademika
Postboks 84 Blindern
NO-0314 OSLO
Tel.: +47 2 218 8100
Fax: +47 2 218 8103
E-mail: support@akademika.no
http://www.akademika.no

POLAND/POLOGNE
Ars Polona JSC
25 Obroncow Street
PL-03-933 WARSZAWA
Tel.: +48 (0)22 509 86 00
Fax: +48 (0)22 509 86 10
E-mail: arspolona@arspolona.com.pl
http://www.arspolona.com.pl

PORTUGAL
Livraria Portugal
(Dias & Andrade, Lda.)
Rua do Carmo, 70
PT-1200-094 LISBOA
Tel.: +351 21 347 42 82 / 85
Fax: +351 21 347 02 64
E-mail: info@livrariaportugal.pt
http://www.livrariaportugal.pt

**RUSSIAN FEDERATION/
FÉDÉRATION DE RUSSIE**
Ves Mir
17b, Butlerova.ul.
RU-117342 MOSCOW
Tel.: +7 495 739 0971
Fax: +7 495 739 0971
E-mail: orders@vesmirbooks.ru
http://www.vesmirbooks.ru

SPAIN/ESPAGNE
Mundi-Prensa Libros, s.a.
Castelló, 37
ES-28001 MADRID
Tel.: +34 914 36 37 00
Fax: +34 915 75 39 98
E-mail: libreria@mundiprensa.es
http://www.mundiprensa.com

SWITZERLAND/SUISSE
Planetis Sàrl
16 chemin des Pins
CH-1273 ARZIER
Tel.: +41 22 366 51 77
Fax: +41 22 366 51 78
E-mail: info@planetis.ch

UNITED KINGDOM/ROYAUME-UNI
The Stationery Office Ltd
PO Box 29
GB-NORWICH NR3 1GN
Tel.: +44 (0)870 600 5522
Fax: +44 (0)870 600 5533
E-mail: book.enquiries@tso.co.uk
http://www.tsoshop.co.uk

**UNITED STATES and CANADA/
ÉTATS-UNIS et CANADA**
Manhattan Publishing Co
2036 Albany Post Road
USA-10520 CROTON ON HUDSON, NY
Tel.: +1 914 271 5194
Fax: +1 914 271 5886
E-mail: coe@manhattanpublishing.com
http://www.manhattanpublishing.com

Council of Europe Publishing/Editions du Conseil de l'Europe
FR-67075 STRASBOURG Cedex
Tel.: +33 (0)3 88 41 25 81 – Fax: +33 (0)3 88 41 39 10 – E-mail: publishing@coe.int – Website: http://book.coe.int